The Act of Judging in Nigeria

Ari Niki-Tobi

The Act of Judging in Nigeria

A Matter of Interpretation and Judicial Discretion

PETER LANG
Berlin · Bruxelles · Chennai · Lausanne · New York · Oxford

Bibliographic Information published by the Deutsche Nationalbibliothek
The Deutsche Nationalbibliothek lists this publication in the Deutsche Nationalbibliografie; detailed bibliographic data is available in the internet at http://dnb.d-nb.de.

Library of Congress Cataloging-in-Publication Data
Names: Niki-Tobi, Ari, author.
Title: The Act of Judging in Nigeria : A Matter of Interpretation and Judicial Discretion / Ari Niki-Tobi.
Description: New York : Peter Lang | Includes bibliographical references.
Identifiers: LCCN 2025004130 (print) | LCCN 2025004131 (ebook) | ISBN 9783631877524 (paperback) | ISBN 9783631936085 (ebook) | ISBN 9783631936092 (epub)
Subjects: LCSH: Judges--Nigeria. | Judges--Nigeria--Decision making. | Judicial discretion--Nigeria.
Classification: LCC KTA3497 .N55 2025 (print) | LCC KTA3497 (ebook) | DDC 347.669/012--dc23/eng/20250202
LC record available at https://lccn.loc.gov/2025004130
LC ebook record available at https://lccn.loc.gov/2025004131

Cover: @ Ari Niki-Tobi
Image of author's late father, Hon. Justice Niki Tobi, JSC (Rtd) CFR (1940–2016)

ISBN 978-3-631-87752-4 (Print)
ISBN 978-3-631-93608-5 (ePDF)
ISBN 978-3-631-93609-2 (ePUB)
DOI 10.3726/b22797

Published by Peter Lang GmbH, Berlin (Germany)

info@peterlang.com

This publication has been peer reviewed.

Contact for General Product Safety Regulation (GPSR): gpsr@peterlang.com

www.peterlang.com

Abstract

Since the formation of the Nigerian judiciary, courts have operated using the Common Law system with the doctrine of judicial precedent (or *stare decisis*). This doctrine has shaped the context of judging in Nigeria, especially as strict adherence to precedent somewhat impacts judicial discretion in interpreting statutes. Judging is not static and does not happen in a vacuum. Instead, judging changes over time and responds to context. However, strict adherence to precedent alone may interfere with the advancement of justice. Therefore, this book seeks to define the act of judging in Nigeria within the context of social realities. It aims to encourage judges to interpret statutes and apply judicial discretion within meaningful social contexts that are considerate of relevant social views, values, and interests (thus interweaving law and society). This book examines various judicial approaches to interpreting statutes and established canons of statutory interpretation. It emphasizes that judges now (more than before) need to use "appropriate" discretion from a social perspective when interpreting statutes or law. This is especially true with ambiguous statutory provisions and constant changes in the law and society. Furthermore, while recommending that judicial jurisprudence changes as culture and social values change, this book explicitly questions judging stereotypically based on strict Common Law principles of precedent currently often used in Nigeria and other Common Law countries. The contention that judges are agents of social change and should be guided more/as much by social interests, social empathy, and changing social circumstances in the interpretation of statutes/law—and less/as by the established canons of interpretation and judicial precedent—will hopefully engender a necessary and robust debate that could lead to a change in practice in Nigerian courts and other courts globally.

Dedication

I dedicate this book to my late father and mentor, Hon. Justice Niki Tobi, JSC (RTD) CFR (1940–2016), and other judges like him (dead and alive, retired and serving) who dare(d) the status quo or precedent to uphold substantial justice over technical justice. Their efforts caused and are still causing social, judicial, cultural, environmental, scientific, economic, and political changes in society.

This is a tribute to their sometimes misunderstood and misinterpreted resilience in taking that lonely path to justice. Some have been accused as corrupt, ignorant of the law, judicial activist/rascals, yet their previous dissenting opinions/deviation from precedent have eventually become precedent, and their judgments that attracted sociopolitical criticisms now advance legal/judicial jurisprudence to develop law and society.

May their legacies endure and thrive for posterity!

Contents

Foreword

It is my pleasure to write the foreword to this book, "The Act of Judging in Nigeria – A Matter of Interpretation and Judicial Discretion" and my delight is for two reasons. The first reason is the author of the book, Ari Niki-Tobi. I became acquainted with Ari about twenty years ago when she took up appointment as a Magistrate-Judge with the Lagos State of Nigeria Judiciary in 2005. I have since then watched and seen her mature, grow and blossom into the intellectual, international scholar and head of a judicial consulting firm she has become today. The second reason for my delight is the topic of the book. It is one that touches upon, and is in respect of, what has been my professional life for the last twenty-four years, since my appointment as a Judge of the High of Lagos State, Nigeria in 2001.

The act of judging refers to the process of making sound decisions, particularly in situations involving complex information, conflicting perspectives, or ambiguous circumstances. It encompasses the ability to analyze facts, apply relevant principles, and reach fair and well-reasoned conclusions. This involves not just knowledge of rules and procedures but also the development of critical thinking, discernment, and empathy. The renowned philosopher, Socrates, suggested that there were four aspects of being a fine judge: "to hear courteously; to answer wisely; to consider soberly; and to decide impartially." The reality is that in practice, there is no formula or science to achieving these ends.

In an article titled "The Art of Being A Judge", Leo R. Yankwich noted that judges administer justice judicially, i.e., not according to some abstract ideas of right and justice, but according to the rules laid down by society in its Code of Laws which it gives its sanctions and that the function of the judge which is primarily adjudication is not a mechanical craft, but the exercise of a creative art, whether we call it legislative or not, which requires great ability and objectivity. In **Rochin v. California**, 342 U.S. 165 at 171-72 (1951), Justice Frankfurter of the United States Supreme Court commented that:

> "To practice the requisite detachment and to achieve sufficient objectivity no doubt demands of judges the habit of self-discipline and self-criticism, incertitude that one's own views are incontestable and alert tolerance toward views not shared. But these are precisely the pre-suppositions of our judicial process. They are precisely the qualities society has a right to expect from those entrusted with . . . judicial power."

Judicial decision-making is described as a complex process influenced by competing values, precedents, societal needs, and philosophical concepts. Judges often face tensions between adhering to precedent and achieving just outcomes. While some judges develop a judicial philosophy over time, their decisions are shaped by experience and the specific circumstances of each case. Differences in judicial outlook, interpretation methods, and approaches to precedent are common, reflecting the diversity of the judiciary. In this book, "The Act of Judging in Nigeria – A Matter of Interpretation and Judicial Discretion", the author focuses attention to the judicial approach to judging with particular emphasis on Nigeria, drawing on her experiences as a Magistrate-Judge and from her interactions with different personalities in the Nigerian Judiciary.

The book consists of seven chapters and each chapter is prefaced with an introduction telling the reader what to expect from the chapter. Chapter One, Historical Perspective of Judging in Nigeria, gives a historical background of the Nigerian Legal System, highlighting the sources of the Nigeria Law and how the interplay of these different sources has impacted on and shaped the approach to judging in Nigeria. The author also talked about the role that judicial norms and the procedural structure of the Nigerian court system play in the act of judging. In Chapter Two, International Law and Judging in Nigeria, the author considered the different sources of international law applicable in Nigeria and how they have affected, positively and negatively, the act of judging in Nigeria and also the backward impact the act of judging in Nigeria has had on the development of international law.

Chapter Three, Judicial Interpretation in Nigeria, discussed the legal framework for interpreting statutes in Nigeria and the rules of interpretation of statutes adopted by the Courts in dealing with statutory provisions. The author suggested the addition of her socio-judicial rule (SJR) as one of the aids to interpretation of statutes. By the SJR rule, the author proposes that statute be interpreted from a societal and judicial perspective in determining the intention of the drafters as legislations are products of social and societal needs, interests or protests, and also of judicial interventions, as per case law. The author is of the view that the court should interpret statutes on the basis of public interest and to take into consideration the relevant constant changes in society in doing so.

Chapter Four is on Judicial Discretion in Nigeria and therein, the author defined judicial discretion and highlighted the five basic principles, deducible from case law, that judges consider or should consider in the exercise of their discretion to enable them arrive at a just determination of a matter. The five principles are that discretion must be equitable and fair, that discretion must be bona fide, that discretion must not be arbitrary or illegal, that discretion must be confined to the facts and circumstances of the case and that discretion must be "judicially and judiciously" exercised. The author also considered the constraints on exercise of discretion, the significance of discretion and the impact of technology on the exercise of discretion. In Chapter Five, Judicial Precedents/Stare Decisis, the author laid out the hierarchy of the Nigerian Courts and discussed how the doctrine of judicial precedents plays out amongst the different tiers of Court. The author considered the impact of the doctrine on the Nigerian Legal System and the challenges it poses to the act of judging and suggested how judges should meander through the challenges.

In Chapter Six, The Impact of Judging in Nigeria, the author emphasized the connection between the Court and the Society and noted that Judges and the law are the connecting cords between courts and society and that while law is designed for social compliance and maintaining order in society, judges are responsible for administering justice by interpreting the law and maintaining social order. In Chapter Seven, the author concluded the book by doing a recap of the discussions in the earlier chapters and emphasised the proposition that judges should approach judging from a socio-judicial point of view as this is the only way to connect the law and courts to society, build public confidence and balance the rule of law with social interests.

These concluding views of the author align with the understanding that while Law originates from societal relationships and aims to regulate and control activities for the common good, judges represent the community in adjudicating disputes and interpreting societal values and standards and they reflect the community's moral outrage in sentencing and assessing credibility based on shared norms. While judges must remain impartial and unaffected by transient public opinion or political campaigns, they are expected to uphold enduring values and principles. Judging is a way of life rooted in truth, values, and connection to society, making judges a manifestation of the people. In the words of Aharon Barak, President of the Supreme Court of Israel, in his treatise, "The Judge in a Democracy (2006)" at page 112;

> "judging is not merely a job but a way of life; ... it is a way of life that includes an impartial and objective search for truth. It is ... not an attempt to please everyone but a firm insistence on values and principles; not surrender to or compromise with interest groups but an insistence on upholding the law; not making decisions according to temporary whims but progressing consistently on the basis of deeply held beliefs and fundamental values .... There should be no wall between the judge and the society in which the judge operates. The judge is part of the people."

The approach adopted by the author in discussing the various legal issues in the book makes for easy understanding and comprehension. The language used is simple, the discussions in the book flow, they are consistent and they are comprehensive, and did not leave out any essential detail. The book is an immense resource material for Judges, lawyers, lecturers and students of Law and it is a good contribution to the legal jurisprudence and materials on the act of judging. I congratulate the author for her resourcefulness in putting the work together. The book is a "must have" and a good addition to the library of everyone.

HONORABLE JUSTICE HABEEB ADEWALE OLUMUYIWA ABIRU
JUSTICE, SUPREME COURT OF NIGERIA

Acknowledgments

All thanks to the Chief Justice of the Universe, who gave me the idea, the grace, and the zeal to begin this research and complete it. I thank God for the wisdom and grace to complete this book amidst several obstacles. My connections to all the wonderful persons below, who supported me with their ideas, perspectives, jurisprudence, skills and time at various stages, were purely divine.

He brought lovey people like Dr. Shawn Marsh, Honorable Justice Adewale Habeeb Abiru, JCA, (as he then was). Judge James Garbolino, and Dr. Johnson Makoba—all members of my masters' degree thesis committee—whose constructive comments helped transform my thesis into this book. I also appreciate Dr. Elizabeth Francis and Dr. Malcolm Feeley for their guidance through the courses that they taught during my master in judicial studies program. Dr. Feeley's constructive comments gave me more insight into researching and writing this book and challenged me for phase two.

Writing is hard work, but writing a good book or paper that others cite is even harder. Therefore, I specially acknowledge and appreciate all the authors I have cited in this book; their work inspired me to share my own thoughts confidently, knowing I had the support of other writers and researchers.

I am especially grateful to Distinguished Professor Taiwo Osipitan, SAN for sending me his articles, presentations and expert opinions on various areas of law, some of which are not yet published. I also appreciate Hon. Justice Benedict Kanyip, my professor from college, and mentor, whose courage to create precedent has established many judgments and articles that align with my socio-judicial reasoning, philosophy, and theory. I also thank Chief Magistrate Eme Uguru, Esq., for the research platform he shared to enable my easy access to caselaw, as well as Hon. Justice Taiwo Taiwo for his valuable professional contributions to this book. I also appreciate Adebayo Akinlade, Esq., Chidi Agbo, Esq., and Henry Nkamuke, Esq., for statutory updates and helping with caselaw research. I sincerely appreciate Professor Festus Emiri, SAN, who took the time to read through my manuscript and commended my unique approach and original research. I am glad that my work inspired him. I am also grateful to Professor Chioma Agomo, Professor Emmanuel Emenyonu for their reviews and comments. I am grateful to Chief Justice Bryan Sykes, Former Chief Justice Babatunde Desmond Edwards,CoRSL, Justice Santiago Otamendi, and several others for their support through this process. All the speakers at my Courts & Society Webinar Series from the first to tenth editions are also thank-worthy as their diverse experiences and valuable contributions were reflected in this writing. Thank you all for volunteering your time to share your knowledge.

This book was originally six chapters, but after a presentation as a guest lecturer in a political science class at State University of New York(SUNY) Oneonta in 2020, I was inspired to expand and include that presentation into this work. Therefore I acknowledge Dr. Brent Heindl and his former students, on whose behest, I prepared that teaching, which conveniently created chapter two of this book. Some questions and comments from them inspired me to write from a global perspective, considering non-Nigerian readers.

Moreover, to the Court of Appeal, and Supreme Court justices who prefer to remain unnamed but supported me with caselaw, practice patterns, and updated (unpublished) information on the modus operandi of their various court systems: I am deeply indebted. Some of the information I gathered from these senior/head judges—often undocumented—reflects practices that have thrived in their courts over the years. These judges granted informant interviews that helped me in getting information on their best practices, which I could not get in any book or document. Non-judges who read my manuscript were enlightened by their contributions. I am especially grateful to retired Honorable Justice Amina Adamu Augie, my mentor and friend, for her unwavering emotional, mental, and intellectual support throughout this process. I deeply appreciate the effort of these judges who, despite returning from hectic hours on the bench, took the time to answer my questions during lunch or dinner. Also mention-worthy is Chief Magistrate Ayo Odugbesan, Rtd., for her experiential contribution to chapter one. Your commitment to advancing judicial jurisprudence has enriched this book. Today, the world will benefit from insights into essential judicial practices and procedures because of your generous contributions. Thank you, my lords and my ladies!

I also thank my publishers for taking the chance to accept this unique book, which some believed was not worth the effort. I especially thank Anja Lee for her consistent support, encouragement, and patience. I appreciate the production team behind the scene that helped Anja to get the work done smoothly. I also wish to thank my invisible team, the peer reviewers, for their detailed and comprehensive critiques, which helped shape this finished work.

I further acknowledge the spouses of these dedicated judges like my mother, Gbegbeto Niki Tobi, who sacrificed a lot behind the scenes to support judges like my late father to research and write outstanding society-changing judgments. THANK YOU!

Last but certainly not least, I am thankful for my loving family's support, especially my mother who constantly prays for me, my Jewel—Edyn—and my Trophy—Ethan—my supportive children who for the most part were well behaved and allowed me to write. You are the bestest!

A special posthumous thank you to my late father, whose act and art of judging I observed closely with keen interest. I thank him for answering all my questions, taking the time to mentor me and explain judging in such a way that it arouse and inspired my keen interest to research about it.

Thank you all for being part of my journey. God bless you all.

Praise for the Book

"Ari Niki-Tobi provides fresh and thoughtful perspectives on an ageless subject, the jurisprudence of judging. Rigid adherence to judicial precedents or a more activist socially conscious approach? Her conclusions are well worth reading."

—Professor Yemi Osinbajo, SAN, GCON
Former vice President of The Federal Republic of Nigeria

"Ari Niki-Tobi, who authored this book, is a woman with extensive knowledge of Nigerian Courts and judicial systems, and this is manifested in the seven chapters of what I call a must-read Court Manual. With an inviting title - *The Act of Judging in Nigeria: A Matter of Interpretation and Judicial Discretion*, the book captures ideologies conceptualized into sections that narrate the history and modus operandi of judging in Nigeria while comparing Nigerian and American case laws, coupled with legal principles that connect Courts to society. The introduction of the author's unique socio-judicial approach is a novel contribution to judicial jurisprudence that reinforces the argument of Courts as agents of social change, and I have no doubts whatsoever that every Judge (Nigerian or not) would find this Book/Court Manual instructive."

—Hon. Justice Amina Adamu Augie, CFR, JSC (Rtd.)
Retired Justice of the Supreme Court of Nigeria

"Springing from an unprecedented access to the inner recesses of judicial decision-making, *The Act of Judging in Nigeria* steps on thorough grounding in time-honoured judicial rules and principles to propound a bold approach to a core art of judging and interpretation– the Socio-Judicial Approach (SJA). While contextualised in the Nigerian setting, the issues thrown up by the book are of universal relevance and bound to reignite old debates on judicial activism and, perhaps, extend the jurisprudential dimensions of the debate. Is SJA a mere rehash of an existing theory or a new approach that democratises judicial decision-making, taking it beyond calls on specific questions of fact to enabling 'We the People" determine what the law is? Does SJA represent a timely appreciation of the demands of the times or an unwarranted expansion of the mandate of judges? May SJA effectively usurp the lawmaking role of elected legislators in favour of appointed judges or rather ensure the actualisation of the elected lawmakers' goals?

The author does not avoid ruffling judicial feathers too. The proposed SJA is not rooted in superficiality but boldly admits and embraces an expansion of judicial discretion, even at the expense of adherence to judicial precedence. How may that play out in the hierarchical judicial setting? The profundity of this work destines its nuances and imports to dissection and discernment in law faculties and schools but also commends itself to serious introspections and deliberations in judges' chambers and conferences of all rungs. Yet the simplicity of its diction and delivery aptly makes it amenable to comprehension by public commentators in this judicialised polity.

Well-grounded in the classic, conventional common law theories but openly challenging their frontiers and redefining the underlying commonality, there is no ignoring *The Act of Judging in Nigeria*."

—Hon. Justice Kashim Zannah
President, Commonwealth Judicial Education Institute (CJEI).
Chief Judge of Borno State, Nigeria

"The book 'The Act of Judging in Nigeria' is a must-read for aspiring as well as current Judges in Africa. It covers a lot that will guide and direct Judges as they set out in this sacred duty of judging. The fresh and unique Principles outlined are of universal application - a great treatise on how to effectively, judiciously, and independently dispense justice. I will recommend it for those undergoing induction courses to being judges in Sierra Leone and Africa as a whole. It covers, inter alia the knowledge and substance of effective judging, judicial discretion, and the impact of judging on society. This in my opinion covers the universality of the principles of judging..."

—Hon. Justice Desmond B. Edwards,
Former Chief Justice, Sierra Leone
Ambassador to Dublin Ireland

"This book is a compelling read for anyone wishing to follow the fortunes of the rule of law of a country that had its own system of law, with the law of a colonial power imposed on it, followed by independence, a succession of military coups, and finally, what appears to be a stable democracy. The

Judiciary of Nigeria demonstrated its resilience and commitment to the rule of law throughout a turbulent and difficult history from 1961 to the present. The writer manages to capture the heart and soul of the many judges who struggled mightily to nurture the fragile and delicate plant of justice in, at times, a very hostile and inhospitable environment. This book is not just about a legal system, neither is it a dry narrative of legal history, but it embodies a not-so-often-spoken-about virtue that all judges need: judicial courage to be true to integrity and fairness, even at great cost to one's life and safety. The invested time reading this work will be well spent."

—Hon. Mr. Justice Bryne Sykes,OJ,CD.
The Honorable Chief Justice of Jamaica.

"In "The Act of Judging in Nigeria," Ari Niki-Tobi draws deeply from lived experience and legal scholarship to explore the delicate balance between interpretation and judicial discretion. As a former magistrate judge in Nigeria, she understands firsthand the weight of judicial responsibility and the nuanced decisions judges must make. This work is both insightful and essential for anyone seeking to understand the art—and burden—of judging within a complex legal system."

—Hon. Benes Z. Aldana (Ret.).
President, The National Judicial College, Reno, Nevada, U.S.A.

"I am honored to present to you this book elaborated by Ari Niki-Tobi. This important work intends to contribute to an ongoing debate that was initiated a long time ago with the emergence of democracy around the world, but is still relevant today, i.e., what are the values and ideas that are essential for the consolidation of a solid, just, and legitimate judiciary? The interactions between judicial precedent and societal changes and development have never been more significant.... To have a direct impact on a better life for society, courts are required to be a beacon of democracy, independence for economic power, and political influence. In this spirit, the author explains in chapter six how the court's role affects society, and how society impacts judicial decisions. This is especially relevant nowadays where the modern models of government are under serious scrutiny and traditional means of communication are being replaced by social media. Furthermore, the author categorizes and explains experience-based techniques of judging, as ten stages of judging, and how they help judicial democracy. For this purpose, it is indispensable that even after their appointments, magistrates and judges continue a rigorous and constant education, both in technical and legal topics as ethical and methodological issues. In today's modern world, where marginalization is rampant and economic inequity often means that many vulnerable groups are virtually left out of the possibility of accessing justice, judges must work towards ensuring everyone their human rights. This is essentially relevant in countries of the Global South like Nigeria and my home country Argentina, which intend to ensure a more prosperous and equal reality for their future generations. The author reinforces this in an open letter to judges about the impact of judicial decisions on posterity. To this end, I recommend this book. Finally, I would like to take this opportunity to recognize especially Ari Niki-Tobi and everyone who generously dedicated their time, knowledge, and dedication to making this book possible. The commitment of such people is what continues to nurture the practice of law and our work as judicial operators."

—Hon. Justice Santiago Otamendi, Ph.D.,
Supreme Court of The Autonomous City of Buenos Aires, Argentina.

"The Act of Judging in Nigeria, demonstrates the dire need for a composition of people-centered judging approach in our courts. As a judge presently sitting in the criminal division, it is my view that applying a "socio-judicial " canon of interpreting statutes will help judges incorporate the perspective of the victim or aggrieved party in a case and give meaningful justice to both the complainant and the state/ society whilst holding true the doctrine of stare decisis, although Ari argues against complete adherence to precedent. Ari's unique Socio-Judicialism theory of judging, which she introduces in this book, especially in chapters three and six, advocates for a human-centered perspective in criminal justice. I believe that we all have something to absorb from this judging handbook."

—Hon. Justice Yetunde Adesanya
Judge, High Court of Lagos State, Criminal Division

"Ari Niki-Tobi dedicated her passion, time, efforts, and enthusiasm to this book and its crucial topic in any society. Although the book relates to Nigerian judges and the judiciary, judges worldwide could recognize themselves in it. There is a lot of misunderstanding between judges, the judiciary, the public, and society. No matter how slow or inefficient courts are, they always represent a true and last frontier and protection for everybody's rights. In doing so, judges and the legal profession neglect that we live in the 21st century. Things have changed dramatically and are changing faster than ever. And the legal profession likes the status quo. Ari and her book appeal to judges to become real agents of change in their societies .... Judges have a unique position to spread their words, individual values, and the values of modern societies, and introduce needed positive changes.... Judges and legal professionals should not only be legal experts and intermediaries between the Law and the parties in a dispute. Judges should start looking beyond the formal and strict Laws. Law, by itself, most of the time, cannot provide justice.... When we bring humanity to the courtrooms, we will gain humanity back—and much more—mutual understanding, trust, and parties' and public confidence, just as Ari proposes in her socio-judicial theory. ....This book will be handy to judges, helping them improve their knowledge and skills and possibly triggering them to acquire new skills unrelated to Law. It will definitely help all those affected by judges' work understand what they do. Ari's late father, Hon. Justice Niki Tobi, would be proud of Ari's great accomplishment. Thank you, Ari, for the great job you have done!"

—Hon. Justice Srđan Šimac, Ph.D.,
High Commercial Court of the Republic of Croatia.

"This is a huge accomplishment, and it doesn't come as a surprise being a former colleague of the author Ari Niki-Tobi when she was a magistrate in the Lagos State Judiciary, Nigeria's judiciary of excellence, that she authored a book of this magnitude. As one who had first-hand experience of her style of judging, I have watched her interactions and also related with her. Upon mere reflection, I can see that the ten stages of judging that she created in chapter six, which exemplifies how judges should adjudicate, and which are not available in any print, are simply her personal way of adjudicating. The author is definitely a chip off the old block as a daughter of late Hon. Justice Niki Tobi, our very much revered retired Justice of the Nigerian Supreme Court, and author of the only known book on judges generally in Nigeria, titled "The Nigerian Judge." I usually say, "you cannot give the right reason for doing the wrong thing, neither can you do the wrong thing to put things right." As judges and magistrates, we are called to set the record straight. So, in our exalted calling, we must always apply our discretion rightly. It is undisputed that the author, Ari Niki-Tobi has set the record straight by giving reasons for doing the right thing in stating the ten stages of judging which she created, which exemplifies how judges should adjudicate, and is indeed the lifestyle she has lived. By authoring this book, Ari Niki-Tobi has also done the right thing to put things right, being a step in the right direction. A disciplined, confident, firm and highly principled individual, the author is indeed a true child of her heroic late father, and one can indeed say, "like father like daughter." I expect to see and hear more positive things about her, given her foundation and experience, and her characteristic involvement in anything justiciable as well as her creation of a theory called "socio-judicial-ism." It's been my privilege to endorse this book being the first of its kind. It is highly recommended for members of the bench as well as lawyers who intend to join the bench."

—Adejumoke Olagbegi-Adelabu (Mrs.)
Chief Magistrate Admin,
Lagos State Judiciary
Chairperson, Steering Committee on
Diversion Community Rehabilitation Program, Lagos State.
Former Chairperson, Magistrates Association of
Nigeria, Lagos State Branch (2019-2023)

"I am happy to endorse THE ACT OF JUDGING IN NIGERIA: a Matter of Interpretations and Judicial Discretion by Ari Niki - Tobi. This is the first of its kind. As an advocate for gender equity and equality, I am particularly excited about Chapter 6 titled, The Impact of Judging on Society. Readers will find the treatment of the landmark decision in Mojekwu v. Mojekwu, a case which successfully challenged the status quo on female inheritance, enlightening. There is something to take away from each chapter."

—Professor Chioma Kanu Agomo, LL. B, LLM (London),
Emeritus. Fulbright Scholar, Honorary Fellow, Queen Mary,
University of London. First female Dean of
the Faculty of Law, University of Lagos March 2021).
Currently, Dean of Law, Anchor University, Lagos, Nigeria.

"This seven-chapter book on the Act of Judging in Nigeria contains impactful and insightful information on how judges and adjudicators decide on cases brought before them for resolution. The book sidelines peer review methodology and embraces what the author describes as a "straight from the mouths of the experts in the field" approach. The author consequently leveraged her experience as a former magistrate in the Lagos State Judiciary, interaction with her father (Hon. Justice Niki Tobi of blessed memory), and some Nigerian judges, whose identities the author strategically conceals. The book frontally disapproves of judicial enslavement to judicial precedent/stare decisis. It x-rays the adverse and suffocating effects of judicial precedent on the development of law and society. Judges and adjudicators are encouraged to take leap of faith, avoid stereotype judgments, be forward looking progressive and be change agents through liberal/purposive interpretation of statutes and in the dispensation of justice. I entertain no iota of doubt, that the book will serve as a useful compass to Judges, lawyers, law professors, law students, law researchers, reformers, and all in search of knowledge on the act of judging. I wholeheartedly recommend the book as "a must-buy" by persons concerned with the study of how Courts and adjudicators administer justice."

—Distinguished Prof. Taiwo Osipitan, SAN, FNIALS.
Department of Public Law,
Faculty of Law, University of Lagos. Nigeria

"This book reminds me of the *Nature of the Judicial Process (1921)*, by the great American Supreme Court Justice, Benjamin Cardozo, published just over one hundred years ago. Like him, Ari is an informed judge (retired), a disciplined scholar, and a wonderful writer. They both explore the same issues: the role of the judge, the nature of precedent, the rule of stare decisis, the challenges of interpretation, the need for discretion, adaption to social change. However, she writes about a judicial process that is an amalgamation of local traditional legal systems and English common law, one that is increasingly responsive to international law, and one that must confront the challenges of rapidly changing technologies. Anyone interested in the Nigerian judicial process will learn a lot. More generally, anyone seeking an analysis of the challenges facing judges in the contemporary world will find her discussions illuminating. Indeed, the book addresses timeless and universal issues confronting judges in all places and at all times. An informative book."

—Dr. Malcolm Feeley, (Emeritus) Claire Sanders Clement Professor of Law, University of California Law School, Berkley.

"This book, authored by Ari Niki-Tobi, the daughter of the esteemed jurist Hon. Justice Niki Tobi (late Justice of the Supreme Court of Nigeria), is a timely contribution, especially in a period when Nigeria's judiciary faces a trust deficit. The contents are engaging and accessible to readers who are non-lawyers. "The Impact of Judging on Society" examines the crucial relationship between courts and communities, emphasizing the role of judges as mediators between law and society. It advocates for judges to exercise discretion, emphasizing the importance of substantial justice over rigid legalism. The book examines how societal needs shape judicial decisions and the need for adaptable legal interpretations that can facilitate social change. It warns against prioritizing procedural strictness at the expense of justice, advocating for a compassionate and flexible approach to law that prioritizes fairness and equity. This analysis, which I found interesting and vital, encourages readers to reconsider the fundamental principles of justice in today's legal landscape. It stands as an invaluable addition to the justice ecosystem, reminding us of the importance of fair judgment, particularly for the poor, oppressed, and marginalized."

—Professor Joy Ngozi Ezeilo, SAN, OON
(BBC recognized 100 Women of Impact in the World 2022)
Professor of Public Law Former Dean,
Faculty of Law, University of Nigeria (UNN), Enugu Campus
Founding Director, Women's Aid Collective (WACOL)
UN International Fact-Finding Mission on
Sudan Former United Nations Special Rapporteur on
Trafficking in Persons

"This book, The Act of Judging in Nigeria: A Matter of Interpretation and Judicial Discretion, by Ari Niki-Tobi, is an excellent work defining the act of judging in Nigeria within the context of social realities in the context of statutory interpretation and the use of judicial discretion. By use of empirical case-law and visuals the author shows how judicial jurisprudence responds to changes in culture and social values, thus questioning received wisdom of formalism dictating strict adherence to common law principles of precedent. Rather the book normatively recommends a flexible adherence to precedent that takes account of social change guided by principles of empathy, and context. If anything, it reminds judges that canon of interpretation are mere means, not ends in themselves.... In all, the book is an eye-opener to new vista in judging, inviting judges to discard old ways of interpreting statutes- formalism- dogmatic allegiance to stare decisis. It says in effect, "judges come down from the high horse." See the reality on ground. Stay concrete. Use the socio-judicial approach in the act of judging."

—Professor Festus Oghenemaro Emiri, SAN
Chairman, Nigerian Bar Association Institute of Continuing Legal Education (NBA-ICLE) Board
Former Director General of Nigerian Law School, Enugu Campus.
Former Dean of Law, Delta State University, Nigeria.

"A concise book on the act of judging in Nigeria, with prospects for shaping the emergence of judicial studies as a field of study."

—Ayodele Atsenuwa
Professor of Public Law, Former Deputy Vice Chancellor, Developments
University of Lagos, Lagos, Nigeria.

"Judge Niki-Tobi's book makes a valuable contribution to the comparative study of law and the interplay of domestic and international law. Her far-reaching analysis shows exemplary attention to nuance and context and draws out the complexities of the actual practice of law in an increasingly interconnected and interdependent world."

—Dr. Brett Heindl,
Chair Political Science Department,
Associate Dean, School of Liberal Arts and Business
State University of New York, Oneonta., U.S.A.

"Ari Niki-Tobi in this timely and robust discussion of judicial interpretation of statutes joins a debate poised to become a defining one for how governance evolves in Nigeria. One honorific heritage of British colonial rule in Nigeria is the tradition of a much-regarded judicial system and quite a number of highly respected jurists. The view on the streets in Nigeria today and from noted commentators like Chidi Odinkalu is that the heritage may have evaporated. Rankings of judicial systems in Africa which have gone viral on social media suggest Nigeria does not make the top ten while judicial systems like Botswana whose Chief Justice was once a judge on loan from Nigeria, Justice Akintola Aguda (1923-2001) made the top 10 cut. Ari's analysis of discretion in judicial interpretation of statutes may have explianary power for understanding the shifting status of Nigerian judiciary in the eyes of the analyst. Whether it is Laissez Faire era writer Caude-Frederic Bastiat, author of The Law, urging Property Rights, or Chidi Odinkalu throwing up evidence of how contemporary judges subvert justice in Nigeria, the matter of trouble of judicial discretion remains valued subject of academic explication in this book. In his book, The Selectorate: When Judges Topple the People, Odinkalu focuses on the trend since 2023 in which the courts determine who emerges 'elected' in Nigeria, prompting political actors to seek to influence the pipeline of judicial appointments. Where in the U.S. a similar trend can be witnessed on ideological basis with the U.S. Supreme Court appointments, in Nigeria, it is about filling the pipelines with cronies who can subvert the will of the people, hiding behind the cloak of judicial robes. Ari explores the jurisprudence on these matters where judges can use precedence and technicalities in pronouncement where Constitutions need clarity or read culture and social trends in becoming a force for positive change. The latter category to which Ari's erudite father, Niki-Tobi (1940-2016) belongs, no doubt about is the general preferences of the liberal. Ari in this intellectual journey, follows in the spirit of her father. As one who teacher's entrepreneurship and celebrates the point that its triumph in countries like the United States can be tracked to judicial pronouncements by Louis Brandeis in the U.S. Supreme Court, by economists like Ragurham Rajan and Luigi Zingales, in the book Saving Capitalism from the Capitalists, identify with the thrust of Ari Niki-Tob's inclination. This book is surely a worthwhile contribution and should be read as part of an effort to throw light on judicial discretion. Current Nigerian experience clearly suggests that judicial discretion in interpretation, even judicial activism, can be used or abused relative to the common good. A journal of instruction' or guidebook is therefore of major need. Therein lies the value of this volume. U.S. Secretary of State Maco Rubio, sanctioning Brazilian judge Alexander Moraes using the Global Magnitsky Act, point to the increasingly 'hot peppersoup' territory judicial discretion has become, and the need for though leadership on it. We therefore owe Ari Niki-Tobi a great debt of gratitude for the focus of this book."

—Patrick Okedinachi Utomi (Prof. Pat Utomi)
Founding faculty, Lagos Business School, Oan Atlantic University.
Former Global Policy Scholar and BCM Fellow at
Woodrow Wilson Center, Washington DC.
Founder, Center for Values in Leadership.
Former presidential candidate, Nigeria's 2021 election.

"Dr. Ari-Niki Tobi has taken on a difficult but important area of law and handled it so dexterously as only someone with her background as a lawyer, judge and an educator with extensive exposure to national and international legal systems can do. I recommend this book to lawyers who want to understand what goes on in the minds of judges as they adjudicate complex cases. I also recommend this book to students, scholars and those interested in how judges, who occupy a prime place of importance in the functioning of the judiciary, go about executing 'the art of judging'."

—Emmanuel Emenyonu, (MBA, Ph.D., LLB)
Professor, Southern Connecticut State University, USA

"I like the practicality of this book "The Act of Judging in Nigeria: A Matter of Interpretation and Judicial Discretion." It recognizes the act of judging as interpretational and discretionary and exemplifies how judges should adjudicate. It is an adjudication-made easy handbook. An interesting read, especially as it gives first-hand narratives from judges themselves as they know and experience the act of judging. Every judge, especially aspiring judges will find this book instructive. Lawyers will find it indicative. Socio-legal scholars will find it illuminating. Legal scholars will find it timely and enlightening. Scholars in the social sciences will find it expository, and the public/court users will find it very helpful. This book offers something to everyone, and it almost offers everything to anyone who is engaged in the judicial craft."

—Dr. Sam Amadi,
Director, Abuja School of Social and Political Thought, Nigeria.

"I have read snippets from Ari's book "The Act of Judging in Nigeria and have no hesitation in endorsing the same. Ari comes from a family of Judges. Her late father was a Justice of the highest Court in Nigeria and her brother is currently a Justice of the Court of Appeal. It was my privilege to have known and appeared before the legendary Niki Tobi, JSC (RTD). He was a Judge famous for his integrity and understanding of the Law. Ari herself was a Judge at the Lower Court in Lagos State Nigeria for many years. This book is revolutionary as it challenges one of the most entrenched principles of the Common Law System - the Principle of stare decisis. I eagerly look forward to reading the entire book."

—Wole Olufon,
Wole Olufon & Co
Chairman, Board of Trustees,
Christian Lawyers Fellowship of Nigeria

"Ari Niki-Tobi's "The Act of Judging in Nigeria" boldly reimagines judicial practices, advocating for interpretation that reflects evolving social realities. This groundbreaking work challenges traditional adherence to precedent, urging judges to weave empathy and societal values into their decisions. With insights from Nigerian judges, it offers a rate and profound look into the complexities of judicial discretion. A beacon of hope for change, this book urges that law must reflect the "spirit and pulse" of the society. It compels legal professionals, scholars, and engaged citizens to rethink justice and its application in a rapidly changing world. Don't miss this seminal work poised to reshape global perspectives on law and society."

—Ope Olusaga
CEO of LawPavillion,
Nigeria's Pioneer Electronic Law Reports.

"I wholeheartedly endorse this groundbreaking book by Ari Niki-Tobi, which offers an insightful and bold re-examination of judging in Nigeria. It thoughtfully challenges traditional doctrines of precedent and advocates for a socially responsive judicial approach. As an advocate for alternative dispute resolution and judicial reform, I commend the author's courage in weaving personal experience, judicial interviews, and pragmatic analysis into a compelling narrative. This work is a vital contribution to judicial jurisprudence and a must-read for judges, lawyers, scholars, and policymakers committed to justice that evolves with society. I am honoured to support this important and timely publication."

—Dr. Adv. D Deepika Saini
Advocate – Supreme Court of India Founder, Chairperson & Mediator
Institute for Alternative Dispute Resolution, New Delhi, India.

"I heartily congratulate Judge Ari on this groundbreaking book, which brings to life real cases narrated by the judges themselves. It's a rare and invaluable resource that deepens our understanding of societal conflicts, justice, and the transformative power of jurisprudence. This book not only sheds light on conflict resolution within the Nigerian context but also offers universally relevant insights, setting precedents and providing guidance for righteous conduct among individuals and institutions worldwide. I'm eagerly looking forward to reading this book and commend Judge Ari for this excellent initiative, which proudly carries forward the legacy of her distinguished family."

—Dr. Harbeen Arora Rai
Founder, G100
ALL Ladies League (ALL) | Women Economic Forum (WEF)
WICCI, Women's Indian Chamber of Commerce and Industry
SHEconomy

"This book's relevance is not just the Nigerian judiciary, but also the English judiciary from where Nigeria obtained her Common Law. It challenges the status quo of precedent and advocates for social change. A timely book for all and sundry. As we learn more about judges, judges must also learn more about the public by showing empathy as the author advocates through her socio-judicial theory. Notable is the author's open letter to judges at the end of the book, quoting the ultimate Judge's admonition to do justice. Indeed, judging is a divine calling. God expects so much from judges and so do we. So, despite the social and political challenges, judges should pursue godly justice."

—Pastor Leke Sanusi, Esq.
Presiding pastor, The Redeemed Christian Church of God,
Victory House, London, UK.

Author's Note

The journey to writing this book started over two decades ago, and it materialized into my master's thesis in 2018. Those days when I engaged my late father in talks about judging and society during and after dinner, I did not know that the notes I took would materialize into a book decades later. That is why this book is to his honor– he worked the work, walked the walk, and talked the talk of judging in Nigeria.

This book is based on my master's thesis, originally submitted to the University of Nevada, Reno, and available at <https://scholarwolf.unr.edu/items/15570e9f-ffa2-486b-a133-fdd404f4fde3>. Significant revisions and additions have been made to adapt it for a broader readership.

It was tough getting research materials to support my hypothesis, especially as I am not based in Nigeria. The scarcity in materials delayed this work, as writing with insufficient online material meant extra work. Collating these materials was challenging as most text and caselaw were not online. In addition, I also needed to verify that whatever I obtained online is from the right source. So, I had to contact experts in Nigeria—several judges, lawyers and court staff to get the correct and up to date information. I also had to travel to base.

The experts in this field of research are not your regular experts. They are not law school professors, researchers or scholars, social or political scientist, or even lawyers who are renowned and celebrated on the Internet as experts of their art. They are the invisible persons behind the scenes. They are the superheroes who often save the day. They are distinguished personalities, a majority of whom have not written or published in the areas of their expertise, because of the nature of their jobs. They are judges. Hence, the informant interviews that I used are key reference materials. My informants are live judges (not AI agents). I had to patiently wait to get their undivided attention and honest opinions, some of which were face to face.

It took over five years to fit into their various busy schedules, but I believe the delay and wait were worth it. Some of these judges, as I indicated in my acknowledgment practically just returned from emptying their dockets from a trial/hearing in court, and recieved my laidback time zone call (New York time is 7/8 hours behind Nigerian time), and in their magnanimity, they still picked my call and answered my tasking questions. I feel honored and privileged. My lords and my ladies, as you read this, I want you all to know the great contributions that you have all made in advancing African jurisprudence globally. I do not take this for granted. Dear Judges, I cannot thank you enough for giving the world, this overdue privilege to read about the modalities of Nigerian courts. I AM GRATEFUL!

Therefore, I employ my academic/intellectual readers and colleagues to discountenance the status quo, which is a tenacious requirement and over-dependence on peer-reviewed published articles or books, as a more reliable academic source. Some information in this book are not peer reviewed but are the real McCoy, straight from the mouth of the key actors themselves—senior, renowned, and respected Nigerian judges with high degrees of experience, integrity, and intellect. What you read here is from outstanding Nigerian judges as they saw it, as they experienced it, as they executed it, and as they still live it. They are my number one experts. One can't get a better source than this.

I am humbled and grateful to say this book is the very first of its kind anywhere globally, so in addition to the informant narratives, I have cited some published materials, which I confirmed are genuine, but not peer reviewed. So, I employ the grace and empathy of fellow scholars who may be ardent about peer-review citations in my bibliography. There is no better peer review out there than the informant narratives that I have reported and quoted in this book. As a pragmatic person, I believe in narratives and up-to-date research materials that give a clear and direct picture. Please don't get me wrong. I have nothing against peer-reviewed articles or books. As I acknowledged above, they have helped me a lot in shaping and reinforcing my ideas, but for the nitty-gritty of my topic, I needed more than publications or articles with information that could have changed from when they were peer-reviewed. I needed "hands-on" narratives on the latest information and for the most part, these narratives are not documented.

Furthermore, in my over ten years of experience, as a magistrate judge in Lagos State, Nigeria, specifically who presided at the Igbosere, Tinubu, and Adeniran Ogunsaya magistrate courts, some of the busiest and most daring magistrate courts in Lagos State, I had first-hand encounters. I had burdensome dockets that gave me the privilege to write over a thousand judgments and rulings. So, I am not a stranger to the act of judging. I also watched and learned from my late father who was one of the finest judges I know. I read a couple of his judgments, all of which could take a lifetime to finish reading. He taught me the skills and art of judging, which inspired the act of judging. So, in understudying him for over three decades from a close geographical space at home, I acquired a lot of knowledge that inspired my research, which produced this book. I particularly recall vital skills he revealed about judging during the famous O.J. Simpson live trial, which we watched together as a ritual (never missed a day of the live coverage). He supported Marcia Clerk, and I Johnnie Cochran. His predications from Judge Alito's act of judging remain with me till today. Accordingly, this book is a combination of my personal experiences as a former magistrate judge, the experiences of my late father and mentor, and the experiences of other judges.

Lastly, I understand that being a unique addition to the jurisprudence of Nigerian texts (and other Common Law countries) on courts and judges, it will be useful to the public, litigants and court users. Hence, I tried to write with simple terms, words, and expressions. I explained words that non-lawyers and students can read and understand. I hope that I achieved my objective. Also, although this is a book inspired by a Nigerian judge, and written about the Nigerian judiciary, it is not tailored to fit only the Nigerian judicial process. It is written for global readers. Judges from other countries will find my theory, principles, the Nigerian caselaw, and jurisprudence very informative, useful, impactful, and instructive in their various acts of judging. In addition, the principles, reasonings, and caselaw this book offers could be a one-stop research hub for students from diverse law schools and judicial colleges and institutes. And to my fellow socio-legal scholars, this is your platform and inspiration to create new research interests. I hope that this book challenges some of you to do more research and expand on my writing and possibly write yours too. I look forward to reading your articles or books.

Thank you for buying, reading, or even glancing through my book!

Respectfully,
Ari Niki-Tobi

About the Author

Ari Niki-Tobi is a U.S.-based Nigerian researcher. She is the founder and CEO of A.T. Socio-Judicial Consulting—a research-based consulting firm focused on advancing judicial jurisprudence and building or rebuilding public confidence in courts through research, literature, presentations, and programs. She taught sociology of law, introduction to law, criminology, and criminal justice as an adjunct.

Ari was a magistrate judge at the Lagos State Judiciary in Nigeria. She retired after twelve years from general jurisdiction adjudication to pursue postgraduate studies in Nevada, U.S., where she obtained both master's and doctorate degrees in judicial studies from the University of Nevada, Reno. Ari also earned a master's degree in law from the University of Lagos, Nigeria.

Following two decades of research on her unique focus—courts and society—Ari developed her socio-judicialism theory for judicial development and initiated the Courts & Society Webinar Series, which addresses international socio-judicial concerns. Through this theory, Ari also developed a socio-judicial pedagogy for teaching socio-legal and interdisciplinary courses, which she is presenting at conferences.

Ari's judicial knowledge from Nigeria and the United States informs her comparative approach. Her combined experiences in pro bono human rights practice, the judiciary, judicial education, as a court user and from society add a unique flair to her work.

Ari has published about ten peer-reviewed articles and three book chapters, including a contribution to the Routledge Democracy and Security Handbook. She has presented at over twenty international conferences on unique research topics. Ari's research and writings are based on personal experiences and informant interview data, including direct narratives from distinguished judges of various courts (a rare privilege she is thankful for).

Her literature features unpublished expert narratives of judges' unique experiences and encounters inside and outside the courtroom.

Ari is the first Nigerian and African woman to earn a master's degree in judicial studies, as well as the first Black woman to obtain a Ph.D. in judicial studies worldwide.

List of Figures

List of Abbreviations

AC	Appeal Court
AI	Artificial Intelligence
CJ	Chief Judge
CJN	Chief Justice of Nigeria
ECOWAS	Economic Community of West African States
E.R.	English Reports
FCT	Federal Capital Territory of Nigeria, Abuja
FWLR	Federation Weekly Law Report
HOD	Head of Department
ICJ	International Court of Justice
J	Judge
JCA	Justice of the Court of Appeal
JSC	Justice of the Supreme Court
KB	King's Bench
LGBTQ	Lesbian Gay Bisexual Transgender Queer
LPELR	Law Pavilion Electronic Law Report
NCLR	Nigerian Courts Law Report
NLR	Nigerian Law Report
NSCC	Nigerian Supreme Court Cases
NWLR	Nigerian Weekly Law Report
NJC	National Judicial Commission
Ors	Others
PCA	President of the Court of Appeal
PJCA	Presiding Justice of the Court of Appeal
Pt.	Part
SAN	Senior Advocate of Nigeria
SC	Supreme Court
SCNJ	Supreme Court of Nigeria Judgments
SCOTUS	The Supreme Court of the United States
UN	United Nations
U.S.	United States
WRN	Weekly Report of Nigeria
WACA	West African Court of Appeal

Chapter 1
Historical Perspective of Judging in Nigeria

The Nigerian Legal System attained sovereignty and republican status way back in October 1963 when the Supreme Court and not the Judicial Committee of the Privy Council became the final Court of Appeal, Section 120 of the 1963 Republican Constitution did it all, thus making section 114 of the 1960 Independence Constitution not only moribund but completely dead. England is English. Nigeria is Nigerian. The English are English as also Nigerians are Nigerians. Theirs are theirs. Ours are ours. Theirs are not ours. Ours are not theirs. We cannot therefore continue to enjoy this "borrowing spree" or "merry frolic" at the expense and to the detriment of our legal system. We cannot continue to pay loyalty to our colonial past with such servility or servitude. After all, we are no more in slavery. While some of our laws make omnibus provisions to fall back on English laws, and English rules of Court, these can only be resorted to in appropriate circumstances where our local laws and rules of court are silent.[1]

—Hon. Justice Niki Tobi, JCA (as he then was).

1 Introduction

This chapter provides a brief history of the Nigerian judicial system, explaining the historical context of judging in Nigeria. It reviews the structure of Nigerian courts and explains the sources of Nigerian law and how these sources empower judging in contemporary Nigerian courts. Further, this chapter will explain the structures, organization, powers, and norms of Nigerian courts, and also details of the selection and appointment of judges, and the procedure of assignment of cases in the various courts. It also explains judging in Nigeria as an act that encompasses judicial interpretation and the exercise of judicial discretion. By the end of this chapter, the readers will better understand the history of judging in Nigeria, the origin of Nigerian

1 Caribbean Trading & Fidelity Corporation V. NNPC (1992) 7 NWLR pt. 252 p. 161.

courts, and the structure, organization, hierarchy, procedures, and norms of Nigerian courts.

2 Brief History of the Nigerian Judicial System

The Nigerian judicial system is unavoidably connected to the Nigerian legal system. Thus, we can trace its history to the history of the Nigerian legal system. Olagunju opines that the Nigerian legal system encompasses the laws that are applicable in the courts.[2] According to precolonial historical records, there existed territories that constituted the entity that eventually became Nigeria, and these entities had a somewhat formal administration of justice, although not as formal or sophisticated as the British. Nevertheless, this system of justice was patterned after the indigenous people and was quite effective until the British took over.[3]

Accordingly, the history of Nigeria's judicial system dates to the traditional colonies from the fifteenth century, which eventually formed the territory of Nigeria in the eighteenth to nineteenth centuries.[4] Thus, the judicial system of the Federal Republic of Nigeria is (somewhat) a hybrid of the English Common Law, some aspects of American law,[5] and aspects of the Nigerian precolonial judicial system. Before the establishment of Common Law principles of adjudication by the British in 1861, traditional Nigeria applied customary arbitration to resolve disputes and maintain order in society.[6] This traditional adjudication system evolved over three political eras: the precolonial, the colonial, and the post-colonial eras, and eventually formed the bedrock of the present Nigerian judicial system,[7] as Figure 1.1 and the following explanations depict.

---

2 Olagunju, G. A. (2006). Historical Development of Nigerian Legal System From Colonialism to Present. In Asaju. D. F. (Ed.) Readings in General Studies Volume Two (pp. 306–314). Lagos State University Press.

3 Ibid: 307.

4 Ibid.

5 The influence of American criminal law on the Nigerian justice system is a recent development in the early–mid twentieth century; see the plea bargaining procedure adopted in Nigeria's criminal justice system.

6 Tobi, N. (1992). The Nigerian Judge. A&T Professional Publishers, Nigeria: 1.

7 Ibid.

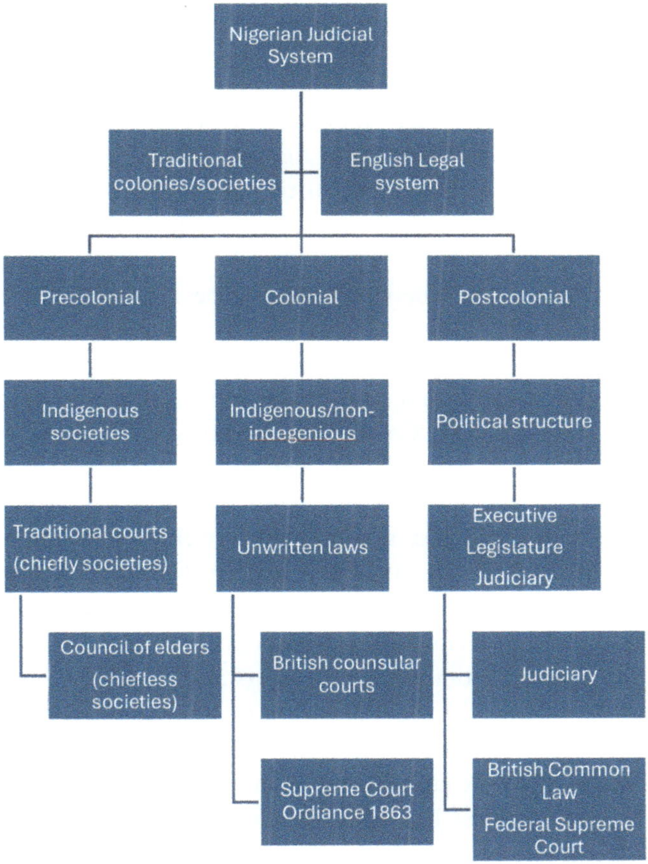

Figure 1.1: The History of The Nigerian Judicial System[8]

2.1 Precolonial Era (1500–1861)

This era though not definite was predicted from the fifteenth to eighteenth centuries.[9] Before the colonization of the entity now known as Nigeria, numerous Indigenous tribes, groups, or territories had their own systems of governance and judicial administration. Traditional courts applied their

---

8 I created this diagram to simplify the historical dimension of the Nigerian judiciary.

9 Tobi, opcit.

respective modes of judging; traditional rulers presided over disputes and resolved them according to the Indigenous governing laws of the land (i.e., laws developed from the customs of the people). This system of justice was informal yet effective. The arrival of the British and colonization led to a more modern adjudicatory system in the communities.[10]

Before the formal arrival of the British, on the Coast of West Africa, which later included some regions of Nigeria, like Lagos, Benin, Bonny, Brass, New Calabar (present Degema), and Old Calabar (present Calabar), there were trading activities between the indigenes and the British and other foreign merchants.[11] The disputes that arose from these trade transactions were usually settled by the Indigenous courts, but the British merchants were usually frustrated with the customary court system as they found the court systems strange to the Common Law court structure they practiced. Thus, the foreign merchants did not believe they could get justice from Indigenous courts, which eventually led to the creation of English courts.[12]

The Indigenous legal systems ensured the convenience of judicial administration and divided traditional societies into *chiefly* and *chiefless* societies—both types influenced the style of "judging" in customary courts. The chiefly societies comprised the Hausa/Fulani communities (in the Northern region) and the Yoruba/Benin communities (in parts of the Southern region). The chiefless societies were the Ibos, also from the southern province.[13] In the Yoruba communities, the Alaafin, the administrative and political head of the Oyo Empire, oversaw the empire with assistance from the council of seven chiefs called the Oyomesi, headed by the Bashorun. The Alaafin in council operated as a traditional royal court, like courts of superior jurisdiction today. The Alaafin judged severe offenses like murder, treason, arson, and armed robbery, while the chiefs presided over minor misdemeanors within their respective regions.[14] This system operated more like courts of trial and

10 Ibid.

11 Ibid.

12 Ibid.

13 Ibid.

14 Adebayo, W. (2014). Yoruba Precolonial Political System. Nigerian History. <https://waidigbenro.wordpress.com/2014/10/27/yoruba-precolonial-political-system/>

appellate jurisdictions.[15] Also, in the Northern region of Nigeria, like the *Alaafin*, the *Emir*, had both appellate and original jurisdiction to preside over serious offenses. Subordinate chiefs known as *Alkalis*, who headed courts in different districts or zones, aided the *Emir*. Further, the *Mufti mallams* who were knowledgeable in Sharia law assisted the *Alkalis* with Sharia law. This system of justice in historic Northern Nigeria resembled the modern court system.[16]

The process of judging in the chiefly societies was more formal and rigid than judging in the chiefless societies.[17] Judging in the chiefless societies was based on institutions, which were republican in structure and function. Tobi gave an example of this when he said that in Iboland, the Council of Elders was charged with the responsibility of administering justice by the customs and cultures of the people.[18] So, the Council of Elders was the fountain of justice, and as a matter of practice, adult male members of the family or village first handled disputes as cases came up.[19]

In comparing the traditional system of judging with the English system of judging, Tobi noted that unlike the English system, which was and is still individualistic, traditional systems were essentially collectivist.[20] In other words, traditional systems did not enact or perceive justice in abstract terms; rather it was equated to moral standards in the society.[21] Hence, traditional systems did not follow legal technicalities. Traditional courts were not established to administer technicalities of law but rather the moral content of law, as social discipline in the fabric of the polity. Therefore, traditional courts were essentially moral courts, as they decided cases based upon local concepts of morality and enforced the moral values of the local people through the decisions they reached.[22] Even though the system of justice in traditional Nigeria was informal, it had a formal structure of judging that was very effective, as

15 Although not the focus of this paper, traditional means of adjudication were argueably more effective in society, especially in the traditional administration of criminal justice.
16 See Ojomo, E. , History of the Nigerian Judicial System, Introduction to Law, opcit:4.
17 Ibid: 2.
18 Ibid.
19 Ibid: 4.
20 Tobi, opcit: 7.
21 Ibid (1992).
22 Ibid: 5.

the chiefs/family heads upheld and applied cultural values, norms, customs, principles, views, and social interests as they judged. The dispensation of justice in traditional settings though different from the British pattern had the same goal of ensuring due compliance to the established law and customs.

2.2 Colonial Era (1861–1963)

As stated above, the traditional justice system, applicable to both natives and non-natives, was based largely on unwritten laws. Hence, it was difficult for non-natives to understand the traditional act of judging because it challenged foreigners when trade ties increased between locals and European traders in the region. Consequently, the British introduced consul courts to preside over trade disputes involving foreigners and natives, while traditional courts continued to administer justice according to precolonial practices.[23] Subsequently, when the nineteenth-century courts of equity were established, they focused on commercial relations and not governance or justice issues, like the consul courts.[24] This led to a divergence of the legal system in those colonies that eventually became Nigeria.

Nigeria became a British colony in 1861 upon the annexation of the colonies that eventually became the Federation of Nigeria. Subsequently, the amalgamation of the protectorate of Southern Nigeria and the protectorate of Northern Nigeria earnestly imported the British system of governance into Nigeria. The Supreme Court Ordinance of 1863 established the Supreme Court in the Territory of Lagos, with both civil and criminal jurisdiction. Subsequently, the Supreme Court Ordinance of 1876 was enacted and established the Supreme Court for the Colony that applied Common Law, doctrines of equity, and statutes of general application, used (in England), on July 24, 1874. In 1887, after Lagos and other surrounding protectorates became a colony, a new Supreme Court was established under a new Supreme Court Ordinance.[25]

Upon colonizing Nigeria, the British system embraced and recognized the society's interests, views, and culture. Thus, in the case of *Laoye & Ors*

---

23 Edefe, *opcit*: 4.

24 In other words, chancery court of equity assumed jurisdiction over trade disputes that was previously the role of consul courts, while the consul courts heard cases of governance and justice issues.

25 Tobi, opcit.

v. Oyetunde,[26] the Committee of the Privy Council said, "the policy of the British in this and other respects is to use for purpose of administration of the country the native laws and customs in so far as possible as they have not been varied by status or ordinances affecting Nigeria." Even though the British system recognized and acknowledged the traditional system outside the framework of English law and jurisprudence, English judicial practice and principles appeared to have replaced traditional practice in many areas of Nigerian courts. For example, the method of swearing in witnesses or taking the oath before giving evidence reflects English influence on the traditional system.[27] Also, the norms and procedures of trials—such as the modern courtroom settings, the witness box, the judge's use of a gavel are all inherited English norms that Nigeria courts still practice.[28]

2.3 Post-Colonial Era (1963–1999)

Nigeria became independent on October 1, 1960, with a Constitution and power to make laws for the protectorate. This established a Federal Supreme Court that consisted of the Chief Justice of the Federation and the federal justices.[29]

After Nigeria's independence from British rule, the political structure experienced drastic changes as the legislature, executive, and judicial arms of government metamorphosed, yet the judiciary maintained significant elements of the British Common Law.

Consequently, the British government established a Federal Supreme Court as the land's highest court. They also established the Judicial Committee of the Privy Council, with high courts, magistrate courts, and customary or native courts in various regions (now known as states). From the above, the impact of the British system and hierarchy in Nigerian courts remain steady until this day.

Since Nigeria's independence, the judiciary has experienced substantial structural changes due to the adoption of various Constitutions. The 1960 Independence Constitution abolished criminal jurisdiction under customary law because criminal offenders could not be convicted of an offense

26 Laoye & Ors v. Oyetunde 1944 A.C 170.

27 In traditional Nigerian courts, oaths were taken, and witnesses were sworn in by customary rituals and not with the Holy Bible or Holy Quran as is today.

28 Olagunju (2006), opcit: 308.

29 Ibid: 312.

unless the offense existed under written law. The sole exception to the written law requirement was contempt of court, for which punishment could be imposed.[30] When Nigeria became a Republic in 1963, the Republican Constitution abolished British rule in Nigeria and terminated Nigeria's allegiance to British rule.[31] The 1963 Constitution replaced the Privy Council with the Supreme Court of Nigeria, making the Supreme Court the highest court in the country. Then, the military coup in 1966 interrupted the constitutional autonomy of the judiciary, and this interfered with the liberty of judges to adjudicate as constitutionally required.[32] Nevertheless, the Nigerian Supreme Court remained resilient to its judicial roles. A lot of positive and negative reforms and changes accompanied the military interference.[33] In 1976, the federal high courts and the Court of Appeal were established under the military regime that ensured appeals ascending from the high courts to the Supreme Court, following the hierarchy of courts. The military also set up ad hoc tribunals as part of the court system. Hence, in place of the 1963 Constitution, decrees and edicts became the ground rule that overrode constitutional provisions in most instances, and the tribunals' decisions in most instances could not be appealed, except to the Supreme Military Council.[34]

Furthermore, the military regime by Decree No. 17 of 1967 divided Nigeria into 12 states, and in 1976, the states were further divided into 19 states and a Federal Capital Territory. In 1987, the states increased to 21, and then to 30 states in 1991. Next, in 1996, 36 states were further created from the four regions in Nigeria (North, South, East, and West). These regions form six geo-political zones (North-central, North-East, North-West, South-East, South-South, and South-West).[35] The categorization of these regions was based on *federal character.*[36] The Nigerian judiciary is structured to fit into the country's federal structure with equal representation of all and sundry,[37]

30 See section 21(10) of the Independence Constitution of 1960.
31 Tobi, opcit: 12.
32 The Constitution that empowered the courts was suspended by the military decree.
33 Olagunju, opcit: 313.
34 Ibid.
35 UN, Sustainable Urban Development and Good Governance in Nigeria, opcit: 4.
36 This means the appointment of judges are region based.
37 This means an equal number or courts and judges from each of the six regions are represented in the federal courts.

which means individual states from the six geo-political zones/regions of Nigeria have quotas in the court system, and judges are appointed according to their respective quotas or regions.

Nigeria's return to democratic rule took several twists and turns but eventually in May 29, 1999, the military regime bantered nation had a safe landing on what now appears as a lasting democracy. Accordingly, the return to democratic rule since 1999 has restored the Nigerian legal system to constitutional governance with the Supreme Court serving as the highest court of appeal, followed by the Court of Appeal as the next court in the hierarchy, and then the high courts, magistrate courts, area courts and customary courts as the lower courts in the hierarchy order.[38]

3 The Sources of Nigerian Law

A combination of the precolonial, colonial, and post-colonial periods of history collectively produced the sources of Nigerian law that have largely influenced the operation of the judicial system. These sources of law dictate the act of judging in Nigeria, as judicial decisions emanate from the sources of Nigeran law, which are part of the Nigerian legal system.

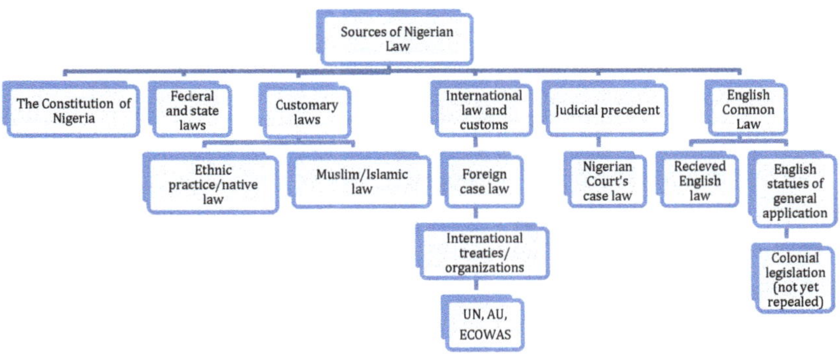

Figure 1.2: The Sources of Nigerian Law[39]

---

38 Olagunju, opcit.

39 I created this diagram to explain the overview of what influences judging in Nigeria.

The sources of Nigerian law explain the origin of judging in Nigeria. These sources impact the judiciary and transform judges in various courts across eras of Nigeria's legal history. The transition through Nigeria's history continues to influence approaches to judging in Nigeria. As Figure 1.2 portrays, the sources of Nigerian law are as follows:

3.1 The Constitution of the Federal Republic of Nigeria

Section 6 of the Constitution establishes the judicial arm of government, which dictates judicial powers that direct the act of judging in Nigeria. In *A.G. Federation v. Abubakar,*[40] the Supreme Court held that the Constitution is the organic law or ground norm of the people. It is the unifying force in the nation, and it apportions rights and imposes obligations on the people who are subject to its operations.[41]

3.2 The Federal and State Legislation

The Constitution empowers the National Assembly and State Houses of Assemblies to make laws that have the force of law in the country. Some of these laws enable the act of judging in Nigeria and empower judicial interpretation. The Supreme Court in *A.G. Federation v. Abubakar*[42] added that the Constitution is the formulation of all the laws from which the institutions of the state derive their creation and legitimacy.

3.3 Customary Laws

These laws developed from the customs, traditions, and usage of the Nigerian people or society. Although there are arguments that customary laws and traditions do not include Islamic law, for this book's arguments and based on precolonial categorization, we will assume that Islamic law is part of customary law. Although Tobi categorized Islamic law under customary law, he argues that Islamic law has a separate and distinct identity from customary

---

40 A.G. Federation v. Abubakar (2007) 10 NWLR (pt.1041) 1 at 118, G-H.
41 Ibid, Walter Onnoghen, JSC.
42 A.G. Federation v. Abubakar (supra).

law.[43] Also, in *Alkamawa v. Bello*,[44] Wali, JSC, argued that Islamic law is not the same as customary law because it does not belong to a particular tribe, and it is more rigid and universal than even the English law. Nevertheless, since Islamic laws codifies customary practices of Islam, this book classifies Islamic law as customary law. Accordingly, Nigeria's customary practices are categorized into ethnic practices and native law, and Muslim or Islamic laws.

3.3.1 Ethnic Practices and Native Law

Ethnic practices and native law were customary to the indigenes before the advent of the British. These laws were the traditional practice of governance in Nigeria (*chiefly* and *chiefless* societies). Each ethnic entity had its own system of governance. Though unwritten, customary ethnic practices or "informal laws" were adopted in customary courts, presently customary/area courts are established in states across the country to hear matters under ethnic practices and native law.[45] The courts administer the appropriate customary law in the land where the court is situated.[46] Customary courts have similar jurisdictions as the regular "English courts," but like the magistrate court, they do not take priority as regular courts in the judicial system.[47] Hence, section 280 (1) of the Constitution states that "there shall be for any state that requires it, a customary court of appeal for that state." Thus, customary courts have taken the back seat in judicial practice. Customary courts are not strictly bound by the rules of evidence or technicalities like regular courts; rather, they are bound by the rules of natural justice, equality, and good conscience.[48] Although judges of these courts are lawyers, they are not necessarily required to be lawyers; neither are they required to be knowledgeable in the law.[49]

---

43 Tobi, opcit.
44 Alkamawa v. Bello (1998) 8 NWLR (pt. 561) 173.
45 Section 6(5) (j) of the Constitution.
46 See *Dada v. Faleye (2007) ALL FWLR (Pt. 349) 1134 at 1146 Paras. A-B (CA).*
47 This shows that customary courts are not as significant to the society as regular courts.
48 See *Ekweghiariri v. Unachukwu & Ors (2013) LPELR-22074 (CA).*
49 See *Oke v. Nwizi (2013) LPELR-21252 (CA).*

In the case of *Ewa Ekeng Inyang v. Efana Ekeng Ita & Ors,*[50] there was a conflict of the headship of the Ewa Ekeng House of Calabar. The defendant was voted into the office at a family meeting, but the plaintiff claimed the leadership as the eldest male in the family, contending that any election was contrary to customary law and therefore ultra vires. In his judgment, the trial court commented as follows:

> Before the government came to Calabar and established law and order, it is certain that the headship of a house belonged as of right to the senior male member of the house … . No doubt in the majority of cases, the senior man was sufficiently suitable and became head without opposition. But when he was not suitable, the family had no hesitation in selecting some other member in his stead. This was only common sense and a natural adaption of custom to make conform to a change in condition. This plaintiff is asking the court to put the clock back. He wishes to deprive the family of any choice in the matter of their head. He ignores the changed circumstances of times and wishes to revert to a custom that safeguards and checks upon which can no longer be applied.

3.3.2 Muslim or Islamic Law

The Muslim or Islamic law is applicable only in the Northern part of Nigeria, where most Muslims reside. This law is based on the Islamic religion as stipulated in the Holy Quran and the teachings of the Prophet Mohammed. Section 275 of the Constitution states that "there shall be, for any state that requires it, a Sharia Court of Appeal for that state." There is a distinction between the Sharia Court of Appeal and the regular Court of Appeal. Other than the Sharia Court of Appeal being strict regarding Sharia law, this court is also not restricted to the issues raised by the parties before them.[51] Hence, unlike the regular Court of Appeal, the Sharia Court can determine issues that are not before the court in a particular case.

Although Islamic law is not widely practiced in Nigeria, its complex and sometimes contradictory norms, practices, and procedures substantially impact Nigerians and the Nigerian legal system. In the controversial case *of Commissioner of Police v. Yahaya Sheriff-Aminu,*[52] an Upper Sharia Court in Kano State of Nigeria convicted a gospel singer of blasphemy and sentenced

50 *Ewa Ekeng Inyang v. Efana Ekeng Ita & Ors (1929) 9 N.L.R.84.*

51 See *Nasi & Ors. v. Haruna (2001) LPELR-7023 (CA).*

52 *Commissioner of Police v. Yahaya Sheriff-Aminu*, (Unreported) Case No. CR/43/2020. <https://cyrilla.org/entity/yrydtdxodfe?file=16986094477028c0l3s3fmg.pdf&page=1>

him to death because he posted statements on social media that accused the revered Prophet Muhammad of bringing "an unforgivable sin to the world." The court held that regardless of the plea that the posted statement was in error, the court reiterated that the blasphemous statement was inexcusable, and since he was "of sane mind," he was guilty of the offense.[53]

3.4 Judicial Precedent/Case Law[54]

It prevails when courts must abide by or follow earlier decisions where the material facts are the same. For instance, British Common Law guided Nigerian laws while Nigerian courts relied on precedents set by Common Law courts. Judicial precedent emanates from case law (i.e., the body of principles and the rules of law that the judges establish). Over the years, Nigerian superior courts have, through their decisions, formulated precedent that establishes principles of law to guide specified legal situations.[55] In *Isaac Madubuago v. Dr. Mudiaga Odje & Ors*,[56] the Supreme Court opined that "In the hierarchy of the courts in this country, as in all other free Common Law Countries, one thing is clear, however learned a lower court considers itself to be, and however contemptuous of the higher court that lower court is, the lower court is still bound by the decisions of the higher court.

3.5 International Law, Customs, Treaties, and Conventions

By Nigeria's affiliation with other nations, through her membership in numerous international organizations like the UN, ECOWAS, etc., the international laws enacted govern Nigerian courts. In *Abacha v. Fawehinmi*,[57] the respondent contended that the African Charter on Human and People's Rights is not applicable in Nigeria. The court held otherwise as the Nigerian legislature had already domesticated the African Charter.

---

53 <https://globalfreedomofexpression.columbia.edu/cases/commissioner-of-police-v-yahaya-sharif-aminu/>

54 This topic will be discussed in detail subsequently.

55 Idahosa, C. O. (2016). "The Doctrine of "Stare Decisis and Judicial Precedent: The Need for Lower Courts to Be Bound by Decisions of The Superior Courts of Record," opcit.

56 *Isaac Madubuago v. Dr. Mudiaga Odje & Ors (1985) 10 SC 267* at pp. 268–269.

57 *Abacha v. Fawehinmi (2000) 4 FWLR 533.*

3.6 English Common Law

The English Common Law is categorized into the Received English Law and the English Law.

3.6.1 The Received English law

These were laws received from England, consisting of The Common Law, the doctrine of equity, statutes of general application in force in England on January 1, 1900, statutes, and subsidiary legislation on specified matters.

3.6.2 The English Law (statutes)

This law consists of English statutes that were enacted before October 1st 1960, before Nigeria's independence from Great Britian. Thus, these laws, which were enacted by the local colonial legislators, were extended to Nigeria and are treated as part of Nigerian legislation, and they are not yet repealed.

English Common Law and tradition formed the basis of the Nigerian judicial system. Nigeria adopted several British laws being a former British colony. Hence, the reception of English law through colonization established several principles of law emanating from the Common Law of England, which Nigerian courts still apply to date. Although some of these principles (laws) did not satisfy Nigeria's legislative scrutiny, English law has had a tremendous influence on the Nigerian legal system and forms a substantial part of Nigerian law. According to section 45 (1) of the Interpretation Act, "the Common Law of England and the doctrines of equity and the statutes of general application which were in force in England on 1st January 1900 are applicable in Nigeria, only in so far as local jurisdiction and circumstances shall permit."[58]

The Supreme Court in *Ibidapo v. Lufthansa Airlines*[59] held that all the received English laws, multilateral and bilateral agreements, concluded and extended to the Federal Republic of Nigeria shall remain valid and enforceable in Nigeria unless expressly repealed or declared invalid by a court of law or tribunal. Thus, a colonial legislation—the Carriage of Goods by Air (Colonies Protectorates and Trust Territories) order 1953 was declared as part of Nigeria law, even though it is not expressly included in the Laws of the Federation 1990.

---

58 The Interpretation Act, Cap 123, Laws of The Federation (LFN), 2004.

59 *Ibidapo v. Lufthansa Airlines* (1997) 4 NWLR 124.

4 The Constitutional Structure of Courts in Nigeria

The Nigerian Constitution's federal character influenced the court system's decentralization.[60] The Supreme Court/the Apex Court is located in Abuja, the Federal Capital Territory of Nigeria. It has original and appellate jurisdictions.[61] This court comprises twenty justices,[62] including the Chief Justice as head of the court.[63] As the final court of appeal, the Apex Court's decisions are binding on all courts.[64] Following the Supreme Court is the Court of Appeal with appellate and original jurisdiction.[65] This court also acts as an intermediate between the Supreme Court and all the other courts or tribunals. The Court of Appeal has twenty-one judicial divisions across the country.[66] Each of the twenty-one divisions has at least three justices, which forms a deciding panel. Next in the hierarchy are the high courts (Federal/Federal Capital Territory and State High Courts), and the National Industrial Court, which has similar jurisdiction with the high courts. The judges of the high courts of various states could be any number from twenty to over fifty. The Customary Court of Appeal and Sharia Court of Appeal are the lowest courts in the hierarchy of courts on record.[67]

The Constitution established these courts, also known as lower courts. They exercise mostly original jurisdiction and minimal appellate jurisdictions.[68] State high courts also exercise considerable appellate jurisdiction, like the customary courts of appeal and sharia courts of appeal which are also lower

---

60 The justices of the Courts are appointed based on the regions their states of origin are located. This is called the federal character principle. However, female judges can also be appointed based on the state of origin of their husbands, which gives them dual opportunities, unlike the male justices.

61 See sections 232–233 of the 1999 Constitution, as amended.

62 There were 21 justices, but one retired in August of 2024.

63 However, section 230 of the Constitution states the National Assembly can appoint such a number of justices in the Supreme Court, not exceeding 21.

64 See section 233(1) of the Constitution.

65 Ibid. See also 240 of the Constitution.

66 Abuja, Akure, Asaba, Awka, Benin, Calabar, Ekiti, Enugu, Gombe, Ibadan, Ilorin, Jos, Kano, Kaduna, Lagos, Makurdi, Owerri, Port Harcourt, Sokoto, Yola, and Gombe.

67 These are the courts as stated in the Constitution, and the Magistrate Courts are also part of the train, but the argument continues as to why magistrate courts, which are very important courts at the lowest hierarchy of courts is not included in the Constitution as a court of record.

68 See sections 251, 154, 262, 267, and 272 of the Constitution.

appellate courts. Although the Constitution did not establish lower courts like the magistrate courts, special courts, family, or juvenile courts, section 6(5) of the Constitution empowers the legislature to establish other courts as the law requires. Hence, the government created magistrate courts, district courts, area courts, customary courts, juvenile courts, corona courts, etc. Section 6(5) of the Nigerian Constitution resembles Article III of the Constitution of the United States, which established the Supreme Court of the United States and grants Congress the option to establish "such inferior courts" as it sees fit.[69]

According to the Nigerian Constitution, the "superior" courts of record are the Supreme Court, the Court of Appeal, the Federal High Court, the Federal Capital Territory High Court, Abuja, the state high courts, the National Industrial Court, the Customary Court of Appeal of the FCT, the customary courts of appeal, the Sharia Court of Appeal of FCT; and sharia courts of appeal. The "inferior" courts[70] include tribunals and special courts, including magistrates' and district courts, juvenile courts, customary and area courts, and courts-martial and Public Complaints Commission.[71] The bifurcation of judicial jurisdictions in Nigeria is based on geographic/cultural alignments, which ensures that individual regions and states have a strong local representation on the federal level.

Ojomo opines that the administration of justice in Nigeria since its early inception, makes a distinction between customary and non-customary jurisdictions, and the extent of that distinction was modified over time.[72] Yet the greatest change occurred with the non-customary system, which has become more sophisticated over time. Also, the wider coverage of the law has limited or restricted reliance on our customary system.[73] For instance, the strict rule of pleadings and provisions of the Evidence Act does not apply to Customary Courts. This is because the area courts and customary courts are vested with

---

69 See section 1, Article 3 of the American Constitution.

70 I oppose the use of the term "inferior courts," as I know that no court that determines the life and fate of people is inferior. I hope that someday that will be replaced with a more appropriate adjective like lower courts, which is already being used.

71 See section 6(1) of the Constitution.

72 Ogomo, E. History of the Nigerian Judicial System, Introduction to Law, opcit:9.

73 Ibid.

the jurisdiction to hear and determine only cases under native law and custom.[74] Accordingly, customary courts still adhere to customary practices and are not strictly bound to apply the Evidence Act in determining evidence,[75] while non-customary courts (basically all other courts in Nigeria) apply the Evidence Act to decide all cases. An example is the transmutation of means of acquiring evidence from an analog age to a digital age, where the use of computers and electronically generated evidence is the order of the day.

Despite the influence of English law, the Nigerian legal system, which is adversarial in nature (like the American legal system), is very complex due to legal pluralism, which was prevalent during the former colonies, and "may" have existed alongside the traditional legal system in Nigeria.[76] This is evident where customary law and practices exist alongside the inherited English legal system. However, Idem submits that the court's resolve that rules of pleadings and the Evidence Acts are inapplicable in the area, customary, or native courts is a positive development. He explained that through this resolve, the courts are attempting to free our Indigenous law, that is, customary laws, from the "straight jacket" made by our erstwhile British colonizers.[77]

---

74 Customary laws of various communities in Nigeria have their own system which the people adhere to. It is based on these customary laws that customary/area courts determine the evidence in a case.

75 Idem, U. J. (2017). The Judiciary and The Role of Customary Courts in Nigeria. Global Journal of Politics and Law Research .5 (.6), 34-49, UK: European Centre for Research Training and Development. Retrieved from https://www.eajournals.org/wp-content/uploads/The-Judiciary-and-the-Role-of-Customary-Courts-in-Nigeria.pdf. According to Idem, "prior to now, for a customary law to have a binding effect, it must be a custom that has been judicially noticed as provided for in Section 14(2) of the Evidence Act 1990 (as amended) … The court may judicially notice a custom if it has been acted upon by a court of superior or coordinate jurisdiction in the same area to an extent which justifies the court asked to apply it in assuming that the person or the class of persons concerned in that area look upon the same as binding in relation to the circumstances similar to those under consideration." Ibid: 41.

76 Legal pluralism is the existence of multiple legal systems within one geographic area. It occurs when different laws govern different groups within a country or where, to an extent, the legal systems of the Indigenous population have been given some recognition, as was the case with the received English Common Law in Nigeria and the establishment of the Privy Council as English courts in Nigeria.

77 Idem, opcit: 42.

According to Abiru, JCA,[78] during colonialism, western countries transported and transplanted their brand of law and legal mechanisms to the territories they annexed. So, they enforced these laws and legal mechanisms in those territories without much regard for existing customary laws that were hitherto prevalent in the communities.[79] For instance, bigamy is still an offense under criminal law of some states in Nigeria, even though polygamy was (and still is) a cultural norm. This clearly demonstrates that Nigerian courts still rely on foreign or English authorities while construing provisions of Nigerian statutes that have English equivalents. In other words, despite the independence of the Nigerian legal system in 1963 within a sovereign Nigerian nation, the English justice system still has a significant impact on Nigerian courts. These impacts are also regarding the legal/judicial culture where Nigerian courts imbibed the British legal culture in dressings, procedure, and nomenclature. Olagunju summarized the above arguments as follows:

> The Nigerian legal system which encompasses all the laws in Nigeria together with their system of application, in and before our courts has a checkered history. The incursion of the British and their other fellow adventures into the shores of Africa on colonialist mission brought with it some pains as well as some gains. In Nigeria as well as in some other African countries, these adventures brought with them their laws which eventually were used to supplant the customs and practices of the Indigenous people under their rule.[80]

Therefore, Tobi's introductory quote in *Caribbean Trading & Fidelity Corporation v. NNPC*,[81] notes that Nigeria is now independent, although the Nigerian legal system attained sovereignty and republican status from the British, "we cannot therefore continue to enjoy this 'borrowing spree' or 'merry frolic' at the expense and to the detriment of our legal system." Tobi frowns at Nigeria's "loyalty to our colonial past with such servility or servitude. After all, we are no more in slavery." While some of our laws make omnibus provisions to fall back on English laws, and English rules of court, Tobi opines and encourages Nigerian judges to apply discretion and

---

78 As he then was, a justice of the Court of Appeal, Nigeria (Akure Branch). Justice Abiru is now a justice of the Supreme court of Nigeria.

79 Abiru, H.A. (2018) The Law as it Is – The Place of Social and Moral Values in Contemporary Nigeria, 60th Birthday Symposium, Celebration of Professor Imran Oluwole Smith (SAN), Lagos. P.3.

80 Olagunju, opcit: 306.

81 *Caribbean Trading & Fidelity Corporation v. NNPC* (supra).

only resort to English laws in appropriate circumstances where our local laws and rules of courts are silent.[82] For example, judges have full discretion to grant bail under exceptional circumstances,[83] but the law did not specify these exceptional circumstances, so in applying its discretion, the Supreme Court in *Gani Fawehinmi v. The State*[84] held health challenges as special or exceptional circumstances for the court to apply its discretion to grant the appellant bail.

5 Judicial Norms and Procedural Structure Through the Act of Judging

Although this section is not central to the act of judging, the norms and procedures of Nigerian courts give a better understanding of the courts' structure that leads to the act of judging.[85] Accordingly, in the act of judging, it is key to understand the judicial compositions, the procedures in assigning cases, the discretionary control over the docket, the criteria that determine the trial judge or decision-making panel for each case, how the majority opinion is assigned, whether unanimity is the norm, and how non-unanimity is resolved.[86] Summarily, this section is key to explaining the procedures that lead to the final stage of judicial decisions and how these decisions eventually impact society.

Although the stages of judging are similar across all courts, the decision-making process differs and depends on the level or hierarchy of the court. At the trial and lower court level, or courts of first instance, it is a single-judge decision without a jury, so the decision-making process is straightforward.[87] From this author's personal experiences, as is with other trial judges at the magistrate and the high court levels (both courts of first instance), the judge's

82 See footnote 1.

83 See Uchechukwu, C. U. (2024). The Administration of Bail in the Nigerian Legal System. SSRN Electronic Journal. 10.2139/ssrn.4795594.

84 *Gani Fawehinmi v. The State (1990) 1 NWLR PT 127*, 486.

85 I want to thank my "invisible person," the peer reviewer who made this comment in his/her review of this book.

86 Most of this section is based on informant interviews of judges (serving and retired) that occupy/occupied leadership roles and positions in the judiciary.

87 Nigerian courts do not practice the trial by jury like the American courts. In Nigeria, the judge is the sole fact finder, hearing officer, decision-maker and sentencing officer.

decisions are based (is supposed to be based) on the facts, evidence, and the law. The trial judge has the sole discretion to make decisions according to the law. Appellate court judges also have the discretion to form an opinion about the facts, evidence, and law regarding the case before their panel, but the final judgment of an appeal court is based on the majority opinion from the panel of justices that preside. For example, if there are three justices in a panel, as is often the case with a regular appeal at the Nigeria court of appeal,[88] and two of these justices take the same position, then the decision of the court, known as the *ratio decidendi*, becomes the court's judgment.

The act of judging is a journey that considers several factors, which determine the outcome of the case and the eventual judgment. These factors could be in form of questions that lead a litigant to understand the modus operandi of the court system from the appointment of judges to case assignments. Some key questions include the following: Who assigns cases? Who determines the specific judge who hears or presides over a particular case? Is there a criterion for assigning cases? Is there discretionary control over the docket? Who determines the final judgment of the court? How do judges arrive at their decisions? Although the procedure differs from court to court as various courts at different levels of hierarchy operate somewhat different procedures as their various court rules stipulate, there is a common practice procedure that cuts across all Nigerian courts.

Suffice it to say, at this point, some lawyers who have been long in the court system of a particular judicial division erroneously believe that understanding the norms and procedural structure/modus operandi of a particular court determines the outcome of their case, as they almost predict the judge's mind from his/her previous decisions/precedent. This may be the case in most courts in the United States where most judges are elected to office and federal appointments are based on political affiliations. Hence, American lawyers and litigants can almost always predict that a Democratic appointee or elected judge would most likely be pro-choice and less conservative, while a Republican elected or appointed judge would be

88 A regular appeal has a three-man panel, and that is where the case involves an appeal on any matter that is not regarding constitutional matters or cases on presidential elections. A full panel constitutes five justices where the appeal involves a presidential election case.

more conservative and give a pro-life verdict. Nevertheless, some judges are still unpredictable. Even the late Justice Antonine Scalia of the Supreme Court of the United States, a Republican appointee and conservative judge, switched sides every once in a while in his verdicts and gave somewhat more realist opinions than he often did.[89] Thus, there is no predicting a judge, even the judge often struggles to predict what he/she would decide. From personal experience, I have changed sides of argument from when I first considered the evidence until my final decision. Judges change their minds all the time and end up deciding something different from what they predicted previously.[90] Although some lawyers and even other judges often accuse such judges who changed their minds as being compromised, several legally justifiable factors account for judges changing their minds in the decision-making process. So even if a Nigerian lawyer closely predicts that a particular judge would be more lenient than another in a case, it is vital for all and sundry to know that there is more to judging than meets the eye. In the act of judging, judges consider various obvious, obscure, and abstract factors. The obvious factors are the written laws, the obscure factor is the judge's approach of interpretation, and the abstract is the judge's discretion that may swing either way.[91]

Typically, the rules of courts stipulate the norms and modus operandi of courts. However, where the rules have not stipulated a procedure, the chief or head judge can give a practice directive. For example, during the COVID-19 pandemic, there was no stipulation in the rules of courts for virtual hearings, so every head judge had to draft a practice procedure to update the inadvertence of their respective rules of courts.

Therefore, to understand the act of judging, in Nigeria, it is key to know the judicial procedure that appoints, forms, or selects the decision-making personnel or panel. Hence, it is incumbent to briefly explain the appointment

---

89 Posner, R. (2012). The Incoherence of Antonin Scalia. <https://www.law.nyu.edu/sites/default/files/Posner%2C%20Richard%20A.%2C%20%27The%20Incoherence%20of%20Antonin%20Scalia%27%20The%20New%20Republic.pdf>

90 Most of my informant judges agree that they often can't predict their final verdicts until they deliver it in open court, as "circumstances may change on the journey to delivering judgment."

91 Although judging has a stipulated expectation, there is no hard or fast rule on the procedure a judge must adopt in the act of judging.

process to give a brief overview of the modus operandi of judicial appointment in Nigeria, which impacts the procedure of assigning cases.

6 Selecting and Appointing Judges[92]

There is no hard and fast rule in the selection and appointment of judges, as different heads of courts adopt different methods, with uniform principles.[93] Nigerian judges are appointed and not elected, as some American judges. In Nigeria, when the searchlight is publicized, the applicants/candidates are short-listed for interviews at the appropriate time. The Constitution of the Federal Republic of Nigeria establishes four institutions vested with the role of selecting and recommending persons for judicial appointments.[94] These institutions are the National Judicial Council (NJC),[95] the Federal Judicial Service Commission (FJSC), the State Judicial Service Commission (JSC), and the Judicial Service Committee of the Federal Capital Territory, Abuja.[96] These institutions are advisory to the appropriate chief executive—the president or the governor.[97]

Accordingly, where there is a vacancy in any of the courts, the head judge in the federal and state courts makes the call for an appointment through separate procedures. At the federal level, the head judge/chief judge notifies the Chief Justice of Nigeria (CJN) of the vacancy or vacancies and the CJN who is also the head of the FJSC informs the president of the number of justices proposed for appointment.[98] If the vacancy is of the head judge/chief judge, the outgoing head judge gives notice to the FJSC which communicates to the NJC and submits the name of the most senior judge in the same court system that is next in line to the outgoing head judge.[99] The next most senior judge also known as number two or the administrative judge would then be

---

92 Judges also include magistrates. Nigerian magistrates are qualified lawyers, some of whom have acquired post graduate and terminal degrees.

93 Tobi, opcit: 22.

94 Konrad-Adenauer, S. (2003). UNODC Working Paper. "Selection and Appointment of Judges in Nigeria, Analysis and Recommendations," p. 6.

95 See section 153 and paragraph 21 of the Third Schedule of the Nigerian Constitution.

96 See Konrad-Adenauer, opcit.

97 Tobi, opcit: 27.

98 Ibid: 8.

99 Seniority at this stage is determined by the next judge's prior appointment into the court. However, at the appointment stage when the judge is newly appointed,

appointed as the acting head judge/Chief Judge (CJ), pending a proper security clearance and protocol to be sworn into office.[100] Usually, the president or the governor has the discretion to initiate the appointment process of the head judge upon advice from the appropriate institutions/heads of courts.[101]

In selecting candidates, the CJ/CJN/various appointment institutions stated above consider two vital factors: the constitutional requirement and the fit and proper requirement. The constitutional requirement is straightforward and any candidate who should be a judge must be a legal practitioner for certain required years.[102] The fit and proper requirement is a bit vague and is either based on the definition as contained in the Rules of Professional Conduct for Legal practitioners, which stipulates a standard of integrity, competence, good and moral character[103] based on the discretion of the head judge and the JSC/NJC.[104]

Generally, the head judge sends a list of the proposed judgeship candidates' names. The JSC conducts an interview and orders a security check or investigation into the "fit and proper" criteria—to ascertain if the candidate has integrity, is competent, and of good character in all ramifications, to occupy the position of a judge of the Federal Republic of Nigeria. Specifically at the state level, the process starts with a recommendation from the head judge/CJ to the SJSC, giving notice to the Governor of the State and the CJN of his/her intention to appoint new judges to occupy a specific number of judicial vacancies. The governor gives the go-ahead, and upon the CJN's advice to proceed, the JSC or FJSC advertises a call for interest through a public notice on the institution's website, the courts' notice boards, and the various Bar Association branches. The advertisement states the application requirements and deadline. After the deadline, the head judge prepares a provisional list of the received applications.[105] These lists are divided into the A and B lists. The A list is shortlisted priority names, and if for some reason the candidates

seniority is based on each judge's age at the bar or roll call as a qualified lawyer and solicitor and advocate of the Supreme Court of Nigeria.

100 Ibid.

101 Tobi, opcit.

102 See footnote 107 and Chapter 7 (Pt. 1 and 2) of the 1999 CFRN, as amended.

103 Rules of Professional Conduct for Legal Practitioners, 2023, Section 10 of the Legal Practitioners Act, Cap. L11 of the LFN

104 Ibid.

105 Ibid: 9.

in the A list fail the interview, or fall short of any other requirement like a security check, then the JSC substitutes his/her name with the next name or most senior candidate (according to post-call years at the bar) from the B list.[106]

Furthermore, the Secretary of the JSC, upon the direction of the CJ/head judge forwards a Form A to all shortlisted applicants. Then, the applicants' completed Forms A and their names are submitted to the JSC/FJSC/NJC for further action. The candidates are called for an interview, and upon passing the interview and other professional requirements, the appointment is made, and the JSC sends the applicants their employment letters, which states their designations and postings. Then the swearing-in ceremony is planned and conducted. The CJ/CJN conducts the swearing-in ceremony as each candidate recites their oath of office, swearing or affirming to the Holy Bible (for Christians) or the Holy Quran (for Muslims).[107] After swearing in and taking their oaths of office according to the CFRN, the newly sworn-in judges are taken to their courtrooms, introduced to their respective colleagues, staff, and given their (retrospective) official entitlements like houses, cars, landed property (if any), etc., as the case may be.[108]

Nigerian judges do not have life appointments like justices of the Supreme Court of the United States. The terms of judicial appointments in Nigeria is until the retirement age of 70 years. There is no specific age required for appointment. However, appointments are based on the applicant's number of years at the bar as a lawyer (post-call to the bar).[109] Judicial appointments are not as straightforward as the books stipulate. Depending on the specific state/region, sometimes the appointment process is rigorous, where candidates

106 Personal knowledge and informant interview confirmation. These informants were retired and current chairs/executive directors/heads of the various institutions that appoints judges.

107 These are the major two religions in Nigeria.

108 These are some of the entitlements that were given to the subsisting judges before the newly appointed came on board.

109 For a magistrate/judge of the magistrate court, some states require five years post-call. For a judge of the high Court, any person that is ten years post-call can apply. If the applicant is from the Ministry of Justice, he/she should have attained the status of a director. If the applicant is from the lower court (magistrate), he/she should be a chief magistrate. If the person is from the bar, he/she must have a combination of superior court appearances. Then, if the applicant is for the appeal court, the applicant must be 12 years post-call and 15 years post-call for the Supreme Court applicants. The above is in addition to a list of criteria that results in a tedious selection and appointment process.

travel to the Federal Capital Territory, Abuja, to attend the interviews regarding federal appointments. In addition to the interview, the candidates are required to submit about ten judgments of cases they have presided over, a fit medical record, a curriculum vitae, proof of birth, and nationality. According to the NJC rules, the governor's permission letter is also required in the selection process. In conducting a security check, the JSC sends the names of the candidates to various security agencies, like the Economic Financial Crime Commission (EFCC), to clear any criminal records. A compilation of the above-required interview documents is bound in volumes and distributed to the NJC members, who are supposed to review and prepare for the interview.[110] Judicial appointments take long processes like three or more months. Practically, different governors could change the process of appointments, depending on their political or legal inclinations. For example, some governors who are lawyers understand the modus operandi of the court system, and they maintain the status quo in the selection and appointment process. Some others could disrupt the status quo and take any format they choose.

Supreme Court appointments are based on zoning by the federal character principle, and the positions are designated according to the six geo-political zones in Nigeria. Therefore, justices are only appointed based on vacancies from these zones. For example, since the former CJN was from the South-West, his retirment opened a vacancy for the South West Zone. Thus, only candidates from that zone will be considered for appointment as justice of the Supreme Court. No appointment can be made from the North or South-East to occupy that vacancy. That will be against the Federal Character rule that the Nigerian government doggedly adheres to. When the vacancy is published, all the court of appeal justices or senior lawyers who qualify from the South-West will express interests, or present Supreme Court justices will make unofficial recommendations. The candidates are required to go through a 'somewhat' merit-based appointment process.[111] Also, the interested applicants could approach the JSCs to recommend them. When the recommendations are received, there is a shortlisting. Then, the JSC picks the candidates for interview. During this process, there is

---

110 Unfortunately, some of these interviews, are politicized and sometimes involve biased panels that ask ridiculous questions that have little or nothing to do with the appointment or interview process.

111 See the Guidelines of the Supreme Court of Nigeria.

a security check, and the candidates' names are sent to the security agents for clearance. Then the candidates face the senate for screening. It is a tedious and comprehensive process. Candidates who do not pass these processes are dropped and replaced with a more qualified candidate. Sometimes, this process takes longer than six months to a year. Like the Nigerian colloquialism would say, *to be judge for Niaja no be moi moi*, which means that to be a judge in Nigeria is worse than the complicated meal. "Moi moi," is a festive traditional cuisine made from beans, which takes a long and very stressful process to prepare. In certain rather unfortunate situations some candidates go through illegal and diabolic means to become a judge.

7 The Procedure for Assigning Cases

Generally, the rules of various courts vest the heads of all levels of courts (CJ/CJN/PJ/PJCA) with the responsibility of assigning cases to individual judges at the trial level and the panel of justices at an appellate level. At the trial level,[112] the head of court who is the Chief Judge (CJ) of every state/the head judge of the high court has the role of assigning specific cases.[113] This role is often shared with the admin judge who is the most senior judge after the chief judge of the state.[114] At the court of appeal level, the head of the court which may be the president of the court of appeal (PCA) or the presiding justice of the court of appeal (PJCA/PJ) of respective appellate divisions often assigns cases. At the Supreme Court, the Chief Justice of Nigeria (CJN) assigns justices in panels to preside over cases.[115]

The procedure in assigning cases in a solo-judge court/high court is different from a panel of judges court/appellate court. It is usually straightforward to get a single-judge decision as there is no need for unanimous decisions. So, our focus is not on the trial courts/high courts or magistrate courts that

---

112 The trial courts include the high court, customary courts, area courts, sharia courts, and magistrate courts. Although some are not courts of record in the Constitution, they are courts of great repute and impact, that deal with and handle cases as the courts of record do, with certain differences.

113 For convenience, we will only discuss the high courts, courts of appeal and Supreme Court. Other lower courts like the magistrate courts have similar procedures with minimal differences.

114 This author is aware of the procedure as I was part of the system for over a decade, but also I confirmed from informant judges and court registrars/clerks.

115 More details on the assignments follow below.

I call solo judging. The focus is more on appeal courts as they determine and create precedent and their process of decision-making is not as obvious to the public as the trial court's decision-making process.[116] Nevertheless, I will discuss the trial court's procedure as there is no appeal without the trial court. At the trial courts, cases are filed at the high court registry. Then, the case file is sent to the head judge/CJ who has the overriding power to assign the case to a specific judge in the judicial division. However, for convenience, the admin judges in the respective divisions can also assign cases. Then, cases go to the appeal court from the high court through a notice of appeal that is filed at the lower/trial court, which is either a customary court, a magistrate court, or a high court. Upon compilation, the records of appeal are transmitted to the registry of the court of appeal.

At the appeal court, the case file from the high court is assigned an appeal court case number. Then, the lawyers file their respective briefs of argument. After the briefs are filed, the PJCA selects a panel of three justices in a regular appeal, or five justices in an appeal on strict constitutional issues and directs the head of litigation to fix a hearing date and issue hearing notices to the parties. The PCA or PJCA, as the case may often be, selects the panel to determine the appeal, and the most senior judge presides as head of the panel.[117] The presiding judge need not be the PCA or PJCA. For an appeal to the Supreme Court, the CJN would constitute the panel and assign the cases. Typically, the panel of the Supreme Court could be either five justices for a regular appeal or seven justices for a rare panel that hears election cases or constitutional cases.[118]

The appeal is heard on the hearing date and if it is a straightforward motion, the presiding judge assigns any of the justices in the panel to prepare a draft of the lead judgment. However, if issues are not straightforward, the justices adjourn to review the case file and convene a conference to give a

116 My knowledge of this is based on informant interviews of several judges (retired and serving) from the courts of appeal who were presiding judges (PJs) and justices of the Supreme Court of Nigeria. I thank all of these justices whose names I may not mention to avoid any media misinterpretations and assumptions. Plus, they asked to be anonymous. So, I do not want to close the doors for future research and education.

117 The most senior judge is often determined by the date of appointment as a judge in the court.

118 Different justices of the appellate court that this author interviewed narrated the same procedure. Some of these justices were heads of courts, PJs, CJs.

unanimous view.[119] After the draft is prepared in a straightforward appeal, the justices convene for a pre-judgment conference usually in the judges' conference room located in a secluded part of the court. Then, the PJ of the panel takes an opinion vote for justices to grant or deny the appeal. If the majority agrees that the appeal succeeds, then the decision of the court is based on that majority opinion, and accordingly, it becomes the court's unanimous decision, and eventually, the ratio decidendi. However, the justices that disagree would state their minority opinions which are also recorded as dissenting opinions and eventually obiter dictums. Interestingly, some dissenting opinions have eventually become precedents. This is the fun thing about law, courts and social change; you never know when the tides will turn. An example is in the Mojekwu v Mojekwu case, which is discussed in chapter 6, where the Supreme Court overturned the Court of Appeal's decision that upheld women's right to inheritance, as overreaching. Although the decision was overruled, several years later in Ukeje v Ukeje,[120] the Supreme Court affirmed the Court of Appeal's decision and established precedent.

The Supreme Court operates a slightly different procedure in "assigning" cases. In the Supreme Court, cases are not necessarily assigned, they are categorized and then fixed for hearing. The CJN fixes dates for the hearing of the cases, which are adjourned in open court or fixed for hearing. Also, the head of litigation upon the CJN's directives may also fix cases for hearing from the registry. The twenty justices (for now, until the remaining one required to complete 21 justices is appointed) form four panels with five justices in one panel. When the cases arrive from the registry, they are categorized into panels A, B, C, and D. These panels, which the CJN fixes every quota,[121] sit for a specific designated week. For example, Panel A and B sit on week one. So, all the cases assigned for week one are shared between panels A and B designated for week one. Panels C and D seats in week two. Therefore, two panels sit/preside every week. The rationale behind these panels is in case a justice in one panel is not able to seat with the rest of the panel for ethical or personal reasons, then he/she will be replaced with another judge

119 The views are not always unanimous as there are often dissenting views.

120 (2014) LPELR–22724(SC)

121 Quota comprises of every four months.

from another panel. Hence, if the panel is supposed to hear an appeal of a judgment of a judge of the same panel when he/she presided as a justice of the appeal court before his/her appointment as a Supreme Court justice, then, in the interest of justice and for ethical reasons, another judge from another panel would substitute him/her to preside in the panel, as he/she can not seat on appeal over his/her previous appeal court judgment. For example, if Judge X was a member of Panel A, and the cases assigned for week one includes a case that Judge X delivered judgment while she/he was in the appeal court, then Judge X is substituted with Judge P from Panel B, just for that case, as Judge X cannot be a judge in 'his own case'. After Judge P finishes that case, he returns to his original panel B, while Judge X returns to her original Panel A.

Therefore, because of this possibility of substituting justices between panels, all the panels cannot preside/sit every week. They need reserves for eventualities.[122] They need free justices to substitute where needed, if a judge gets sick or dies, especially as neither the CJN nor the JSCs have prior knowledge of the specific cases that would be filed in the registry. Also, where the court is seating with a seven-man panel, there will be need for substitution in the same way. It is a clear and uncontrolled/uncontrollable procedure that every panel gets what they get. For example, while I was talking with my informants from the Supreme Court, they explained that the present panel seating was selected a while ago, while the panel for April, 2025 etc has been constituted to handle any future cases that are being filed or will still be filed. The panels' seating in November 2024 were constituted months ago. Then, by December 2024, the CJN constituted another panel that would seat from January to March 2025. Then the panel for April, etc has been constituted to handle any future cases that are being filed or will still be filed. Thus, it is not possible for the justices to influence the panels they belong to based on a future case yet to be assigned, and this gives little or no room for corruption as some lawyers insinuate, because the judges are not aware of the case before their panels were formed. The CJN constitutes the election or constitutional cases as they are ad hoc cases that bother on national security, which are time sensitive. So, when a gubernatorial or presidential election case is filed, the CJN adds two justices to the panel that

122 Informants are retired and current justices of the Supreme Court of Nigeria.

was already assigned for that week to constitute the seven-man panel that must seat for such special cases.[123] The CJN reviews the cases every week to ensure that the HOD litigation adheres to her instructions. The CJN signs off on the list for hearing to authenticate the list.

Therefore, the assigning of cases, play a fundamental role in the act of judging in Nigeria, as the specific judge or justices in the panel determine the nature of the judgment/decision. The judge's personality, which includes his/her history and culture, and judicial perceptions, which include his/her training and educational background, influence their reasonings, opinions and eventual decision. Accordingly, the combination of the Nigerian tradition which is the judge's tradition, and the English Common Law, which the judge imbibed from education, are key factors in the act of judging. Furthermore, based on the globalization of different governments and their procedures, the Nigerian judiciary has further adopted a global perspective. Therefore, even though the Nigerian judicial system originally emanated from Nigeria's tradition and customs, the jurisprudence of Nigerian case law, which originated from the British Common Law through the doctrine of precedent dominates the act of judging in Nigeria. Accordingly, the globalization, societal changes and advancements has long transformed the Nigerian judicial system with the combined influence of customary practices, English Common Law, aspects of the American criminal justice system, and international law and treaties. Interestingly, international law keeps shaping and influencing Nigeria's legal system, and it impacts judicial discretion and interpretation in the act of judging.

---

123 I use this opportunity to thank immensely the retired and seating justices of the various courts that assisted my research to document these very important facts that are not readily available in any material for the public to see and know.

Chapter 2
International Law and Judging in Nigeria

> Certainly, it will not only be ridiculous but an abuse of statehood with all its attendant ramifications in international law, for courts of a sovereign country operating an equally sovereign and independent legal system to be bound by decisions of courts of another country having the same status in international law and practice. The United Nations Charter clearly recognizes the equality of States as subjects of international law, even the smallest States, and so the question of one sovereign nation succumbing to the judicial decisions of another sovereign nation should not arise at all, no matter the historical tie or connection. Viewed from this angle, it is submitted that decisions of English courts, whether by the House of Lords or the Court of Appeal, should be persuasive authorities in Nigeria, and this applies to all Nigerian courts.[124]
>
> — Hon. Justice Niki Tobi, JCA (as he then was.)

1 Introduction

This chapter discusses international law's impact on the act of judging in Nigeria. It briefly defines international law and explains the sources of international law. It also outlines the advantages and disadvantages of international law and explains international law's impact on Nigerian courts, and the courts' impact on international law in Nigeria. In addition, this chapter elucidates how Nigerian case law reflects the impact of international law on judging in Nigeria through the influence of international organizations and treaties, and the extent of judges' discretion in applying international law. Through limited comparative analysis, this chapter also highlights the dilemma between domestic and international courts, in developing the law and society. Therefore, by the end of this chapter, readers will understand how international law influences judging and how judges determine international law's interactions with Nigerian law.

---

124 Tobi, N/ (1996). Sources of Nigerian Law I, p. 94: opcit.

2 What Is International Law?

International law is the set of rules that most countries abide by when dealing with other countries.[125] Cornell Law School's Legal Information Institute defines international law as "a set of rules and principles governing the relations and dealings of sovereign states with each other, as well as with international organizations and individuals."[126] According to Simmons, international law is a body of principles, customs, and rules recognized as effectively binding obligations by sovereign states in their mutual relations.[127] This author defines international law as a set of rules, procedures, and policies that different countries deliberate upon and agree to regulate and bind all signatory countries as law.

International law is indispensable in the 'borderless' world we live in today. A judge coursemate who presides over one of the municipal courts in Canada argued during one of our doctoral classes in public policy, that the world is not borderless. He is entitled to his opinion, and so am I. I believe that the internet and cross-cultural marriages are fast breaking down the invisible border barriers. Through human rights and technological advancements, international law has created a borderless community where national territories are de-territorialized by judicial pronouncements or executive policies to fit the common good of a global community. International law is affiliated with the legal system of most democratic countries, which were either colonized by foreign or international governments. This historical connection automatically establishes and links the laws of the colonizing country to the colonized country, as is the case of Britain and Nigeria. Thus, one way or the other, international law make up the sources of Nigerian law.

---

125 Legal Information Institute. <https://www.law.cornell.edu/wex/international_law>

126 Wex Legal Dictionary. (n.d.). <https://www.google.com/url?sa=t&rct=j&q=&esrc=s&source=web&cd=10&cad=rja&uact=8&ved=2ahUKEwiGmJaao8PkAhUk01kKHRpjBu4QFjAJegQIARAB&url=https%3A%2F%2Fwww.law.cornell.edu%2Fwex%2Finternational_law&usg=AOvVaw1UtKwdipT8c_Y11a8TJIm8>

127 Simmons, B. International Law Handbook of International Relations. <https://www.google.com/url?sa=t&rct=j&q=&esrc=s&source=web&cd=&ved=2ahUKEwiogaey_O71AhVwRN8KHXuMBb4QFnoECAYQAw&url=https%3A%2F%2Fscholar.harvard.edu%2Ffiles%2Fbsimmons%2Ffiles%2Fch_14_-_international_law.pdf&usg=AOvVaw0OILhm2I--9ZsowZ_6o6Nr>

3 Sources of International Law

Article 38 of the International Court of Justice (ICJ) Statute gave five sources of international law for courts to follow during proceedings involving member states or countries that are signatories to the United Nations (UN) or the ICJ statute. These sources are as follows:

1. Treaties between states are binding only on states that become party to them.[128] Only a state/country signatory to a treaty can operate and apply such a treaty in its regions.[129]
2. Customary international law is often derived from the conventional practices of various state parties.[130]
3. General principles of law are recognized by civilized nations and as subsidiary means for the determination of rules of international law.[131] International law seldom adopts in its entirety a legal concept from a particular national legal system; instead, the search is for a principle that, in one form or another, is recognized in a wide range of national legal systems.[132]
4. Judicial decisions of various states also form parts of international law where the doctrine of precedent does not operate. According to Article 38(1)(d), judicial decisions are alternative means of determining the rules of law.[133]
5. The research and writings of "the most highly qualified publicists"[134] or various authorities in their respective fields of international law in the specific region, state, or country also determine the contents of intentional law.

---

128 Greenwood, C. Sources of International Law. <https://www.google.com/url?sa=t&source=web&rct=j&opi=89978449&url=https://www.studocu.com/row/document/university-of-zimbabwe/human-rights-law/greenwood-outline-sources/94920012&ved=2ahUKEwifhsSuu7uKAxW8kYkEHUHrAT8QFnoECBoQAQ&usg=AOvVaw2PWY4qJGts67nMgJPMZSUf>

129 See Article 38 of the ICJ Statute.

130 Ibid.

131 Ibid.

132 Ibid.

133 Ibid.

134 Ibid. <https://www.google.com/url?sa=t&rct=j&q=&esrc=s&source=web&cd=19&cad=rja&uact=8&ved=2ahUKEwjR3ZDU587kAhVuoFkKHdxtAE0QFjASegQICBAC&url=http%3A%2F%2Flegal.un.org%2Favl%2Fpdf%2Fls%2Fgreenwood_outline.pdf&usg=AOvVaw0LNeMRxht3hV9SHBnHxnNu>

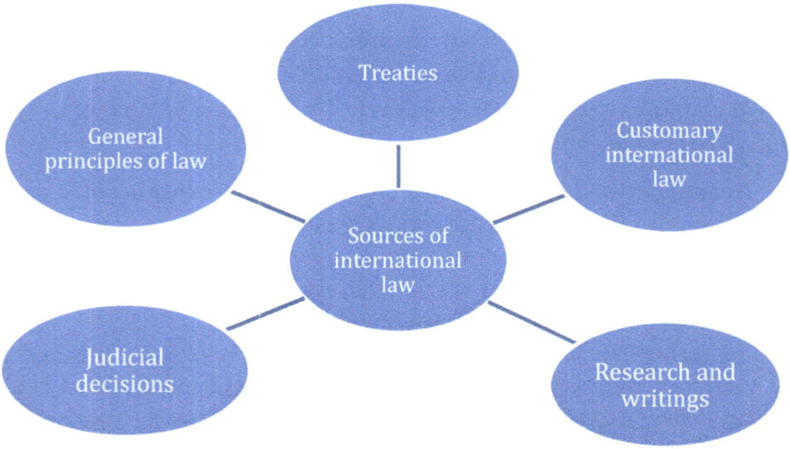

Figure 2.1: Sources of International Law

4 Advantages/Benefits of International Law to Judging in Nigeria

1. International law helps the courts to define law from a broader perspective.[135]
2. International law supports a global judicial connection that enables the development of national and international courts/laws.[136]
3. International law gives judges a loophole out of a dilemma where domestic law does not have an appropriate provision in a pending case.[137]
4. International law breaks cultural barriers to human rights and democratic development by fighting cultures like patriarchy in many societies and recognizing women's rights.[138]

---

135 An example is the history of judicial activism from the United States case, *Marbury v. Madison 5 U.S. 137 (1803).*

136 Ibid. Some cases in Nigeria are decided based on the influence of international law.

137 The National Industrial Court of Nigeria has adopted international law in many cases.

138 The Beijing conference, which reinforced the UN treaty– the Convention on the Elimination of All Forms of Agianst Discrimination Against Women (CEDAW) was an outshoot of international law, and the courts gave it credit in the case of *Mojekwu v. Mojekwu*, opcit.

5. International law reinforces ideal constitutional democracy as a platform for courts[139] and supports the Constitution and domestic laws through silent or salient provisions.[140]
6. International law is a consulting medium that judges consult or run to for back-up.
7. International law acts as a check and balance that exposes the anti-democratic laws in many member states and monitors the rule of law in such countries.[141]
8. International law defines the roles of courts.[142]
9. International law demonstrates the indispensable value of courts in the global development agenda.[143]
10. International law delineates culture and appreciates cultural diversity.[144]
11. International law advances socio-legal jurisprudence.

International law is indispensable for any democracy's judicial system to thrive. As Prasad rightly stated, "the modern state can't live in isolation. The means of transport, communication, and other scientific inventions have brought the states of world closure to each other."[145]

5 Disadvantages of International Law to Judging in Nigeria

1. International law disregards the roots, customs, and traditions of the Indigenous laws, tribes, and thereby causes a dilemma for judges.[146]
2. International law interferes with local, cultural, and traditional practices entrenched in the local statutes.[147]

---

139 Through international treaties, like ICESCR and CEDAW, courts establish a platform to enforce unenforceable laws in Nigeria.

140 Ibid.

141 Ibid.

142 The International Court of Justice defines the role of international courts.

143 Tobi-Aiyemo, A., (unpublished), student, University of Nevada, Reno. Paper presented at the International Law and Organizations Seminar, State University of New York, Oneonta. September 17, 2019, at 109 Schumacher Hall, SUNY Oneonta, New York State.

144 Ibid.

145 Prasad, B. B. (2019). "Sources of International Law," *International Journal of Scientific Research in Multidisciplinary Studies*, *5* (11), pp. 80–88.

146 Ibid.

147 Ibid.

3. International law does not represent the fair court as international law organizations like the UN are not as fair as required.[148] The UN is considered biased in its sanctioning of different countries.[149]
4. International law disrupts the uniformity in building precedent.[150]
5. International law reinforces borderless restrictions and may challenge foreign policies and national security.[151]
6. International law is unable to sustain a uniform global justice system.[152]
7. In applying international law, international court judges are bound to decide the cases based on international law that is foreign to litigants' culture, which may mean injustice in certain circumstances, as the same standards in their specific countries may not be applicable in international forums. Some international court judges are oblivious of cultural or customary implications that may impact the actions of the parties. For example, in the famous International Criminal Court Dominique Ongwen case, a Ugandan war load was charged with 61 crimes. He was eventually convicted. His defense alleged that he was influenced by supernatural forces to commit the gruesome offenses, but the international judges who were not conversant with African diabolic cultures and manipulations did not believe that there were supernatural forces that could influence the defendant's criminal mind and actions.[153]Although some of the judges from other continents may not understand the cultural impacts on crime, the African judges in the panel may know that there is a likelihood for that defense to hold, but because they are required to comply with the western culture of adhering to international standards, they join the bandwagon.

6 International Law's Impacts on Courts in Nigeria

Nigeria is a significant part of the international community that has become a global village, in my opinion. Thus, as a member of various international

---

148 Ibid.

149 UN Press 8962 MEETING. SC/14788. <https://press.un.org/en/2022/sc14788.doc.htm>. 7 February 2022.

150 Ibid.

151 Ibid.

152 Ibid.

153 *The Prosecutor v. Dominic Ongwen (ICC-02/04-01/15)*. <https://www.icc-cpi.int/uganda/ongwen>

organizations, Nigeria has ratified numerous international laws, treaties, and conventions. By Nigeria's affiliation with other nations, she applies numerous international laws enacted by the UN, ECOWAS, etc., as part of the laws of the Federation (LFR). According to *Hon. Justice* Wali, *JSC* in *Ibidapo v. Lufthansa Airlines*[154]:

> Nigeria, like any other Commonwealth County, inherited the English Common Law rules governing the municipal application of intentional law. The practice of our courts on the subject matter is still in the process of being developed, and the courts will continue to apply the rules of international law, provided they are found to be not order-ridden by clear rules of our democratic law. Nigeria, as part of the international community, for the sake of political and economic stability, cannot afford to live in isolation. It shall continue to adhere to, respect and enforce both the multilateral and bilateral agreements where their provisions are not in conflict with our fundamental law.

In *Abacha & Ors v. Fawehinmi*,[155] the Supreme Court stated that courts would not interpret a statute intending to violate rules of international law. In other words, the courts should construe statutes to avoid conflicts with international laws. This is one of the reasons that some judges adopt international perspectives in judging. However, not all Nigerian judges apply international law in judging, as some like Tobi advocate that the judges should only resort to international law where domestic laws are silent on the legal issue.[156] Also, in the absence of Nigerian precedent, in any case, judges can apply foreign law from any other Common Law jurisdiction like the United Kingdom, the United States, or India.[157] Therefore, international law impacts Nigerian courts and influences the act of judging in diverse ways—through judges, laws/international norms, and treaties; foreign jurisprudence/case law; and culture/human rights.

7 International Law's Impact on Judging

International law impacts the act of judging in diverse ways, as judges consult international law and perspectives while interpreting the law to determine the case. Through judicial discretion judges apply international law in decision-making. Judges also consider the parties' rights through consulting

154 *Ibidapo v. Lufthansa Airlines (supra).*

155 *Abacha & Ors v. Fawehinmi (2000) LPELR-14(SC).*

156 See *Olafisoye v. Federal Republic of Nigeria (2004) 4 NWLR (Pt 864) 580.*

157 See Chapter 1

international law and perspectives. The Judge's choice/personality often determines the level of international law's impact on the court, as different judges apply different philosophies and approaches in judging.[158] The personal choice of a specific judge and the nature of the case before the court determines the extent international law is applied in a case. Under Nigerian law, courts can apply international law if it does not conflict with local laws and vice versa.[159] Some judges adopt international perspectives in deciding cases, especially when international law will determine justice in the case.[160] For example, in *Folarin Oreka Maiya v. The Incorporated Trustees of Clinton Health Access Initiative, Nigeria & 2 Ors*,[161] Hon. Justice Kanyip adopted the International Labor Organization (ILO) convention in the case, despite the existing law that Nigerian courts can only apply an international treaty that Nigeria laws domesticate. This judge's decision is based on his choice and philosophy on the fundamental human rights of the applicant. In his judgment, the judge cited the Canadian case of *Brooks v. Canada Safeway Ltd*[162] and the European Court of Justice case to support his submission that the respondent wrongfully terminated the applicant's employment on the grounds of pregnancy.[163]

Nigerian judges encounter major obstacles to upholding economic, social, and cultural rights because Chapter IV of the Constitution only recognizes fundamental human rights like the first generation rights as enforceable.[164] In other words, only the civil and political rights enshrined in Chapter IV of the Constitution are justiciable or enforceable in Nigerian courts. However,

---

158 Some judges cite international laws in their decisions more than Indigenous laws.

159 *Abacha & Ors. v. Fawehinmi (supra).*

160 In the case of *Folarin Oreka Maiya v. The Incorporated Trustees of Clinton Health Access initiative, Nigeria & 2 Ors*, opcit, delivered on December 21, 2011, the NICN adopted the ILO Convention in the case, despite the existing law that Nigerian courts can only apply an international treaty that has been domesticated into our laws. The Honorable Judge was more concerned in ensuring justice in the case. Rightly so.

161 *Folarin Oreka Maiya v. The Incorporated Trustees of Clinton Health Access Initiative, Nigeria & 2 Ors* (2012) 27 NLLR (Pt. 76) 110 NIC.

162 *Brooks v. Canada Safeway Ltd (1989)1S.C. R.*

163 See footnote 72, opcit: 21.

164 The first generation rights are the civil and political rights like the right to life, freedom of speech/expression, right to property, freedom of movement, right to fair hearing, freedom of religion, and freedom from discrimination.

the socioeconomic rights stated in Chapter II of the Constitution, labeled as fundamental Objectives of State Policy are not enforceable in Nigerian courts.[165] Hence, the choice of some judges to resort to international law for answers to the fast-growing Chapter II-related suits in Nigerian courts. In *Archbishop Anthony Okogie and Others v. The Attorney General of Lagos State*,[166] the court held that no court has "jurisdiction to pronounce any decision as to whether any organ of government has acted or is acting in conformity with the Fundamental Objectives and Directive Principles." Hence, for decades, human rights attorneys and civil society organizations continue to challenge the constitutional restriction of this provision.[167]

This writer, who served as a pro bono attorney litigating violations of social and economic rights, participated in a conference where a team of lawyers and human rights advocates discussed possible tactics to convince judges to defend and uphold economic, social, and cultural rights.[168] Thus, several human rights lawyers argue that the right to development and a clean and healthy environment are fundamental human rights as well and should be enforceable like civil and political rights.[169] Also, in her article, "The Right to Adequate Housing," this author explained that the right to housing is tantamount to the right to life and should be enforceable.[170]

Another case where international law impacted judging in Nigeria is *Mojekwu v. Mojekwu*,[171] where the Nigerian judge condemned a custom that prohibited a female child the right of inheriting her late father's estate. In his judgment, Justice Tobi said:

---

165 See section 6 (6) (c) of the 1999 Constitution (as amended).

166 *Archbishop Anthony Okogie and Others v. The Attorney General of Lagos State (1981) 2 NCLR 350.*

167 *Building Nigeria's capacity to implement Economic, Social and Cultural Rights: Lessons Learned, Challenges and the Way Forward*, organized by SERAC (September 27–28, 2006).

168 Ibid–Stakeholders meeting invoving the National Human Rights Commission, Nigeria, at Lagos State, Nigeria.

169 In one of such cases, *Samuel Adeyemi & Others v. Government of Lagos State*, SERAC intervened against the displacement of occupants of the largest slum community in Nigeria, Maroko. We argued that the government owed the evictees a duty of care as citizens to provide them with housing, as the right to housing is a human right and is tantamount to the right to life.

170 See Tobi, A. "Right to Adequate Housing," The Guardian National Daily Newspaper (December 2, 2003), p. 56.

171 Hon. Justice Niki Tobi, JCA (as he then was). Ibid: 305.

> We need not travel all the way to Beijing to know that some of our customs, including the Nnewi "Oli-Ekpe" custom relied upon by the appellant are not consistent with our civilized world in which we all live today ... On my part, I have no difficulty in holding that "Oli-Ekpe" custom of Nnewi is repugnant to natural justice, equity and good conscience.[172]

Although another judge of the Supreme Court overturned this Mojekwu decision, subsequently, more Nigerian judges began to accept international laws, jurisprudence, and arguments regarding women's rights. Thus, in subsequent decisions with similar facts on discrimination against a girl child, the Supreme Court upholds the same principles as the Mojekwu court.[173]

8 International Law's Impact on Human Rights

International law protects human rights in Nigeria. It is the courts' duty to uphold human rights. It is also a judicial responsibility to respect and safeguard international law, especially if the court's country is a signatory to the international treaty, policy, or law. In an international conference, this writer enunciated how international law impacts judging through human rights as follows:

> Ladies and Gentlemen, in the domain of litigating economic social and cultural rights, ... we have gone past the era where arguments are based strictly on local legislation or local agencies.... We have entered an era where the Supreme Court is fast losing its status as the final Court of Appeal in Nigeria,... In this era of incessant armed conflicts, and unfortunate spates of suicide bombings, it has become expedient for various nations to jettison the antiquated hold on state autonomy and embrace the global strategy or pursuit of the actualization of economic social and cultural rights. What determines the kind of sovereignty we all aspire to attain, or build is a grasp of the regional /international laws and practices. The world is now a global village, and we are all clans and communities in it.... Whether we like it or not, we are getting to the era where the only option available to development, is by looking at developmental issues, which include economic social and cultural rights, through regional/ international lenses.[174]

---

172 This case was decided at a time after the Beijing Declaration and Platform for Action, adopted at the UN's Fourth World Conference on Women (Beijing, China, 1995), with an agenda for women's empowerment, at which Nigeria participated.

173 This case influenced a major part of this writer's life and commitment to developing judicial jurisprudence in Africa. Incidentally, the same judge who encouraged Nigerian judges to apply domestic laws/cases, saw the need to resort to international law to interpret and nullify a discriminatory traditional practice.

174 Tobi, A. (2008). *Looking Through the Regional Lenses*, an introductory talk presented at a three-day seminar with the broad theme, "Economic, Social and Cultural Rights

In the above statement, this writer made it clear that human rights have become a borderless concept that connects nations worldwide, making international law indispensable in interpreting human rights in all democratized nations. Thus, courts have various roles in upholding human rights, and it is a judge's duty to shape human rights in the society.[175]

Abul-Ethem opines that one of the vital ways to keep human rights safe is by preserving the judiciary's prevailing role.[176] According to him, the standards judges/courts develop in interpreting human rights and establishing principles will benefit society, improve people's welfare, and efficiently accomplish the government's goals.[177] In addition, these standards may ensure a better understanding of the relationship between the people and their government, on the one hand, and among the members of the international community, on the other.

International law impacts how judges shape, define/ redefine, interpret, and expand human rights from cultural, personal, and unique societal perspectives when they apply judicial discretion in the specific circumstances of each case. International law impacts judicial discretion and opinions as human rights keep advancing with societal changes. Human rights have come a long way from the first to fourth-generation rights because human interests and human desires keep changing. Nigerian courts now apply or resort to international law more than before.

(ESCR) litigation seminar," organized by the Social and Economic Rights Action Center (SERAC) in conjunction with the Banjul-based Institute for Human Rights and Development (IHRDA) with the support of the MacArthur Foundation at Lagos State, Nigeria. This speaker, then a former staff attorney of SERAC, chaired a panel consisting of two renowned speakers from the Gambia and the United States. The panel discussed the jurisprudence, strengths, and weaknesses of litigating economic, social and cultural rights at the regional level. The panel also discussed complaint procedures at the African Commission, the ECOWAS courts, the African Committee of Experts on the Rights and Welfare of the Child, and the African Court on Human Rights.

175 Tobi-Aiyemo, A. (2022). "The Role of Courts in Shaping Human Rights in a Borderless World." Critical Perspectives on Human Rights Conference. The City University of New York, April 21, 2022.

176 Abul-Ethem, opcit: 770.

177 Ibid.

9 International Law's Impact through Norms and Treaties / International Law Organizations

In upholding human rights, courts adopt international norms and apply international treaties based on the country's membership status and statutory requirements. The international, regional, and domestic treaties and organizations have immensely influenced judging in Nigeria and thus contributed to promoting democracy. Hence, judges, as "agents/defenders" of democracy, defend human rights and protect individual/corporate rights from governmental intimidation or threats.[178]

To this end, the UN has developed a body of binding conventions from the 1948 Universal Declaration of Human Rights.[179] These conventions dictate the protection of human rights and sustainable democratic development globally. The UN also promotes human rights through international courts like the ICJ or the World Court; the International Criminal Court (ICC), the ECOWAS Court of Justice (ECJ), the regional Court in Africa, and the Inter-American Human rights Court (IAC), and the regional Court in America. These international courts are instrumental in influencing human rights outcomes in member-state courts worldwide.

International courts' decisions continues to lay the platform for various judges/courts to apply precedent in interpreting human rights to be enforceable in their countries. However, under Nigerian law, international laws, treaties, and conventions remain unenforceable until the National Assembly recognizes them as enforceable. In other words, a Nigerian court can only rely on international law, treaties, or conventions that the Nigerian government ratifies, and the National Assembly accepts.[180] According to the Nigerian Supreme Court in *Abacha v. Fawehinmi*,[181] no matter how

---

178 Some of them are set up and put in jail; some are persecuted for their role in ensuring transparency (the media).

179 International Human Rights Conventions <https://www.google.com/url?sa=t&rct=j&q=&esrc=s&source=web&cd=6&cad=rja&uact=8&ved=2ahUKEwijg4PYn8XkAhWqd98KHcyDDGYQFjAFegQICBAB&url=https%3A%2F%2Fwww.eda.admin.ch%2Feda%2Fen%2Fhome%2Fforeign-policy%2Finternational-law%2Fun-human-rights-treaties.html&usg=AOvVaw1C1w02RLlW2fZGLgG3H3NT>

180 See section 12(1) of the Constitution.

181 *Abacha v. Fawehinmi (2001) WRN vol. 51*, pp. 165–166.

beneficial an international treaty is to Nigeria until Nigeria becomes a signatory to that treaty, it remains unenforceable, and until the National Assembly endorses it as the law of the country. However, some Nigerian judges have, in the interest of justice, applied discretion to make enforceable such conventions that the National Assembly has not accepted yet. More Nigerian judges are adjusting to enforce supposedly non-justiciable rights by citing international treaties that Nigeria ratified. For example, in the case of *Abacha & Others v. Fawehinmi*,[182] the Supreme Court held that where the National Assembly enacts a treaty into law as was the case with the African Charter, the courts must give effect to that treaty as it becomes binding like other Nigerian laws that fall within the courts' judicial powers. Thus, the African Charter is now part of Nigeria's laws and, the courts must uphold it like all other Nigerian laws.[183]

A more instructive case is *Defense & Assistance Project (LEDAP) GTE & LTD v. Federal Ministry of Education & Another.*[184] In this case, the appellants sought a declaration at the Federal High Cour, to enforce the constitutional provisions on the right to free, compulsory, and universal primary education up to junior secondary school for all Nigerian citizens, as stipulated under Section 18(3)(a) of the Constitution (which is under the seemingly non-justiciable Chapter II of the Constitution). They argued that the alleged provision is constitutionally enforceable under the Compulsory, Free Universal Basic Education Act, 2004, which the National Assembly enacted into law. The appellants relied on section 2(1) of the Constitution, which stipulates that the government "shall provide free, compulsory and universal basic education for every child of primary and junior secondary, school age" and Section 3(1) of the Constitution, which states that the "services provided in public primary and junior secondary schools shall be free of charge." The Court held that although, section 18(3) (a) of the Constitution is ordinarily non-justiciable, as incorporated under Chapter II of the Constitution, but the Compulsory,

182 *Abacha & Others v. Fawehinmi* (supra).

183 See also *Nemi v. The State* (1994) 1 LRC 376, where the apex court also affirms that "the Charter has become part of our domestic law" and "the enforcement of its provisions like all our other laws falls within the judicial powers of the courts as provided by the Constitution and all other laws relating thereto."

184 *Legal Defence and Assistance Project (LEDAP) GTE & LTD v. Federal Ministry of Education & Another (Judgement) (FHC/ABJ/CS/978/15) [2018] NGFCHC 1 (17 April 2018).*

Free Universal Basic Education Act of 2004, being an enactment by the National Assembly, confers justiciability to that provision of the Constitution, notwithstanding Section 6(6)(c) of the Constitution, and, therefore, failure by the government to provide free primary and junior secondary education would amount to a violation of the Constitution.[185]

10 Courts' Impact on International Law

As international law impacts courts, courts/judges also impact international law. Courts impact the development of international law in diverse ways through culture, and judges' unique approaches to judging. These judicial approaches include the judges' philosophies, discretion, attitudes, notions, viewpoints, ideas, values, tradition, and beliefs. These approaches dictate judges' application of discretion and depict a judge's or a group of justices' personal or judicial philosophies.[186] The two primary ways that judicial discretion impact international law is through the judge's personality/idiosyncrasy and the culture of the society where the court is located.

10.1 Judges' Impact on International Law in Nigeria

Judges' notions, views, perspectives, and personalities differ in their applications of international law. Thus, judges influence the development and advancement of international law through their personal experiences, proclivities, cultural notions, ideologies, and judicial views/discretions. Judges are constantly called upon to exercise their discretionary power in any judicial process.[187] Sometimes, in the absence of statutory direction, judges encounter a "clay-like" situation where they mold their views, ideas, ideologies, or perceptions into the law and interpret it appropriately. Judicial discretion is vital to the due administration of justice; it develops international law's application on both domestic and international courts.

Therefore, a judge can apply discretion to rely on international law or not. The extent of judicial discretion is not specific. I repeat the Court's

---

185 See also *Femi Falana v. Attorney General of the Federation* (2014).

186 Philosophies of judging also mean theories of interpretation or decision-making.

187 See a detailed discussion of the broad concept of judicial discretion in Chapter 4 of this book.

opinion in *Caribbean Trading & Fidelity Corporation v. Nigerian National Petroleum Corporation*,[188] as follows:

> The Nigerian Legal System attained sovereignty and republican status way back in October 1963 when the Supreme Court and not the Judicial Committee of the Privy Council became the final Court of Appeal,... England is English. Nigeria is Nigerian. The English are English. So also, the Nigerians are Nigerians. Theirs is theirs. Ours are ours. Theirs are not ours. Ours are not theirs. *We cannot, therefore, continue to "enjoy" this borrowing spree" or "merry frolic" at the detriment of our legal system*. We cannot continue to pay loyalty to our colonial past with such servility or servitude. After all, we are no more in Slavery. While some of our laws make omnibus provisions to fall back on English laws, and English rules of Court, these can only be resorted to in appropriate circumstances where our local laws and rules of court are silent.

It is clear from the above quote that judges can impact international law through culture. Tobi advises Nigerian judges to resort to Nigerian laws as much as possible, and interpret the law and apply discretion from the Nigerian perspective, not from the British or English viewpoint. According to Tobi, if citing or referring to foreign or international law will be "detrimental" to the Nigerian legal system, Nigerian judges should desist from "borrowing" foreign law/case law. He admonishes judges to rely on Nigerian law/case law. In a Court & Society Webinar Series that this writer convened, Sam Amadi argued that Nigerian judges are now influencing customary practices, cultural changes, and development through their modes of interpretation, and they still retained the substratum of culture.[189]

Judges should always abide by the principles of justice to retain the Nigerian legal system or culture in judging. So, if applying Nigerian law will be detrimental to the case, then citing foreign law will be justified. However, if applying a foreign decision will be detrimental to justice in a case, the judge must avoid that angle and apply a Nigerian law/caselaw.[190] It is often at the

---

188 *Caribbean Trading & Fidelity Corporation v. Nigerian National Petroleum Corporation (supra).*

189 Amadi, S. (2022, July 21). The Courts as Agents of Social Change. (Courts and Society Webinar Series, Second Edition.) A.T. Socio-Judicial Consulting. <https://youtu.be/ORYwQjNW-mc?si=trvweq_WiX57sPWR>

190 There are circumstances where foreign decisions/law may be unjust in a Nigerian court. Such laws do not take our unique lawful custom and traditional practices into consideration.

judge's discretion to weigh the scale of justice and determine the appropriate and fair approach that interprets justice to the case/parties.

10.2 Cultural Impact on International Law in Nigeria

Culture is a very strong component in any society, as it affects socio-legal/judicial development in multiple dimensions. Culture impacts the application of international law in Nigeria. A judge's culture—the court's culture, the legal culture/legal system, or the culture of the society where the court is located, or even where the judge lives, guides the judge's choice in applying or ignoring international law in a case. Nigerian practices, beliefs, ethos, customs, and traditions impact (should impact) the law that serves them. Culture inadvertently affects the application/development of international law in Nigeria. The introductory quote to this chapter emphasizes the importance of culture to Nigerian law, stating that it will be "an abuse of statehood for … an equally sovereign and independent legal system to be bound by decisions of courts of another country."

An example of how culture impacts the courts' application of international law in Nigeria is regarding marriage/same-sex relationships. The Nigerian culture and legal system prohibits same-sex relationships. Thus, Nigeria's Same Sex Marriage (Prohibition) Act 2013 considers same-sex relationships illegal.[191] It is punishable by up to 14 years in prison.[192] Even though most Nigerian courts now apply discretion to interpret non-justiciable human rights as justiciable, by applying international law and treaties, judges are still unwilling to recognize LGBTQ rights and relationships as human rights, because it is not considered as Nigerian cultural practice.

Furthermore, the Marriage Act defines marriage as a relationship contracted between a man and a woman, and thus valid marriage in Nigeria. Although the refusal to recognize same-sex marriages in Nigeria contravenes international law standards, Nigeria's refusal to recognize same-sex relationships reflects

191 Nigeria Bans Same Sex Marriage. (January 14, 2014). <https://www.google.com/url?sa=t&rct=j&q=&esrc=s&source=web&cd=&ved=2ahUKEwjwlY38qP-f7AhVPE1kFHdU3Bas4FBAWegQIDBAB&url=https%3A%2F%2Fwww.cnn.com%2F2014%2F01%2F13%2Fworld%2Fafrica%2Fnigeria-anti-gay-law%2Findex.html&usg=AOvVaw3RCfdgD2icA1itPQqT4JKR>

192 ibid

Nigeria's sociocultural and religious heritage. However, it is likely that as society changes, Nigerian judges may begin to adopt exceptions to the rule and consider LGBTQ rights, as the UN High Commissioner anticipates.[193]

International laws impact the approach or system of judging in many countries. Courts interpret and apply international law/case law through human rights to relevant decisions. The society's culture or the nature of the case determines whether the judge will apply international law or sustain domestic law.[194] Since international law is 'supposedly' an optional resort to domestic laws in Nigeria, it is necessary that judges apply international law in cases where there are no Nigerian precedents. Therefore, in the event of a new case or principle to support an existing precedent, courts should not hesitate to resort to international law or foreign law in the interests of justice and society like the National Industrial Court of Nigeria in *Folarin Oreka Maiya v. The Incorporated Trustees of Clinton Health Access initiative, Nigeria & 2 Ors.*,[195] where the applicant brought an action for wrongful termination of her employment. She urged the court to enforce her fundamental rights against discrimination, claiming that the first respondent terminated her employment because she became pregnant. She argued that the second and third respondent's approval of the termination violated her fundamental rights to human dignity and freedom from discrimination. The rationale for the applicant's conclusion was that she was employed through a competitive process, as the most suitable for the job. In the course of her employment, she was never reprimanded, queried, or told that her work was unsatisfactory. However, after she informed her immediate supervisor about her pregnancy, the supervisor replied by saying that she would try her best to ensure the applicant kept her job. A few hours later, after the supervisor had informed the company's director of the pregnancy, they terminated

---

193 UN Human Rights Chief Denounces New Anti-Homosexuality Law in Nigeria. <https://www.google.com/url?sa=t&rct=j&q=&esrc=s&source=web&cd=&ved=2ahUKEwjsv9_3qff7AhXCK1kFHc52ARo4FBAWegQIBRAB&url=https%3A%2F%2Fwww.ohchr.org%2Fen%2Fpress-releases%2F2014%2F01%2Fun-human-rights-chief-denounces-new-anti-homosexuality-law-nigeria&usg=AOvVaw3dX8Y8GqsAwqGIx5AVlJlm>

194 Some judges cite international laws in their decisions more than Indigenous laws.

195 *Folarin Oreka Maiya v. The Incorporated Trustees of Clinton Health Access initiative, Nigeria & 2 Ors* Supra.

the applicant's employment. Hence, she concluded that the respondents terminated her appointment because of her pregnancy. In supporting the applicant's case of wrongful termination, the Court referenced foreign law, like the Discrimination (Employment and Occupation) Convention 1958 (No 111), and concluded that termination on the grounds of pregnancy must attract an award of heavy damages.[196]

Everything that judges interpret are as they see it, as they know it, as they observe it and inadvertently, as they experienced it. The judge's personality dives full force into the act of judging. Every part of the judge is focused on the case and its likely outcome. According to a retired Nigerian Supreme Court Justice, "each judgment I write, takes a part of my soul. Then I move unto the next without ever looking back."[197] This narrative is not unique to this judge; it applies to most judges in diverse levels and areas of their judicial careers. Several intellectual interactions webbed in the judge's mind regarding the balance between the law, the drafter's intention, culture, international law, and the justice of a case, create a platform for interpreting the facts and statutes applicable to each case. These subconscious interactions in judicial interpretation are key to the act of judging.[198]

---

196 https://nicn.gov.ng/view-judgment/1536>

197 <Justice Amina Adamu Augie (2023, July 27) Courts and Society Webinar Series, Eighth Edition, A.T. Socio-Judicial Consulting, LLC. Available at https://atsjconsulting.com.

198 Thus, in a follow-up research, this author delves into the lives of various judges and obtained informant narratives, perspectives, and experiences from different Nigerian judges who narrate how the act of judging impacts their lives and roles in society.

Chapter 3
Judicial Interpretation in Nigeria

A judge by the very nature of his judicial function, gets into contact with statutes every day in court. He is faced daily with the interpretation of statutes coming before him. In some cases (most cases actually) the particular statute had earlier been interpreted by judges of the superior courts. In such cases the job of the judge of the inferior court is much easier. He simply uses the decided cases on the particular statute if it is appropriate in the circumstances of the case before him. This is the whole essence of stare decisis. There are however certain cases where statute had not received judicial interpretation. The statute is coming to the court for the first time for the interpretation of the judge. The judge must exercise his interpretative jurisdiction to vindicate the intentions of the legislator. He has no jurisdiction to interpret the statute the way he feels it should be. He has no power to re-write a statute. All he has to do is to interpret the statute to bring out its intended meaning and no more.[199]

— Hon. Justice Niki Tobi, Judge of the High Court of Nigeria (as he then was)

1 Introduction

This chapter focuses on the central role of judges in interpreting laws/statutes. It analyzes the legal framework for interpreting statutes in Nigeria. It also states the classic canons or rules of statutory interpretation applied in Nigerian courts. Through reviewing case law, to show how Nigerian judges interpret statutes, the author classifies twelve principles of statutory interpretation that guide the application of rules of interpretation.[200] This chapter also introduces a novel canon/rule of interpretation, which is the author's socio-judicial rule of interpretation. At the end of this chapter, readers will comprehend the approach(es) judges adopt in interpreting statutes, that is, the how, the why, and when of judicial interpretation in Nigeria. Although judicial approaches to interpreting statutes may overlap with the rules or principles of interpretation,

199 Tobi, N. (1992). The Nigerian Judge, opcit: 218.

200 I gleaned these principles from several decided authorities.

the judicial approaches to interpretation operate in isolation, and they are key in directing the court's decision-making philosophy.[201]

2 The Legal Framework for Interpreting Statutes

No law specifically states the judge's role in interpreting statutes in Nigeria. However, the judge's core role is to settle disputes by interpreting statutes according to the regulations that establish and govern the court and the justice system. Justice Ukeje aptly states that the importance of interpreting legislation cannot be over-emphasized, as a good understanding of the rules and principles of law is an indispensable tool for the legal draftsman.[202] Judicial pronouncements about statutes generally determine the conclusive meaning of the law and its effects until the legislature amends the law.[203] America's former Chief Justice John Marshall said in *Marbury v. Madison*,[204] "it is emphatically the province and duty of the judicial department to say what the law is."[205] Hence, the most prominent and challenging task of the judge is interpreting statutes to determine what the law is.[206]

In the absence of rules or procedures to guide judges in interpreting statutes, case law provides the only legal framework governing statutory interpretation.[207] Through interpreting statutes and establishing principles in case law, Nigerian judges create their Common Law.[208] The Court in *Okumagba v. Egbe*[209] held that courts ought to find out the intention of the

201 Rules of interpretation are slightly different from principles of interpretation.

202 Ukeje, R. N. (2018) Intrinsic and Extrinsic Aids to the Interpretation of the Constitution, Statutes and Private Documents. ECOWATCH Publications (Nig) Ltd, Lagos, Nigeria. p. 4.

203 Brannon, V..C. (2018) Statutory Interpretations: Theories, Tools and Trends, opcit:2.

204 *Marbury v. Madison 5 U.S. (1 Cranch) 137 (1803).*

205 Cited from Brannon, opcit: 2.

206 This onerous task requires judges to decipher the intention of lawmakers and mentally transmute into the minds of the framers and "repeat" what the drafters had in mind when drafting the specific statute, despite circumstances that are completely different from the reason that established the said intention of the drafters.

207 Even the Interpretation Act does not state how judges can interpret statutes.

208 See *A.G Abia State v. A.G Federation (2002) 3 SC 106 at 164*; no special provision of the Constitution gives to the court any power of interpretation greater than that which flows from the ordinary rules of construction. Hon. Justice Kutigi, JSC.

209 *Okumagba v. Egbe (1965)1 All NLR 62 at 65.*

legislature/lawmakers while interpreting the provisions of a statute.[210] This rule has remained central through Nigeria's rapidly changing socio-legal system.[211] The celebrated case of *Chief Awolowo v. Alhaji Shagari*[212] established the legal framework of interpreting statutes in Nigeria. In this case, the Supreme Court extensively discussed the rules/canons (and principles) of interpretations as follows:

> A statute should always be looked at as a whole. Words used in a statute are to be read according to their meaning as popularly understood at the time the statute became law. A statute is presumed not to alter existing law beyond that necessarily required by statute. It is necessary to emphasis that a decision on the interpretation of one statute generally cannot constitute a binding precedent with regard to the interpretation of another.
>
> The three rules of statutory interpretation which dominate the historical perspective are:
>
> (1) The Mischief Rule
> (2) The Literal Rule and
> (3) The Golden Rule.
>
> They have been useful aids in the interpretation of statutes in Common Law countries for centuries. It has been said that they have been fused so that we now have just one rule of interpretation, a modern version of the literal rule which requires the general context to be taken into consideration before any decision is taken concerning the ordinary meaning of words. The Mischief rule is now used to explain what was said by Parliament....The object of the statute is relevant on all occasions not only when the meaning is doubtful as was said in the Sussex Peerage case (1884)CL and Fin 85 at p. 143 (6–8 E.R.)The golden rule can only be invoked when there is internal disharmony in the statute, not in cases in which a literal interpretation would produce results which are absurd or inconvenient for other reasons....There is need to emphasis the point that the proper application of the Literal rule does not mean that the effect of a particular word or phrase, clause or section is to be determined in isolation from the rest of the statute in which it is contained. The Golden Rule allows for a departure from the literal rule when the application of the statutory words in the ordinary sense would be repugnant to or inconsistent with some other provisions in the statute or even when it would lead to what the courts consider to be absurdity. The usual consequence of applying the Golden rule is that the words, which are in the statute, are ignored or words which are not there are read in....It should be emphasized that when the Golden Rule is used as a justification for ignoring or reading in words, resort may only be made to it in the most usual cases....There are some dicta flatly denying

---

210 See Tobi, E., JCA, in *Ola Animashaun Oluwabukola v. Attorney General of Lagos State & Ors at (2002) 2 NWLR (Pt. 1815) 499 p. 29.*

211 Also, in *Ugwu v. Ararume (2007)12 NWLR (pt. 1048) 367 at p. 498*, the court said that its function is to interpret legislation according to the intent of those who made it.

212 *Chief Awolowo v. Alhaji Shagari (1979) 6–9 SC 51.*

that the courts have any power to reject the natural and grammatical meaning of a word or phrase on the ground that it leads to some result which cannot reasonably be supposed to have been intended by the legislature....The words used in the statute must not be given a meaning they cannot by stretch of imagination bear.... The duty of a court is to interpret an Act of Parliament so as to give effect to its intention. the court does not claim the right to order Parliament or its draftsman to observe the rules which judges laid down.... The ordinary meaning of words is a question of fact. It is however very far from being an ordinary fact for legal purposes as it is the subject of judicial notice and the decisions on them become binding precedents so far as the construction of the statute in question is concerned. This question of fact so far as law of statutory interpretation is concerned, is not one which evidence can be called on each side.... when it is agreed or contended that statutory words have a technical meaning, evidence with regard to that meaning is unquestionably admissible and it is generally preferred to information gleaned from other sources such as dictionaries.

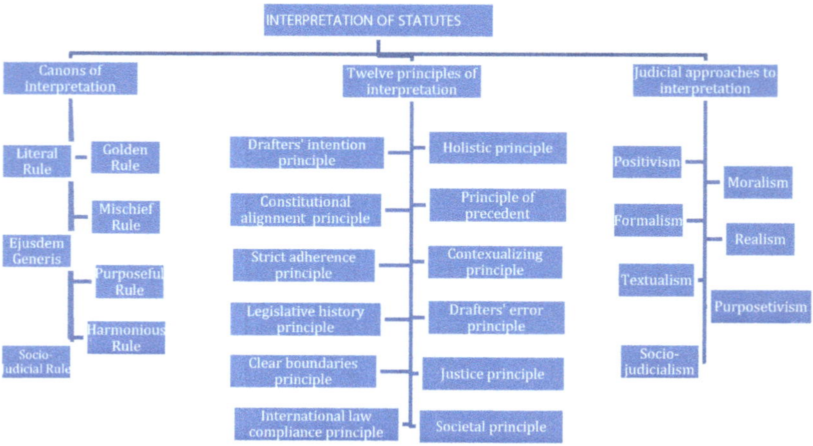

Figure 3.1: Judicial Interpretation

3 The Canons/Rules of Statutory Interpretation in Nigeria[213]

From the above case, the basic Common Law rules that guide Nigerian courts in interpreting statutes are called canons or rules of interpretation.

---

213 It is imperative to note that rules of interpretation are different from principles of interpretation although they are often used interchangeable. See subsequent discuss on principles of interpretation in this chapter.

Historically, Nigerian courts adopted and continue to apply these classic rules of interpretation.[214] These rules are the literal rule, the golden rule, the mischief rule, the *ejusdem generis* rule, and the purposeful approach rule.[215] And the author would be introducing her socio-judicial rule.

3.1 The Literal Rule

This is the starting point of statutory interpretation in Nigeria. Also known as the plain meaning rule, it simply states that the words of the statute best declare the intention of the law giver, hence these words should be the first point the interpreter must consider.[216] Where the words of a statute are plain, clear, and unambiguous, the court shall give effect to their literal meaning.[217] The general principle under this rule is that judges should construe words used in a statute in their usual grammatical sense.[218] This rule posits that the courts' primary responsibility in applying and interpreting the law is to determine the intent of the legislature from the words used in the statute. In *Okumagbae v. Egbe*,[219] the Supreme Court declared that once the meaning of a word in a statute is clear, a judge is bound to give effect to it.[220] Under this rule, a judge cannot and should not defect to another meaning outside the clearly stated meaning in the statute. Similarly, in *Sebelius v. Cloe*,[221] the American Supreme Court held that if the statute's language is plain and unambiguous, it must be applied according to its terms.

It is settled law that courts should apply the literal interpretation of the statute unless such application leads to absurdity and inconsistency with the statute's provisions at stake. This was the opinion in *Onashile v. Idowu*,[222]

---

214 See Chapter 1.

215 As propounded by Lord Denning, M. R.

216 See *Chief Awolowo v. Alhaji Shagari (Supra)*.

217 See *Ogbunyiya v. Okudo (1976) 6–9 Sc.32; Ogunmade v. Fadayiro (1972) 8–9 SC.1; Global Excellence Communications Limited & Ors v. Mr. Donald Duke (2007) LPELR-1323 (SC); Lawal v. GB Ollivant (1972) 2 SC 124; Okotie-Eboh v. Manager & Ors. (2004) LPELR-2502 (SC); Adejumo v. Military Governor Lagos State (1972) 3 SC 45; Agwuna v. A.G. Federation (1995) LPELR-258 (SC).*

218 See *R v. Bangaza (1960) 5 FSC 1.*

219 Okumagba v Egbe (*Supra*).

220 Tobi, N. (1994) The Nigerian Judge, opcit: 218.

221 *Sebelius v. Cloe 569 U.S. 369 (2013).*

222 *Onashile v. Idowu (1961) All NLR 313.*

where the court reiterated that if the literal interpretation of the statute would lead to the result that the legislators would never have intended, the courts must reject the interpretation and seek for some other interpretation.[223] Also, in *Ola Animashaun v. Attorney General of Lagos State & Ors.*,[224] the Court of Appeal states that its duty is to interpret the law by applying the literal rule of interpretation. However, if applying this literal rule leads to absurdity, a court should consider other rules of interpretation, including the golden and the mischief rules of interpretation.[225]

The notion is that words used in a statute, except with scientific meanings, should be construed as they are understood in a common language. However, the exception to the general rule is that if the literal meaning may result in ambiguity or injustice, the judge can only seek internal aid within the statute or external aid from other similar or relevant statutes to resolve the ambiguity or injustice.[226] This is where international law comes handy, and it is at the judge's discretion to consult or not. This rule is commonly applied by the Nigerian courts, but it obstructs a progressive interpretation and may impact the justice of the case.[227] Rigid adherence to this literal approach to interpretation may hinder adapting to the current needs of society and may result in decisions contrary to the spirit of the Constitution or any other law.[228]

3.2 The Golden Rule

Nigerian courts adopted a version of the golden rule established in the English case of *Becke v. Smith*,[229] where Judge Parke stated that "it is a very useful rule in the construction of a statute to adhere to the ordinary meaning of the word used, and to the grammatical construction, unless it is at variance with the intention of the legislature to be collected from the statute itself, or

---

223 Oshio, P.E (n.d) Towards a Purposeful Approach to the Interpretation of the 1999 Constitution, opcit: 16.

224 *Ola Animashaun v. Attorney General of Lagos State & Ors (Unreported) Appeal No: CA/L/1046/2015*, delivered on 30/10/2018.

225 Ibid: 30.

226 See *Mobile v. F.B.I.R (1977) 3 SC 53.*

227 The Constructionist school of jurisprudence also apply this rule of interpretation.

228 Sokefun, J. & Njoku, N. C. (2016). The Court System in Nigeria: Jurisdiction and Appeals, opcit: 11.

229 *(1936) 150 E.R 724 A.T. 736.*

leads to any manifest absurdity or repugnance, in which case the language may be varied or modified so as to avoid such inconvenience, but no further." The Supreme Court said in *Ejike Okoye v. Commissioner of Police*[230] that "the golden rule of interpretation of statutes is that if the words used in a statute are clear and ambiguous, they must be given their natural and ordinary meaning unless to do so would lead to absurdity or inconsistency with the rest of the statute."[231] This rule gives courts an alternative to literal interpretation.[232] The golden rule enables judges to alter the meaning of a statute to fit the statutes assumed intent. According to Ukeje,[233] in applying the golden rule, the court gives words a secondary meaning they are capable of bearing, with the aim that the lawmakers would not have intended an unreasonable result.[234]

3.3 The Mischief Rule

Heydon's case[235] by the barons of the exchequer in 1584 established the mischief rule. This case predicates the mischief rule on four factors: 1) the Common Law as it stood before the legislation in question was enacted, 2) the mischief and defect that gave rise to the legislation, 3) the remedy provided by the legislation, and 4) the rationale for the legislation. However, where the mischief rule does not cure the "mischief" in the law, or give it a clear meaning, the court can look outside the statute to construct a meaning that defines the drafter's intent.

Therefore, in order to interpret a statute properly it is necessary to consider how the law stood when the statute was passed; what the mischief

---

230 *Ejike Okoye v. Commissioner of Police (2015) LPELR, SC 279/2011.*

231 See also *SPDC (Nig) Ltd v. KATAD (Nig) Ltd (2006) 1 NWLR (PT.960) 216 PARA D-G.*

232 In *R v. Princewill (1963) 2 All NLR 31*, where the words to be interpreted are ambiguous, it is the court's duty to interpret the words in such a manner as to avoid absurdity.

233 Ukeje, R.N, (2013) Instrinsic and Exrinsic Aids to the Interpretation of the Constitution, Statutes and Private Documents. opcit: 39.

234 In *Bronik Motors Ltd & Anor v. Wema Bank (1983) 1 SCNLR 296*, Idigbe, JSC, stated that "where a judge is of the opinion that the application of the words of an enactment in their ordinary meaning would produce an absurd result which cannot reasonably be supposed to have been the intention of the legislature, he may apply the words in any secondary meaning which they are capable of bearing."

235 *3 Co. Rep. 7a at 7b.*

was for which the old law did not contemplate or provide; and the remedy provided by the statute to cure the mischief or defects.[236] In *A.G Lagos State v. Mamman Keita*,[237] Ekyegh, JCA, applied the mischief rule in interpreting the Administration of Criminal Justice Law, 2011.[238] Hence, the duty of the Court is to adopt an interpretation that will suppress the mischief and promote the remedy within the legislations' true intent.[239]

Eig states that to understand the mischief that a law may be designed to prevent, the courts may consult explanatory documents to gain a better feel for context or to shed light on the specific language in a statute. In the United States, courts may consult legislative history.[240] A proper construction frequently requires consideration of a statute's wording against the background of its legislative history and in the light of the general objectives Congress sought to achieve.[241] In *Shell Oil Co. v. Iowa Dep 't of Revenue*,[242] the court reiterates reliance on legislative history to guide broad congressional purposes.

3.4 The Ejusdem Generis Rule

This rule is coined from the Latin maxim *ejusdem generis*, which means "of the same kind of nature."[243] In other words, when words in a statutory text are flanked by restricted words, the meaning of the general words are taken to be restricted by implications of the meaning of the restricted words.[244] On the application of this rule, the Supreme Court held in *Ehuwa v. Ondo State I.E.C & Ors*[245] that the rule means that in interpreting the provisions

---

236 See Heydon's Case *Balogun v. Salami (1963) 1 All NLR 129.*

237 *A.G Lagos State v. Mamman Keita (2016) LPELR-40163 (CA) 15–16.*

238 *Wilson v. A.G of Bendel State (1985) 1 N.W.L.R (pt. 17) 572,* "to arrive at a reasonable construction of a statute, the court is entitled, following the Rule in Heydon's case to consider how the law stood when the statute was passed, what the mischief was for which the old law did not provide and the remedy which the new law has provided to cure that mischief."

239 Tobi, opcit: 221.

240 Eig, M. E. (2014). Statutory Interpretation: General Principles and Recent Trends, opcit: 47.

241 See *Wirtz v. Bottle Blowers Ass'n, 389 U.S. 463, 468 (1968).*

242 *Shell Oil Co. v. Iowa Dep 't of Revenue 488 U.S. 19,26 (1988).*

243 Ukeje, opcit: 48.

244 Ibid: 49.

245 *Ehuwa v. Ondo State I.E.C & Ors (2006) 10 NWLR (pt1012) 544 at 595, paras A-C.*

of a statute, general words which follow particular and specific words of the same nature as themselves take their meaning from those specific words. The *ejusdem generis* rule confines the construction of general words within the genus of special words in the statute or document.[246]

3.5 Purposeful Approach

Under this rule, Common Law courts interpret enactments based on the purpose for the enactment.[247] Lord Denning established this rule of interpretation in *Seaford Estates Ltd v. Asher, Denning.*[248] According to Lord Denning, the literal method is now out of date; it has been replaced by the purposeful approach, which will promote the general legislative purpose underlying the provision.[249] It is developed from the use of the purpose clause commonly found in statutes—a clause that may help the reader interpret the statute in the event of any uncertainties in the statute.[250] It is essential that in interpreting the words of a statute, the court must consider the statute's object.[251] The court must guide itself with the essence of a provision in giving meaning to words of that provision. Once an interpretation meets the purpose of the provision of an enactment, then it is fine, and it is irrelevant that other possible interpretations of the provision exist. So said the court in *Rivers State Government v. Specialist Konsult.*[252] Also, in *A.G of Lagos v. A.G of federation & 35 Ors,*[253] Uwaifo, JSC, reiterated this principle as follows:

> This court is entitled to take account of and use such material or information which it considers will help it to determine the true intendment of a statutory or constitutional provision in a purposive interpretive approach; or which will lead it to access the correctness of a meaning it has, through the usual canons of interpretation, given to such a provision. This is particularly so of a provision which is either ambiguous or seems to have become controversial.

---

246 *Fawehinmi v. I.G.P & Ors (2002) LPELR-1258(SC) 36, Hon. Justice Uwaifo, JSC.*

247 *Garba Kyos & Anor v. Kwaturu & 41 Ors (Unreported APPEAL NO CA/K/EPT/ SHA/01/2015*, p. 16. Delivered September 21, 2016.

248 *Seaford Estates Ltd v. Asher, Denning (1947) 2 K.B 481.498.* It is a recent rule adopted by Nigerian courts.

249 Ibid.

250 Ukeje, opcit: 56.

251 *Elabanjo v. Dawodu (2006) 15 NWLR (Pt 1001) 76 at 138H.*

252 *Rivers State Government v. Specialist Konsult (2005) 7 NWLR (Pt 923) 145.*

253 *A.G of Lagos v. A.G Of federation & 35 Ors (2003) 35 W.R.N97.*

The advantages of the purposive approach are numerous in defining the justice system—the approach enables the court to consider the letter and the spirit of the statute.[254] Oshio opines that perhaps the greatest advantage of the purposive approach is the prevention of excessive legalism through undue adherence to the doctrine of judicial precedent, whereby the case before the court must be decided according to the principles in an earlier case regardless of the different surrounding circumstances.[255]

After strict adherence to conservative approaches, even English courts have become comfortable with the purposive approach. The House of Lords in *Pepper (Inspector of Taxes) v. Hart*[256] said: "The days have long passed when the courts adopted a strict constructionist view of interpretation which required them to adopt the literal meaning of the language. The courts must adopt a purposive approach which seeks to give effect to the true purpose of the legislation."[257] The purposive approach is the rule that judges apply with the realist philosophy of judging.[258]

3.6 Harmonious Rule of Interpretation

Ukeje proposed this rule in her book Intrinsic and Extrinsic Aids to the Interpretation of the Constitution and Private Documents.[259] According to her, "the rule of harmonious construction is the "thumb rule" to the interpretation of any statute. The aim of the Court is to construe the legislation as a consistent whole to avoid inconsistency or repugnancy between the various sections or parts of the statute."[260] This rule suggests that words should not be construed in isolation but interpreted in light of the general context.[261] Accordingly, the court examines various and other relevant provisions of the statute before explaining the meaning to the expression being

---

254 Oshio, ibid: 20.
255 Ibid: 28.
256 *Pepper (Inspector of Taxes) v. Hart (1993) 1 All E.R 42.*
257 Cited from Oshio, opcit: 1.
258 In the case of *Amaechi v. INEC*, the court seemed to have adopted the purposeful approach of judicial interpretation. A more detailed argument will be discussed in Chapter 4.
259 See Ukeje, opcit: 52–56.
260 Ibid: 53.
261 Ibid.

interpreted.[262] The Supreme Court in *Dantsolo v. Mohammed*[263] held that the Court is bound to consider any other parts of a statute that throws light upon the drafters' intention, in construing the statute or any provision therein.

3.7 The Socio-Judicial Rule[264]

By this concept of judicial interpretation, the author proposes social and judicial reasoning in interpreting statutes or any document before the court. This rule recognizes the value and rightful place or impact of interpreting statues with the plain meaning rule,[265] the assumed intent of the drafters,[266] while attempting to resolve the mischief of the law.[267] It also appreciates adopting the same nature rule,[268] the purpose of the statute concept,[269] and the general context rule—[270] all of which aids judicial interpretation. In addition to supporting previous canons of interpretation, the socio-judicial canon stipulates interpreting statues from both societal and judicial perspectives. It emphasizes the place of society in a democratic state and enjoins judges to consider the drafters' intention from both societal and judicial perspective, as the drafters enacted the law based on social needs, interests or protests, and also from judicial interventions as per case law.

This socio-judicial rule loops all canons of interpretation as connected and interdependent concepts in interpreting statutes, equitably. It argues that as important as a plain meaning is to interpreting statutes, the plain meaning may not do justice to certain cases as the society may have changed since that plain meaning was enacted. Hence, the need to deviate from the literal interpretation to assume the statutes' intent and apply the golden rule. Also, certain statutes/provisions may include "mischief," which requires consulting explanatory documents to gain a better contextual understanding to cure

262 Ibid: 54.

263 *Dantsoho v. Mohammed (2003) 6 NWLR (pt.817) 457 at 492.*

264 This socio-judicial rule of interpretation is this author's coinage and a new jurisprudence for judicial interpretation. It is a concept birthed from this author's socio-judicialism theory, which she created over two decades ago.

265 The literal rule.

266 The golden rule.

267 The mischief rule.

268 The ejusdem generis rule.

269 The purposeful approach.

270 The harmonious approach.

the mischief. In this context, Ukeje outlines intrinsic and extrinsic guides to interpreting a statutes/document.[271] The intrinsic guides include the preamble,[272] the heading and the title,[273] the marginal notes,[274] the explanatory notes,[275] the long title.[276] The extrinsic guides are the Interpretation Act, language or law dictionaries, and renowned textbooks.[277]

Furthermore, the intrinsic or extrinsic guides to cure a mischief may not suffice to interpret some statutes/provisions of law and may require the interpreter to construct general words within the genus of special words in the statute or document. Hence, the ejusdem generis rule applies. Additionally, one fundamental clue to interpreting statutes is understanding the purpose of the legislation, but if the purpose in not very clear from certain provisions in the statute, there will be discrepancies, which will confuse and mislead the interpreter. Thus, a harmonious interpretation valuably steps in for a comprehensive understating of the purpose and intent of the statute.

However, literal, intentional, curative, contextual, explanatory, purposeful, and harmonious the interpretation of a statute is, the statute's impact on the respondents of its enactment should determine and guide its interpretation. In other words, if the statute passes all the above canon checklists and it is not impactful to society or the public (directly or indirectly), the statute makes little or no impact on the people, society, and democracy. Therefore, the socio-judicial rule reinforces the implication of society to the act of judging.

As judges engage in the onerous task of applying canons of statutory interpretation, they encounter several challenges. There is no single, all-

271 Ukeje, opcit: 64–68.

272 Ibid: 64. According to her, the preamble is a useful guide to the history of the legislation and in ascertaining the legislative intent. It is most useful in the mischief rule.

273 Ibid: 65. Ukeje asserts that the heading and title of the statute is most useful in interpreting unclear provisions of statutes.

274 Ibid: 66. Marginal notes, which are for "ease of reference," are helpful "when considering the general purpose of a section and the mischief."

275 Ibid. Ukeje states that "in the absence of any other aid, they serve as a weak pointer to the intention of the legislature."

276 Ibid: 67. "The long title delimits the purpose of the statute and may be relied upon as explaining its general scope."

277 Ibid. The Interpretation Act is a law of the Federal Republic of Nigeria that aids in interpreting the Constitution's provisions, and judges often consult dictionaries to clarify the words or use of language, while textbooks of renowned authors assist in understanding the legislation to interpret.

encompassing canon of interpretation that binds judging. Hon. Justice Fatayi-Williams, JSC, observed that "some of these canons of interpretation take the form of broad principle only; consequently, a common feature of most of them is that they are of little practical assistance in settling doubts about interpretation in particular cases. This is partly due to vagueness but also because in many cases, where one canon appears to support a particular interpretation, there is another canon, often on equal status which can be invoked in favor of an interpretation, which could lead to a difficult result."[278] Similarly, some judges in the United States (depending on their judicial philosophies) are also critical of canons of interpretation.[279]

Therefore, this author introduces her unique socio-judicialism approach for judicial interpretation. However, before discussing this unique approach coined from this author's socio-judicial research, spanning into its third decade, it is vital to lay a proper foundation with the principles of interpretation and judicial approaches to interpretation.[280] These will give a better understanding of the author's reasoning and philosophy.

4 Basic Principles of Interpretation of Statutes in Nigeria[281]

Every statute that applies to cases in court requires interpretation or construction, and it is vital that principles guide judicial interpretations. As courts follow the rules/canons of interpreting statutes in Nigeria, these principles (inadvertently) establish the form or standards that courts adopt in interpreting statutes. Some judges see principles of interpretation and canons of interpretation as the same,

---

278 See *Awolowo v. Shehu Shagari (1979)6–9 SC51 at 64.*

279 See Posner, R. A. & Gluck, A. R. (2019). Statutory Interpretation on the Bench: A Survey of Forty-Two Judges on the Federal Courts of Appeal, *opcit*: "The younger judges, who attended law school and practiced during the ascendance of textualism, are generally more formalist and accepting of the canons of construction, regardless of political affiliation. The older judges that are less focused on canons, take a broader view of their delegated authority, and appear to grapple more with questions of judicial legitimacy."

280 This author's theory, socio-judicialism, is published in her dissertation, which will be the second volume of this research/book. This book introduces the theory.

281 The author created these principles as she gleaned from various Nigerian cases/case law.

but they are different.[282] Thus, before we proceed with this discussion, it is vital to understand the difference between the principles and canons of interpretation. Canons of interpretation are rules that judges apply in interpreting statutes, while principles of interpreting statutes are the foundational base to applying the canon. The principles of interpretation are like a compass/roadmap that directs courts on how to apply the rules to interpret statutes. These principles also dictate the judges mind and thought pattern. They basically answer what, how, and why of judicial interpretation. These principles are support mechanisms that guide judges on what rule or canon fits a specific case, how judges should apply the rule, and why the rule makes sense to the justice of the case.

The principles of statutory interpretation are preliminary conditions that resonate in judges' minds and aid them in applying the appropriate canons of interpretation. They direct judges to adopt the right approach in each case. The Court in *University of Lagos & Ors. v. Professor Luke Uka Uche*[283] states that it is the court's duty while construing the statutory provision to have regard to basic principles depending on the words and phrases the statute uses.[284] Therefore, it has become a standard requirement for Nigerian courts to adhere to these basic principles while interpreting statutory provisions. The courts have laid down these principles in numerous cases.[285] Also, Ijaiye[286] outlined four principles of interpretation similar to the canons/rules of interpretation:[287]

---

282 In *Tejumade A. Clement & Anor v. Bridget J. Iwuanyanwu & Anor (1989) Nigerian cases/ case law LPELR-872 (SC)*. Oputa, JSC, explains that principles are wider than rules. Rules apply in all or nothing dimension. Principles merely inclines a decision one way but not conclusively. Principles are distilled from the facts of the case in which they were promulgated. As principles draw their inspiration and strength from the facts which framed the issues for decision, it follows that when the facts are not similar, the principle need not apply or be applied to the new case. See also *Adegoke Motors Ltd. v. Dr. Babatunde Adesanya & Anor (1989) LPELR-94 (SC)*.

283 *University of Lagos & Ors. v. Professor Luke Uka Uche (2008) LPELR-5073 (CA)*.

284 See *Ugwu v. Arurume (2007) 31 WRN 1 at 60–61*.

285 See *A.G Bendel Sate v. A.G federation (1981) SC 1; Agbaje v. Fashola (2008) All FWLR (pt.443) 1302 at 1337 B-C; PDP v. Ugba & Ors (2011) LPELR-4838 (CA)*.

286 He recommends that to avoid judges applying different conflicting personal nuances and predilections, the legislature should indicate in an enactment the principles that must be used in its interpretation.

287 Ijaiye, H. O. (2017). Constitutional Approach to Interpretation of the Constitutions in Nigeria, Australia, Canada, and India, opcit: 145.

- The language of the Constitution must be given its plain meaning.
- The provisions of the Constitution must be read together as a whole.
- Words of the Constitution must be given a broader interpretation.
- The provisions of the Constitution should not be interpreted to have retrospect.[288]

Therefore, gleaning from the above and several other cases, this writer creates and categorizes twelve principles that (inadvertently) guide judges in interpreting statutes. These inexhaustive principles are not mandatory but recommended.

5 Twelve Principles that guide Judicial Interpretation

These principles confine judge's discretion to the specific cases, parties, and adverse circumstances that precedent does not consider. Hence, in applying these principles, the judge gets a leeway to think outside the box and patterns his/her decision according to each cases unique demands. Some of these principles overlap and contradict another, which is typical and one of the challenges in the act of judging. The principles are as follows.

5.1 Drafters' Intention Principle

This principle is a pointer to the literal rule of interpretation and directs judges to ascertain the true intention of the legislature, so they do not import words into legislation that is contrary to the legislators' intentions.[289] This principle indicates the aspect of the law that legislators' clearly interprets the true intention of the drafters with unambiguous words.[290] So, where the judge observes an unambiguous word in the statute, he does not resort to another rule or canon. An example is that the word "shall" is a clear command and does not require another interpretation or an attempt to understand

288 Ibid: 187.

289 See *Federal University of Technology, Akure & Anor v. Asuu (2013) LPELR-20323 (CA)*.

290 Also, in *Attorney General, Federation v. Attorney General, Lagos State (2013) 16 NWLR (Pt 1380) 249*, the court states that in interpreting a statute, a court must not give the statute an interpretation that would defeat the intention and purpose of the lawmakers and should not read a particular provision of the statute in isolation; rather, the whole statute should be read so as to discover the intention of the lawmakers.

the drafters' intention. The case is different when the statute used the word "may," which gives room for judicial discretion. In *A.G Bendel State v. A.G federation*,[291] Obaseki, JSC, summarized ten principles that judges should consider in interpreting statutes. His principle four stated that "the language of the Constitution where clear and unambiguous must be given its plain evidence meaning." Similarly, in *Agbaje v. Fashola*,[292] the court's first of four principles reads: "a liberal approach to the interpretation of the Constitution or statute should be adopted." Also, in *PDP v. Ugba & Ors*,[293] the first of the five principles from the Court, states: "it is the intention of the Legislature that should be sought, and same is to be ascertained from the words of the statute alone and not from other sources." Obaseki's eight principle caps up this principle as follows: "Words are the common signs that mankind makes use of to declare their intention one to another and when the words of a man express his meaning plainly and distinctly and perfectly, there is no occasion to have recourse to any other means of interpretation."[294]

5.2 Holistic Principle

This principle streamlines the relevant aspect of the law that the judge should concentrate on in interpreting. It stipulates that the relevant provision of the statute be read together with the rest of the statute to arrive at a comprehensive interpretation.[295] This principle comes handy when the judge encounters an ambiguous or verbose statute. It reiterates the harmonious rule of interpretation. Obaseki's tenth principle reads: "Words of the Constitution are therefore not to be read with stultifying narrowness."[296]

According to Sokefu and Njoku, the words of an Act should be read in the entire context, in their grammatical and ordinary sense, harmoniously with

---

291 Supra.

292 Ibid.

293 Ibid.

294 See *A.G Bendel State v. A.G federation*, ibid.

295 In *A.G Federation v. Alhaji Atiku Abubakar (Appeal No. CA/A/21/07, delivered on 5th April 2007)*, "one of the basic principles of interpretation of all Constitutions and statutes is that the lawmaker will not be presumed to have given a right in one section and take it in another."

296 See *A.G Bendel State v. A.G federation*, supra.

the scheme of the Act, and the intent of the parliament.[297] Words alone, do not exist in a vacuum; they exist along with other words which the interpreter should consider together with the other words and aspects of the statute.[298] The Court in *Ibrahim v. Mohammed*[299] states that as a rule of interpretation, statues should be read together with all related provisions and the entire statute.[300] The courts also state that it is imperative when interpreting a section to read the entire subsections together, have a comprehensive perspective, and discover the legislators' intention in enacting the said provisions.[301]

In addition, Muhammad, JSC, stated in *Akpamgbo-Okadigbo v. Chidi & 7 Ors*:[302] "Lest we forget, it is a cardinal principle of interpretation that provisions of a statute should not be read in isolation ... the provisions must be read together. Thus, in ascertaining the true meaning of the provisions of a statute, the statute must be read as a whole."[303] Similarly, in *PDP v. INEC*[304], Uwais, CJN, stated that in interpreting the provision or section of a statute or indeed the Constitution, statute provisions or section should not be read in isolation from the other parts of the Constitution; in other words, the statute or Constitution should be read as a whole to determine the intendment of the makers of the statute or the Constitution.[305] Also, in the American case of *United Sav. Ass'n of Tex v. Timbers of in wood Forest Assocs. Ltd*,[306] Scalia, J, stated that courts should refrain from interpreting statutes in isolation. Thus, where an optional word like "may" is used in a statute, this holistic principle

---

297 Sokefu & Njoku, (2016), opcit: 18.

298 Ibid.

299 *Ibrahim v. Mohammed (2003) LPELR-1409 (SC) at 23.*

300 In *Skye Bank v. Iwu (2017) LPELR-42595 (SC)*, the Supreme Court reiterates interpretation of a statute is a holistic endeavor.

301 See *Eboreime v. Olagbegi & Ors (2018) LPELR-44816 (CA)*. Also, in *Olatunbosun v. Odunjo & Ors (2016) LPELR-40542 (CA)*, the court reinforced the purport of interpreting a statute together with the entire and not in isolation.

302 *Akpamgbo-Okadigbo v. Chidi & 7 Ors (2015) LPELR-25464 (SC) 28.*

303 *See Obayuwana v. Governor Bendel State & Anor. (1982) 12 SC. 147 and Action Congress (Ac) And Anor v. INEC (2007) 12 NWLR (PT. 1048) 222 at 259.*

304 *PDP v. INEC (1999) 7 SC (pt. 11) 30.*

305 Also, in *Odutela Holdings v. Ladejob (2006) 12 NWLR (ot.994) SC 321*, the courts held that when a section has more than one subsection, all must be read carefully to ascertain whether it should be interpreted conjunctively in line with the principles of construction of statutes with many subsections.

306 *United Sav. Ass'n of Tex v. Timbers of in wood Forest Assocs Ltd 484 U.S 365, 371 (1988).*

directs the judge to an all-inclusive procedure to adopt in interpreting. The judge becomes more alert and applies caution to understand what the drafters meant by asking "why," and what the drafters expect the judge to do.

Are there moments that may require the judge to interpret a word in isolation of the rest of the statute? I believe so. Quite rear but likely, especially as exceptions to the general rule may apply. For example, if the specific provision gives an unclear perspective on an issue that has no precedent like the application of AI in court proceedings, the judge could isolate that provision and not resort to the rest of the statutes as the statute may not be up to date on technology procedures. So, where the word "may" or "shall" is the bone of contention in interpreting the statute one way or the other, the judge can make an exception, again with the latitude of discretion and considering the unique circumstances of a new technology like AI and interpret the statute distinctively. However, this must be done with every sense of caution and as a last resort. The contextualizing principle explains this point more succinctly.[307]

5.3 Constitutional Alignment Principle

This principle is one of supremacy. It directs courts to ensure that the rules of interpretation applied in a case align with the spirit of the Constitution—the preamble. Obaseki's fifth principle states: "The Constitution of the federal Republic of Nigeria is an organic scheme of government to be dealt with as an entirety; a particular provision cannot be severed from the rest of the Constitution."[308]

Judges have the duty to avoid interpretations that would raise serious doubts about the statute's constitutionality or legality. They must ensure that the interpretation they give aligns with the Constitution's essence. Obaseki's third principle states: "a constitutional power cannot be used by the way of condition to attain unconstitutional result."[309] Similarly, in *Abegunde v. The Ondo State House of Assembly & Ors*,[310] the Court of Appeal held that the general principle of law that governs interpretation of the Constitution or

307 See principle 6 below.

308 See *A.G Bendel Sate v. A.G federation, supra.*

309 Ibid.

310 *Abegunde v. The Ondo State House of Assembly & Ors (2014) LPELR-23683 (CA).*

any statue should be the interpretation that serves the Constitution's/statute's aim or that best carry out its objective and purpose. In *Nwali v. Ebsiec & Ors*,[311] one of the principles suitable to the Constitution's *sui generis*[312] nature is that judges give a benevolent, broad, liberal, and purposive interpretation.

Furthermore, according to Obaseki's seventh principle, "A constitutional provision should not be construed so as to defeat its evidence purpose."[313] To promote its underlying policy or purpose, courts must avoid a narrow, strict, technical, and legalistic interpretation to accommodate the democratic essence of the Constitution's preamble. Thus, if the use of the word "shall" in a statute indicates discrimination against a citizen's gender, race, nationality, etc., this principle directs the judge to a more superior law that gives the judge discretion to disregard that law as contrary to the Constitution and to reiterate the human rights provisions that discourages discrimination.[314]

5.4 Precedent Principle

This principle reiterates adherence to precedent, which indicates Nigeria's judicial norm and culture. It directs judges to apply the appropriate precedent where necessary. The status quo requires Nigerian judges to rely on precedent in deciding cases.[315] So, when a judge is interpreting a statute, the first point of call is resorting to precedent. If precedent exist, the lower court is bound by law to adhere to the precedent. If the lower court disregards the precedent, the higher court deems this as judicial deviance, and an affront to the existing norm.[316] In *Dalhatu v. Turaki*,[317] Katsina-Alu, JSC, stated that the Supreme Court is Nigeria's highest and final Court of Appeal. Its decisions bind every court, authority, or person in Nigeria. Thus, where a lower court judge refuses to comply with such a decision, he/she is

311 *Nwali v. Ebsiec & Ors (2014) LPELR-23682 (CA).*

312 *Sue generis* is a Latin maxim that means "of its own kind."

313 See *A.G Bendel Sate v. A.G federation, supra.*

314 See Chapter 4 of the CFRN, as amended.

315 See *Kobia Osumanu v. Kofi Amadu & 2ors (1949) 12 WACA 437; A.G Ogun State and Anor v. Dr. L.C. Egenty (1986) 1 C.A. (pt. 11) page 162; Nwangwu v. Nwangwu (2000) Pt. 2 FWLR Page 273.*

316 Tobi, The Nigerian Judge, opcit: 42.

317 *Dalhatu v. Turaki (2003) 15 NWLR Pt. 843 page 310 at 323.*

considered a judicial misfit or a "judicial rascal."[318] Thus, according to this principle, judges must first consider the existing precedent in interpreting a case before resorting an alternative. The alternative is an exception to the general rule, where the judge can distinguish the case and disregard the precedent because it has certain aspects of the present case that differ from the precedent.[319] For example, if the precedent, which was established under the old Constitution, requires the judge to comply with the word "shall," and contravenes a constitutional requirement of equal treatment, the lower court judge can refer to the revised Constitution and re-interpret the statues accordingly.

5.5 The Strict Adherence Principle

This principle enjoins judges to abide strictly by the meaning of words used in a statute and not add to or remove any language from the statute. This principle differs from the drafters' intention principle as it helps judges to focus on the drafters' words and not their intentions. Afterall, nobody, except God, can really tell one's true intentions. The court's third principle in *PDP v. Ugba & Ors* states that "the court must not import into legislation words that the legislature did not use and words that will give a different meaning to the statute's text as enacted by the Legislature." This principle informs judges to highlight the specific words used in the statutes and directs them on how to connect the words to the whole statutes to interpret the drafters' intentions. It emphasizes the importance of words and semantics in interpreting statutes. According to the court's fourth principle in *PDP v. Ugba & Ors*, "the court must not bring to bear on the provisions of a statute its prejudices as to what the law should be, but rather should interpret the law from the clear words the Legislature uses."

Thus, to understand the statute's purpose, the judges should detect the semantics that applies to the specific word or set of words being interpreted. In *Awolowo v. Shagari & Ors*,[320] the court stated that anybody called upon to interpret any kind of statute should not, for any reason, attach to its statutory provision a meaning which the words of the statute cannot

318 Ibid.

319 See Chapter 5 for detailed discussions on judicial precedent.

320 *Awolowo v. Shagari & Ors (1979) LPELR-653(SC) P. 22para B-C.*

reasonably bear.[321] However, if the words have more than one meaning, then the person interpreting the statute can choose between the meanings that fit the circumstances of each case but not beyond. This calls for strict judicial discretion.

In *Kolawole v. Alberto*,[322] the court reiterates that courts should assume that the legislator intended a different meaning where the legislator uses words differently from those originally used. When the statute's words are clear and unambiguous, they are interpreted as is. Still, if the words or the entire statute are ambiguous and vague, the courts attempt to construct a meaning that defines the drafters "original meaning or intention."[323] Nigerian courts warn against a voyage of discovery in interpreting statutes.[324] In *Johnson v. Mobil Producing (Nig) Unlimited*,[325] the court stated that a court is not entitled to read anything into or remove anything from statutes unless there are adequate grounds to justify the inference that the legislature intended something which it omitted to express.

5.6 Contextualizing Principle

This principle means that the words in a statute should be used within the context of the specific situation or case. It helps judges to streamline the drafter's intention where there is mischief or ambiguity, within a context. The court's fourth principle in *Agbaje v. Fashola*[326] states that in interpreting statutes, the judge must bear in mind that "the mischief which the legislation was made to deter is arrested."[327] Obaseki's second principle stated: "A construction nullifying a specific clause will not be given to the construction unless absolutely

---

321 The Court of Appeal supported this point in *Mwana v. UBN (2003) 28 W.R.N 62* when Muhammed, JCA, said, "if the words of the statute are in themselves precise and unambiguous, no more is necessary than to expand those words in their natural and ordinary sense, as the words themselves in such case best declare the intention of the legislature."

322 *Kolawole v. Alberto (1989) 1 N.W.L.R (pt98) 382.*

323 Karibi-Whyte, JSC, ibid.

324 See *A.G Abia State v. A.G Federation (2006) 16 NWLR (pt. 1005) 265.*

325 *Johnson v. Mobil Producing (Nig) Unlimited (2010) 7 NWLR (Pt 1194) 462.*

326 See *Agbaje v. Fashola (2008) All FWLR (pt.443) 1302 at 1337 B-C.*

327 This position was restated in the case of *Skye Bank v. Iwu (supra).*

required by the context."[328] Also, in *Tinubu v. I.M.B Securities*,[329] Karibi-Whyte, JSC, held that the facts of the case should guide the interpretation of the Constitution. The meaning of a word can only make sense from the facts accompanying it. Thus, words best explain the statute's meanings within a context of facts or evidence and not in isolation.

In *Federal Republic of Nigeria v. Osahon*,[330] the Supreme Court stated that where a statute makes the meaning of a provision difficult to discern properly, it is the court's indispensable right to explore deeper and to attempt to make sense of it in the context of the primary law. The court's attempt following the construction of the words will eventually carry meaning which would help to promote the statute to optimize the cause of justice and to advance the sociological jurisprudence of the rule of law. The case of *Nigerian Navy v. Lambert*[331] explained this principle. The Supreme Court held that in interpreting statutes that restrict the citizen's rights, any doubt, gap, duplicity, or ambiguity regarding the meaning of words used in the enactment should be resolved in favor of the person who should be liable to the penalty or deprivation of his right.[332]

5.7 The Legislative History Principle

This principle comes from the statute's history and what led the drafters to enact the law. It directs courts to consider more than the strict application of plain meaning and refers to the history of a statute to confirm the plain meaning or intended meaning. The third principle from *Agbaje v. Fashola* states "the historical facts which are necessary for the comprehension of the subject matter may be called in aid."[333]According to the Supreme Court, it is sometimes helpful to look into the history of the legislation to ascertain the mischief in the statute properly.[334] About interpreting the 1979 Constitution, Nnanami, JSC, suggested that "should there still be any lingering doubts as to the proper meaning of section 230 (1) (b), I would suggest that it is

328 *A.G Bendel Sate v. A.G federation(supra).*

329 *Tinubu v. I.M.B Securities (2001) 8 NWLR (PT 740) 192.*

330 *Federal Republic of Nigeria v. Osahon (2005)25 NSCQR512 at 537.*

331 *Nigerian Navy v. Lambert (2007) LPELR-2026 (SC).*

332 See also *Nwosu v. Imo State Environmental Sanitation Authority & Ors. (1990) 2 NWLR (pt.135) 688 at 723; Peenok Investment Ltd. V. Hotel Presidential Ltd. (1982) 12 SC 1 at 25.*

333 *Agbaje v. Fashola (supra).*

334 *Ifezue v. Mbadugha & Anor (1984) LPELR-1437 (SC).*

legitimate to look back at the history of the process which brought the 1979 Constitution, and particularly section 230 into being."[335]

Furthermore, in *Nkwocha v. Governor of Anambra State & Ors.*,[336] the Nigerian Supreme Court cited the American case of *Knowlton v. Moore*[337] and emphasized that it is a legitimate principle of interpretation for the history of legislation to afford some assistance in determining the proper meaning of the legislation. In another American case, *Green v. Bock Laundry Machine Co.*,[338] Justice Scalia agreed on the appropriateness of consulting legislative history to determine whether what appeared to be an absurd meaning of a key statutory term was indeed considered and intended. Similarly, another American court in *Thunder Basin Coal Co. v. Reich*[339] held that "the legislative history of the Mine Act confirms its interpretation."[340] This principle comes in handy when there is no other option to explain the drafter's intention to the judge.

5.8 Drafters' Error Principle

This principle guides judges to be circumspective in interpreting statutes or in assuming the drafters' intents. It reminds us that the drafters are human beings who can commit errors in legislative drafting and that the drafters may have included certain provisions in the statutes for selfish or political reasons, or even from limited experience or understanding. For example, statutory law originally/historically defined crime, criminals and deviance as committed by low-incomed/low-class/low-social status members of the society. However the definition of crime has now advanced to include white-collar crimes and political crimes, which are crimes committed by persons of high social status, and political leaders who possibly enacted the statutes or influenced the enactment.[341] This principle also highlights that judges are also human and since no

335 *Bronik Motors Ltd & Anor v. Wema Bank Ltd (supra).*

336 *Nkwocha v. Governor of Anambra State & Ors (1984) LPELR-2052 (SC).*

337 *Knowlton v. Moore 178 U.S 41 (1990).*

338 *Green v. Bock Laundry Machine Co., 490 U.S. 504 (1989).*

339 *Thunder Basin Coal Co. v. Reich,510 U.S. 200, 209 (1994).*

340 However, in *Darby v. Cisneros, 509 U.S. 137, 147 (1993)*, "recourse to the legislative history of S.10(c) was considered unnecessary considering the plain meaning of the statutory text, when the Court considered the legislative history, nevertheless, and found nothing inconsistent between it and the Court's reading of statutory language."

341 See Sutherland, E.H, "Differential Association Theory and Differential Social Organization." Encyclopedia of Criminological Theory. (2010) Sage Publications.

human is infallible, erroneous interpretations are inevitable. Therefore, there should be an expectation that statutes may include drafting errors likely to create ambiguities and confusion for judges to interpret. Although, technically it is not the judge's role to amend such drafters' errors, judges may, in the interest of justice, comment on drafters' errors to instigate legislative amendment.

Technically, though inadvertently, this principle helps judges to correct drafters errors while interpreting the mischief. However, the court must be cautious. In *United States v. Locke*,[342] the Court dealt with a drafting error in a statute that required the claimant to file a case "prior to December 31." Even though Congress meant to say "on or before December 31," the Court held that dates have a plain meaning. It was the legislature's responsibility to be more careful, not the court's job, to rescue Congress from its error.[343] The second principle in *PDP v. Ugba & Ors* states: "the court is not concerned with the results of its interpretation, that is, it is not the court's province to pronounce on the wisdom or otherwise of the statute but only to determine its meaning."

5.9 The Clear Boundaries Principle

This principle reiterates the doctrine of separation of powers and emphasizes that the courts maintain their judicial limits and does not encroach on legislative functions to draft laws. This writer gleaned this principle from the case of *SETRACO (Nig) Ltd v. Kpaji*,[344] that courts are guided by a clear boundary beyond which, they cannot enter. Thus, while the courts have power to interpret the law, they have no license to veer into the legislative arena or assign themselves the legislative role, regardless of how unfair or unsatisfying the legislation may be.[345] This is because once the words are plain and unambiguous, the court is duty-bound to give effect to those words and not interpret the law as it ought to be. The Court,[346] in *Dickson v. Sylva*

---

342 *United States v. Locke 471 U.S, 84 (1985).*

343 Ibid.

344 *SETRACO (Nig) Ltd v. Kpaji (2017) LPELR-41560 (SC) Hon. Justice Peter-Odili, JSC, PP 25–26 paras D-A.*

345 Ibid.

346 The Chief Justice of Nigeria.

& Ors,[347] stated that a court cannot embark on a voyage of legislating while interpreting a statute. The court further stated that courts ought to expound and not expand the law, that is, to decide what the law is and not what it should be; it should tow the path of objectivity and not be subjective.[348]

Also, in *A.G Bendel State v. A.G Federation and 22 Ors*,[349] Fatayi-Williams, JSC, held that Nigeria courts have the power and indeed the duty to ensure that there is no infraction of the exercise of legislative power, whether substantive or procedural, as stated in the relevant provisions of the Constitution. Nevertheless, this writer argues the courts' role could be contradictory as judges often decide what the law is and what it should be—this is how precedent is created. In the second volume of this research, this writer categorized and defines the real and ideal roles of courts and explained judges' impactful roles to include expanding the law.[350] After all, that was how the British Common Law that Nigeria applies was created. However, the courts should not exceed their required statutory roles.

5.10 TheJustice Principle

This principle directs judges to the path of equity, which states that judges should interpret statutes from a fair perspective and decide according to the best interest of justice. This principle should prevail over rules of judicial[351] or mental[352] technicality when interpreting statutes.[353] In *Nafiu Rabiu v. The State*,[354] Udo Udoma, JSC, stated that where the issue is whether the Constitution has used an expression in a wider or narrow sense, the court should always lean where the justice of the case so demands—to the broader

347 *Dickson v. Sylva & Ors (2016). LPELR-41257 (SC) JSC P. 78, paras C-F.*

348 With all due respect, this writer disagrees with this statement, as the role of judging entails both expounding and expanding the law, despite how we look at it. However, to avoid deviating from our focus, details of this will be reserved for future discussions.

349 *A.G Bendel State v. A.G Federation and 22 Ors (1983) NCLR 1 at 40.*

350 The second volume of this research will be available as soon as possible.

351 Judicial technicality as this author defines it is procedural technicality as per the court system and all the procedures that accompany the justice system.

352 Mental technicality is in the judge's mind—the judge's mindset.

353 *A.G Lagos v. A.G Federation*, "in interpreting the Constitution, we should avoid technicality." Hon. Justice Uwais, CJN.

354 *Nafiu Rabiu v. The State (1981)2 NCLR 326.*

interpretation unless there is something in the context or in the rest of the Constitution to indicate that the narrow interpretation will best carry the Constitution's object and purpose. Obaseki's ninth principle says: "The principles upon which the Constitution was established rather than the direct operation of literal meaning of the words used, measure the purpose and scope of its provisions."[355]

In explaining the value of equity in interpreting laws, Abiru, JCA, stated that there is a presumption against the legislature intending what is unreasonable and inconvenient in interpreting statutes. He argued that judges apply common sense and adopt reason in construing statutes and the construction agreeable to justice. Thus, where words used in an enactment are open to two interpretations, in which one will lead to an absurdity while the other would give effect to what common sense shows was intended, courts should apply the interpretation that accords with common sense.[356]

5.11 International Law Compliance Principle

This principle enables the court to apply international law standards in interpreting statutes when necessary. It guides the court to ensure that judicial interpretation complies with international law standards. In *Abacha & Ors. v. Fawehinmi*,[357] the Supreme Court stated that statutory interpretation should not violate international law. In other words, judges should interpret statutes in compliance with international law standards. Accordingly, the court should apply international law, where international standards and perspective give the statute relevant meaning, and depicts justice to the parties. An example will be cases on human rights, where the parties seek the court's intervention to uphold chapter two of the Nigerian Constitution.

5.12 The Society Principle

This principle emphasizes the democratic principle of "We the People." It helps the court to interpret statutes based on public interest. This principle directs the courts to take into consideration the constant changes in society and interpret laws according to the relevant changes in society. In *A.G Bendel*

---

355 See *A.G Bendel Sate v. A.G federation (supra).*

356 Abiru, ibid: 17.

357 *Abacha & Ors. v. Fawehinmi (supra).*

Sate v. A.G federation,[358] Obaseki's sixth principle says: "while the language of the Constitution does not change the changing circumstances of a progressive society for which it was designed, it yields new and fuller imports to its meaning." This principle complements all others and guides judges to question the relevance of the statute to the people and their present predominant social circumstances. According to the Court's second principle in *Agbaje v. Fashola*,[359] "the court must employ care and take the circumstances of the people into consideration."

There is no hard and fast rule in applying or adopting the above principles. So, in summary, before interpreting a statute, judges must first ask suggestive questions to guide their choice of the specific principle(s) to adopt and the relevant canon to apply. Accordingly, the suggestive questions are as follows:

1. What is the drafters' intention? That is, the drafters' intention principle.
2. Is there a prior superior court decision interpreting these provisions? That is, the precedent principle.
3. Does this provision or statute have strict application clauses like "shall," "must," "should," "requirement," "mandatory," etc.? That is, the strict adherence principle.[360]
4. Does this word/phrase/paragraph stand on its own or does it require more explanation from other aspects of the law? That is, the holistic principle.[361]
5. In what context is/are the word(s) being used? That is, the contextualizing principle.[362]
6. Does the drafters' choice of words depict a historical framework? That is, the legislative history principle.
7. From the holistic view of the provision/statutes, are there possible errors on the drafting intentions? That is, the drafters' error principle.[363]

---

358 Opcit.

359 See *Abaje v. Fashiola (supra)*.

360 Does this provision/statute depict a strict meaning that drafters intended? The strict adherence principle comes as support to the drafter's intention and gives it more clarity.

361 In some statutes, certain words stand alone, while other words cannot be used in isolation until connected to other words in the same document.

362 This contextualizes the words as part of the statutes and facts. It complements the holistic and strict interpretation principle.

363 This principle inadvertently helps judges to correct drafters' errors, while interpreting the mischief.

8. Does the provision/statutes have a caveat or clear instruction that restricts judges to a specific interpretation? That is, the clear boundaries principle.[364]
9. Will this form of interpretation serve the justice of this case? That is, the justice principle.[365]
10. Does this provision/legislation comply with international standards/ treaties that Nigeria is signatory to? That is, the international law compliance principle.[366]
11. Does this provision align with constitutional requirements? That is, the constitutional alignment principle.
12. How do these provisions/statutes impact social change/the public/society? That is, the society principle.

These principles are not mandatory but highly recommended and necessary to ease the act of judging, and to guide judges, especially newly appointed judges. Some of these principles, like the international law compliance principle, are conditional principles. Judges may resort to any or all of the principles somewhere within the proceedings. For example, if the drafters intention does not make sense, a holistic analysis would be necessary, however, the three most important and indispensable principles are the precedent principle, the constitutional alignment, and the justice principle. In no particular order, these trio are intertwined in application, as judges must comply with existing precedents, interpret statutes that speak the Constitution's language, and ensure justice in the case.

Notably, the type or nature of the case, and/or the party in the case determines the applicable principle. For example, a case with the government as a party would most likely require the judge to consider the historic principle, the society principle in addition to the three mandatory principles discussed above.[367] Also, cases on judicial review, writ of mandamus, would require the constitutional alignment and historic principles, in addition to the mandatory principles.[368] So, "like the hero who saves the day," courts should interpret the statute using any appropriate principle of interpretation to adopt a canon, to

364 The boundaries will be crossed if interpreting in a particular way.
365 This is the final recap where the principle helps judges determine justice from the facts, evidence,and statutes of the case.
366 This principle is most relevant with human rights cases.
367 See the previous paragraph.
368 Ibid.

save society and government from the "villain" of unnecessary ambiguous statutes or statutory errors, which could lead to unprogressive caselaw, societal frustration, lack of public trust, and eventually democratic crisis.

6 Judicial Approaches to Interpreting Statutes

Judicial approaches to interpreting statutes involve judges' attitudes, viewpoints, ideas, values, and beliefs. Judges adopt various approaches to aid statutory interpretation. These approaches depict the personal or collective philosophies of the individual judge or a group of judges, as precedent stipulates. Philosophies of judging also mean schools of statutory interpretation. Different schools or philosophies adopt various approaches to interpreting statutes.[369] Also, judges apply practical standards to the facts of a case to ensure that the drafters' intended design/objective captures the facts and ensures justice in the case.

Accordingly, their assessment or review of the case follows principles that direct or influence modes of interpretation. The judge's perception or the precedent in a case often influences the philosophy the judge adopts in interpretation.[370] These approaches are not specifically noted or known as such in Nigeria, as the Nigerian courts are not necessarily interested in the semantics but in the actions/outcome which the principle dictates. In addition, no known literature intentionally connects the Nigerian practical mode of judicial interpretation to a specific judicial philosophy/approach of interpretation. So, for a more comprehensive perspective, and for the purpose of this book's thesis, I discuss the more prominent and established approaches/philosophy of judicial interpretation.

Generally, there are four modern jurisprudential theories of judicial decision-making. They are positivism,[371] moralism,[372] formalism,[373] and realism.[374] Positivism and moralism are diametrically opposed; formalism and realism are

369 Eig, opcit.
370 No doubt these philosophies are gleaned from precedent.
371 According to the positivist, "law" is what the law says and nothing more; it is simply rules.
372 To the moralist, "law" is what is right; it is simply morality and justice.
373 To the formalist, the application of law is mechanical.
374 To the realist, the application of law is dynamic.

antithetical.[375] However, Nigerian courts informally apply two similar approaches/ philosophies to interpreting statutes—the formalist (constructionist, textualist, or originalist) approach and the realist (purposive or proactive) approach.

6.1 Formalism

Formalism is a philosophy that restricts statutory interpretation to the exact text of the law.[376] The formalist judge aims to transfer the literal meaning of the word or statute from the legislation to the bench. Formalist judges are somewhat conservative, and they believe that they can use established forms of logic, based on fundamental Common Law principles to determine the meaning of any text of a statute.[377] According to Posner, "'formalist' can mean narrow, conservative, hypocritical, resistant to change, casuistic, descriptively inaccurate (that is 'unrealistic' in the ordinary language sense of the word) Ivory-towered, fallacious, callow, authoritarian,—but also rigorous, modest, reasoned, faithful, self-denying and restrained." Strict construction of a statute does not expand the law by implication or equitable consideration; strict construction confines its operation to cases clearly within the statute's letter and the statute's (supposed spirit) or reason.[378]

6.2 Realism

Realism is driven by logic and social improvement. It theorizes that courts should adhere to interpretations that advance the importance of moral ideas and human values in society.[379] For legal realists, there is "no single right and accurate way of reading a case."[380] Realists believe that a text's sense of purpose should guide interpretation. Hence, if the purpose of the text is discernible, the text's literal meaning is unnecessary.[381] The realist judge has a distaste for legal jargon and wants non-lawyers to be able to read judicial opinions with no ambiguity.[382] According to Hines, "the proponents of traditional realism and

---

375 Hine, K. D. (1997). The Rule of Law is Dead, Long Live the Rule: An Essay on Legal Rules, Equitable Standards, and The Debate Over Judicial Discretion, opcit: 1779.

376 Scalia, the arch formalist of statutory and constitutional interpretation.

377 Brannon, opcit: 6.

378 Black's Law Dictionary (8th ed.), opcit.

379 Monahan, J. & Walker, L. (2002). Social Science in Law: Cases and Materials, opcit: 24.

380 Ibid: 7.

381 Posner, R. A. (2013). Reflections on Judging, Harvard University Press, USA, opcit: 120.

382 Ibid.

critical legal studies, the 'law' is what the law says. Judicial pronouncements and legislative directives provide the building blocks for judicial decision making. But what the law 'says' is unclear. Ambiguities, contradictions, and exceptions in the positive law leave room for (and indeed) selective interpretation. For these scholars, the ultimate application of the law is dynamic and indeterminate."[383] Unfortunately, it is this belief in the indeterminacy of legal decision-making that leads realist scholars to reject rule of law.[384]

The formalist and realist approaches are most prominent in the U.S. courts. In Nigerian, more judges seem to apply the liberal approach.[385]

6.3 Liberal Approach

The *liberal approach*, also called "broad interpretation," is interpretation according to what the reader believes the author reasonably intends, even though inadvertently, the author failed to think of how his/her reader may perceive, interpret, or understand the words.[386] Hence, the text carries a narrow meaning compared to originalism.[387] Liberalism takes a convenient spot somewhere between formalism and realism.[388] The Nigerian Supreme Court instructs the adoption of a liberal approach.[389] According to Udo Udoma, JSC, the courts' approach to the construction of the Constitution should be (and so it has been), one of liberalism, as it is not the duty of the courts to defeat the obvious aim of the Constitution under the guise of interpretation.[390] Also, in *Ali v. Albishir*,[391] courts were enjoined to adopt a liberal approach and, in doing so, give the provisions an interpretation that portrays the intentions of the document's framers.[392]

---

383 Hine, K. D., opcit: 1781.

384 Smithburn, J. E. (2006). Judicial Discretion, opcit: 49.

385 The difference may just be based on nomenclature.

386 Also termed *mixed interpretation*. Blacks (4th ed.), Henry Campbell Black, M. A., p. 2399.

387 Ibid: 2400.

388 However, liberalism adheres more to the strict constructionist approach than to precedent.

389 The liberal approach could also be seen as a formal approach/formalism, as they have the same meaning but different terms.

390 See *Rabiu v. State (1981) 2 NCLR 293 at 326.*

391 *Ali v. Albishir (2008) 3 NWLR (Pt. 1073) 94 at Pp. 130–131, paras. H-A.*

392 See *NURTW & Anor v. RTEAN & Ors. (2012) LPELR-7840 (SC).*

6.4 Proactive Approach

The *proactive approach* was proposed by Ijaiye.[393] According to him, this approach to constitutional interpretation confers more certainty to the purpose of the legislation, as no words have a single and definite meaning without drawing from the values, bias, perceptions, prejudice, and training of the interpreter (the judge).[394] This approach does not confer an additional duty on the judge. Judges still act within their judicial enclave, but they should look beyond the literal meaning of the words construed to ensure that the interpretation does not defeat the policy objectives of the enactment.[395]

The rules and principles of interpretation appear intertwined or dependent on one another, and Nigerian courts understand this, hence the greater use of the liberal approach. Duxbury stated that "all that is certain is that some so-called realists, despite their opposition to the tradition of legal formalism, did not, in their writings, extricate themselves once and for all from the clutches of that tradition. Legal realism, we might say, was not entirely anti-formalist; for legal formalism, often heavily disguised, persisted under the realist banner."[396] However, Brannon opines that although judges have taken various approaches to resolving a statute's meaning, proponents of formalism and realism theories generally share the goal of adhering to Congress' (legislature's) intended meaning but disagree about how best to achieve that goal.[397] Now to this author's jurisprudence- the soico-judicial approach.

7 Introducing the Socio-Judicial Approach to Interpreting Statutes

The socio-judicial approach (SJA) to interpreting statutes is this author's concept from her socio-judicialism theory (SJT)—the crux of her research, introduced in Chapter 6.[398] The SJT lays the foundation for this socio-judicial approach to interpretation. SJT found formal expression during this writer's

393 Ijaiye, opcit.

394 Ibid.

395 Ibid: 183.

396 Duxbury. (1995). Patterns of American Jurisprudence, opcit: 64.

397 Brannon V. C. (2018). Statutory Interpretation: Theories, Tools, and Trends, opcit: 2.

398 This author has been researching this theory (inadvertently) since the 80s and intentionally since 1995 as an undergraduate law and sociology student. The semi-formal

postgraduate program in judicial studies at the University of Nevada, Reno, U.S.A.[399] This author discussed a detailed historical base of this theory in her dissertation, which is the second phase and volume of this research.[400]

The SJA to interpreting statutes emphasizes the significant impact of courts on society and the impact of society on judicial decisions. It promotes the democratic principle of "We the People" and the predominant role of public interest over the literal rule of interpretation. This approach feeds off the purposeful approach and reiterates society's influence on the act of judging. Hence, it stipulates that in giving meaning to words of a statute/provision, judges should consider how the statute's essence impacts the public interest, principles, and culture.

The SJA empowers the democratic essence, which emphasizes the government of the people, for the people, and by the people. Thus, the people's interest and welfare is (or should be) a key component in judicial interpretation. This non-conservative, realistic approach to statute depends largely on a judge's discretion (no matter how limited) to develop the law for the public interest. This approach campaigns for more courageous judges to think outside the box in a fast-changing world.

The approaches or philosophies of judges in interpreting law often depend on the type/hierarchy of the court,[401] the nature of the case,[402] the principle of interpretation required in the case,[403] or even the judge's personality.[404] The approach to statutory interpretation is similar across board, worldwide. As Breyer puts it aptly, "most judges start in the same way. They look first to the statute's language, its structure, and its history in an effort to determine the statute's purpose. Then, they use the purpose (along with the language, structure, and history) to determine the proper interpretation. Thus far, there is agreement."[405] However, judges still disagree over the plain

establishment of this research went on with diverse intellectual exposures from my late father and my teachers at various levels from my undergraduate to postgraduate studies.

399 This book gives an introduction into a "lifetime research."

400 See Tobi, opcit.

401 Whether it is a high court or appellate court.

402 Whether it is a civil or criminal case.

403 This writer has categorized principles of interpretation gleaned from case law.

404 The judge's personality or judicial philosophy.

405 Breyer, S. (2005). Active Liberty, Interpreting Our Democratic Constitution, Vintage Books, New York, USA, opcit: 86.

meaning of the statute.[406] Some judges are more sanguine than others in their approach to interpreting a statutory text. As some judges resort to the "extrinsic" aid of legislative history, others limit themselves to a narrow focus on the clarity or ambiguity of a particular statutory phrase.[407] Some judges look broadly to statutory context for insight into phrases that may seem ambiguous in isolation, and inevitably, tensions may arise between apparently clear language and perceived intent.[408] Yet, other judges argue about abstract interpretations to hide their implicit biases.

Ultimately, case law encourages Nigerian courts to discountenance frivolities and adopt a liberal approach to avoid construing law to produce an outcome where one section defeats the intent or purpose of another.[409] The court in *Standard Trust Bank Plc v. Olusola*[410] summarized its duty in interpreting any Act as adopting a liberal interpretation. Sometimes, the strict adherence to precedent or the literal rule of interpretation leads to absurd results and injustice. Hence, where a liberal interpretation will result in absurdity or injustice, the court may seek internal or external aid.[411] Consequently, discretion comes in (hopefully) to correct the injustice/ the mischief and undue adherence that precedent creates.[412]

---

406 See *Corley v. United States, 556 U.S. 303 (2009).*

407 See Ukeje, opcit.

408 Eig, opcit: 44.

409 See *Ugoji & Ors v. Iwuagwu (2013) LPELR-20810 (CA).*

410 *Standard Trust Bank Plc v. Olusola (2007) LPELR-4978 (CA).*

411 The internal aid is within the body of the statute itself, and the external aid is from other statutes in *pari materia,* or same matter or subject, with the statute being construed to avoid absurdity or injustice.

412 Judicial discretion has evolved into the framework for statutory interpretation in other English-speaking countries that apply Common Law.

Chapter 4
Judicial Discretion in Nigeria

> It is now a notorious principle of law that as courts of equity that we are, we should not pursue technical and abstract justice at the expense of dealing with the merits of the matter, but rather ensure that substantial justice is done to the parties. The primary function of any court of law is to do justice to the parties and where any procedural rules antithesis to justice and fair play, maneuver that harsh rule of law in pursuit of justice. If in the course of pursuing justice, the court errs, it has "erred" in the right direction.[413]
>
> —Hon. Justice Niki Tobi, JCA (as he then was)

1 Introduction

This chapter defines the meaning and scope of judicial discretion in Nigeria. It reviews case law about judicial discretion and examines how judges apply discretion in extenuating circumstances of a given case, especially in the absence of precedent or where precedent is outdated. This author categorizes five basic principles that should guide judges' exercise of discretion. This chapter also outlines the constraints of judicial discretion and the significance of judicial discretion. With the socio-technological changes and advancements in society, this chapter further discusses AI's impact on judicial discretion. At the end of this chapter, readers will appreciate how judicial discretion impacts judging in Nigeria, and appraise the indispensable role of judicial discretion in a world of AI.

2 What is Judicial Discretion?

Black's Law Dictionary[414] defined judicial discretion as the exercise of judgment by a judge or court, based on what is fair under the circumstances

413 *Busari v. Ose (1992) LPELR-14981 (CA).*
414 Black's Law Dictionary, opcit: 1405–1406.

and guided by the rules and principles of law; a court's power to act or not act when a litigant is not entitled to demand the act as a matter of right.[415] According to Abhulimhen-Iyoha, judicial discretion is the power to make a choice between alternative courses of action or the right to make official decisions using reason and judgment to choose from acceptable alternatives.[416] The Supreme Court in *Celtel Nig B.V v. ECONET Wireless Ltd & Ors*[417] held that discretion knows no bounds. In its general usage, judicial discretion is the freedom or power to decide what should be done in a peculiar situation.[418] Also, in *UBN Plc. v. Astra Builders (W.A.) Ltd*,[419] the court states that an exercise of discretion is an act or deed based on one's subjective judgment according to one's conscience, free and unfettered by any external influence or suggestions. A more befitting definition in *Airhiavbere v. Oshiomhole & Ors*[420] is that discretion of a court or judge is the power or right conferred by the law, on a court to act in certain circumstances, according to the judge's dictates or the court's judgment and conscience, that is uncontrolled and unfettered by others' judgments or conscience.[421]

Judicial discretion is a very broad concept because of the different kinds of decisions judges make and the different limits the law places on these decisions.[422] A judge is constantly called upon to exercise his/her discretionary power in the judicial process.[423] Sometimes, in the absence of any direction in statutes, courts encounter a "play-doh" or "clay-like" situation where the judge molds his or her own view, ideas, or perceptions from the statute, to give it an appropriate interpretation. Such molding is judicial discretion—where the judge

---

415 See *Akinyemi v. Odu'a Inv. Co. Ltd (2012) LPELR 3270 (SC) 39.*

416 Abhulimhen-Iyoha, A. (2015). Judicial Discretion of Judges in Criminal Cases in Nigeria: Prospects and Challenges, 2–3.

417 *Celtel Nig B.V v. ECONET Wireless Ltd & Ors (2014) LPELR 22430 (CA).*

418 "It is indeed a type of amour, speaking metaphorically, which a judge should and ought to employ judicially and judiciously whenever the need arises." See *Ajuwa v. SPDC Ltd. (supra)*. See also *Odusote v. Odusote (supra); Olatubosun v. Texaco Nigeria Plc (2012) 14 NWLR (Pt.1319) 200; Achi v. Ebenighe (2014) 4 NWLR (Pt.1397) 380.*

419 *UBN Plc. v. Astra Builders (W.A.) Ltd (2010) LPELR-3383 (SC).*

420 *Airhiavbere v. Oshiomhole & Ors (2012) LPELR-19787 (CA).*

421 See *Suleiman v. Commissioner of Police (2008) 3 SCNJ 1 at 9–10; Johnbull Adams Nig. Ltd & Ors. v. Isoko Community Bank Ltd (2013) LPELR-20730 (CA).*

422 Kana, A. A. (2014). Perspectives and Limits of Judicial Discretion in Nigerian Courts, opcit: 160.

423 Tobi, opcit: 128.

interprets statutes as the judge understands (it is about what the judge perceives as right and just), given the prevailing circumstances in each case.[424] The choice of deciding which canons or principle of interpretation to apply in any case is a matter of discretion, which judges should exercise judiciously and judicially.

Judicial discretion is a vital tool for the due administration of justice. By its purpose and implications for substantial justice, it is a sacred power that grants judges unfettered opinions in suitable and deserving cases. However, such discretion must be within the confines of the law to make fair decisions. Judges' application of discretion indicates their commitments to their judicial role and oaths of office. According to section 6(6) (a) of the 1999 Constitution, "the judicial powers vested in accordance with the foregoing provisions of this section shall extend, notwithstanding anything to the contrary in this Constitution, to all inherent powers and sanctions of a court of law." This provision enables courts the latitude to carve the niche that guides their discretion. Accordingly, Judges have formulated basic principles from respective "documentary" and historical sources to support judicial evolution and adventures.[425] An example is section 45 (1) of the Interpretation Act, which empowers the courts in Nigeria to apply the Common Law of England, the doctrine of equity together with the statutes of general application in resolving disputes in Nigerian courts.[426] The constitutional powers of courts in Nigeria are like that of the United States,[427] where the court noted that trial judges have broad discretion to take steps to ensure that they protect the Sixth Amendment rights of criminal defendants.[428]

In its legal usage, the concept of discretion implies the power to choose between alternative courses of action; therefore, where and when judges test or apply discretion, it follows that there is no absolute procedure to solve the issue in question. As Adekeye, JSC, stated, "there is no hard and fast rule to the exercise of a judicial discretion by a court for if that happens a discretion becomes fettered."[429] The judge's discretionary power is judicial power that is

---

424 Which could also be social interests and views.

425 See Dantosho v Mohammed (supra).

426 Interpretation Act CAP 123 L.F.N 2004.

427 *U.S v. Noriega 917 F.2d 1543 (11th Cir. 1990).*

428 However, the Court also noted that the discretion the court wrote includes steps that might negatively affect First Amendment interests.

429 See *Iwuju v. Federal Commissioner for Establishment and Anor (1985) LPELR-1568* (SC).

not inherent.[430] Judges can only exercise judicial discretion according to legal requirements and the justice of the case. So, the judge cannot act according to his judgment willy-nilly.[431] In other words, judicial discretion is not a judge's free ticket to act as he or she pleases; rather, it is an opportunity to interpret justice fairly from a personal yet objective perspective.

Figure 4.1 gives an overview of the court's discretion as is and as should be.

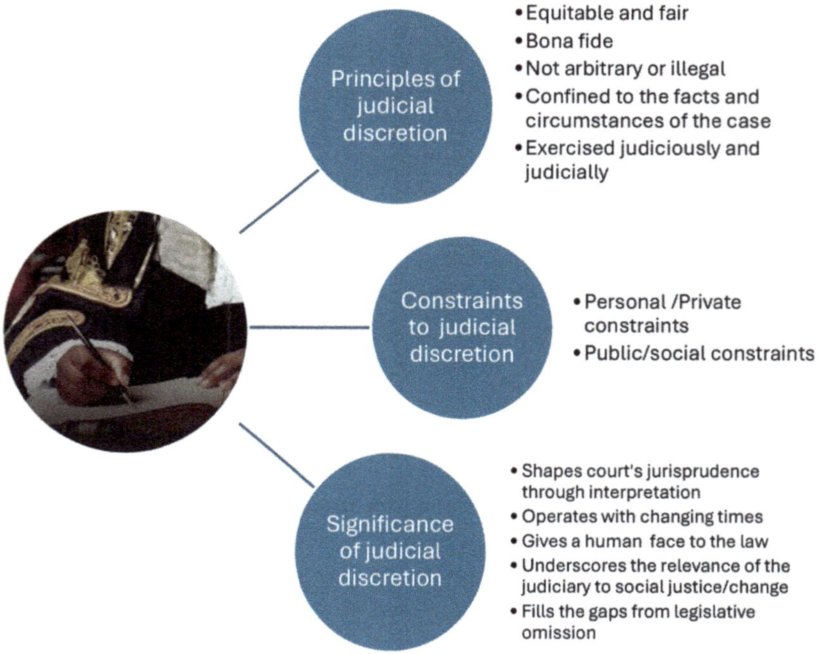

Figure 4.1: Judicial Discretion

430 "... which means that power which is itself essential to the very existence of the court as an institution. They are the powers the court is born with, more or less and such powers can only be exercised in respect to matters within the court's jurisdiction." Tobi, ibid: 124–125.

431 Ibid.

3 Five Basic Principles of Judicial Discretion in Nigeria[432]

These five principles define what judges consider or should consider when applying their discretion, to arrive at a just determination. Since no law specifically guides a judge's use of discretion[433] or codifies the way judges should exercise discretion, case law has created guiding principles that the trial court may consider in exercising their discretion. These principles are fundamental to the act of judging. So, courts rely on text guidelines and numerous judicial pronouncements that define the scope of discretion (although still with some form of restraints). For example, Judge Zonay[434] outlined ten guidelines to judicial discretion in his text on judicial discretion.[435] In *Tell Communications Limited v. Colonel Mohammed Buba Marwa*,[436] the court states that since no authority binds the exercise of judicial discretion, judges establish certain principles and guidelines to consider in applying discretions. Accordingly, this author categorized five basic principles gleaned from numerous Nigerian cases, as follows.

3.1 Discretion must be Equitable and Fair

This principle is the most important of all the principles that guide judicial discretion, as it basically caps up and defines the context of judging that hinges on the rules of equity, justice, and fairness. This is similar to Judge

---

432 The author categorized these principles from Nigerian case law.

433 Even the Constitution does not give the courts guidance on how to weigh or measure discretion.

434 Judge Zonay offered ten guidelines to aid judges make discretionary decisions: (1) establish the record; (2) apply the correct law; (3) consider different ways to exercise your discretion; (4) consider doing nothing; (5) consider the equities of the situation; (6) consider the results of your decision; (7) take time to think over any decision; (8) clearly and logically explain your decision; (9) do not unnecessarily look back; and (10) do not make a decision just because you can. His guidelines, although generic, were fashioned after the courts in the United States. Nevertheless, they are also applicable to Nigerian courts, just like this book's, although about the Nigerian courts, is generic and applicable to courts of other countries.

435 Zonay, T. A. (2015). *Judicial Discretion: Ten Guidelines for Its Use*. The Judicial Edge, The Reno, Nevada: National Judicial College. <https://www.judges.org/judicial-discretion-ten-guidelines-for-its-use/>

436 *Tell Communications Limited v. Colonel Mohammed Buba Marwa (2005) LPELR-6148 (CA).*

Zonay's fifth guideline, to consider the equities of the situation, and sixth guideline, to consider the results of your decision. The court in *Onovo & Ors v. Mba & Ors*[437] explained that discretion means equitable decision of what is just and proper under the circumstances, or the liberty or privilege to decide and act according to what is fair and equitable under the particular case as the law dictates.[438] In this case, the appellants, Geofrey Mba, Francis Mba, and Oneche Mba (all brothers) challenged the ruling of the high court and filed an appeal against the respondent (their mother) over the property of their late father. The appellants contended that the trial court ought to have adjourned to deliver a considered ruling, and that the judge should not have allowed the affidavit filed by the respondent after submission of appellants' counsel. Therefore, the issue before the court was whether the court properly exercised its discretion to allow use of affidavits after hearing arguments. In dismissing the appeal as frivolous (against the appellants), the Court of Appeal held that the court can apply its discretion to determine the appropriate stage to file an affidavit to determine the justice in the case. Also, in *Obidiegwu Onyesoh v. Nze Christopher Nnebedun & Ors*,[439] one of the grounds of appeal challenged the lower court's exercise of discretion, asserting that the lower court wrongly exercised its discretion in dismissing the appeal against the lower court's decision. The court said that an overriding principle in exercising judicial discretion is to maintain a balance of justice between parties and bearing in mind the right of parties.

3.2 Discretion must be Bona Fide

Even though judges have the freedom to exercise their discretion at will, it is fundamental that judges apply such discretion for bona fide reasons. Judicial discretion must be genuine and not ingenuine. According to Judge Zonay, judges should clearly and logically explain their decision and not unnecessarily reflect on a decision already taken.[440] In *Etokhana v. Progress*

---

437 *Onovo & Ors v. Mba & Ors (2014) LPELR-23035 (SC).*

438 See *Artra Industries Nigeria Ltd v. The Nigerian Bank for Commerce and Industries (1998) 4 NWLR (Pt. 546) 381 SC; Doherty v. Doherty (1960) 1 All NLR 299.*

439 *Obidiegwu Onyesoh v. Nze Christopher Nnebedun & Ors (1992) LPELR-2742 (SC).*

440 Ibid, guidelines 8 and 9.

Bank of Nigeria Plc.,[441] the court emphasized this principle thus: "It is well settled that if judicial discretion has been exercised bona fide, uninfluenced by irrelevant considerations and not arbitrarily or illegally by the lower court, the general rule is that an appeal court will not ordinarily interfere."[442] It is a well-established principle that an appellate court, does not as a matter of course, interfere with the trial court's exercise of discretion unless it is not exercised in according to the law or it was exercised perversely.[443] In *Okon Bassey Ebe v. Commissioner of Police*,[444] the appellant along with three other persons were charged before a Chief Magistrate's Court, with unlawful forcible entry on a parcel of land and the trial Magistrate dismissed the charge for want of diligent prosecution, as a result of the absence of the prosecuting counsel. The respondent (the Commissioner of Police) was dissatisfied with the order dismissing the charge and appealed to the high court. The high court upheld the magistrate's order. The respondent further appealed to the court of appeal and then to the supreme court. The issue for determination before the Apex court was whether the appeal court rightly held that the trial magistrate adequately exercised its discretion to dismiss the case for want of diligent prosecution. In dismissing the appeal and sustaining the trial magistrate's order, the Supreme Court held as follows:

> For a judicial discretion to be properly exercised, it must be founded upon the facts and circumstances presented to the court from which the court must draw a conclusion governed by law and nothing else. The exercise of that discretion must be honest and in the spirit of the statute, otherwise, any act so done will not find solace in the statute and such a discretionary act must be set aside.

3.3 Discretion must not be Arbitrary or Illegal

As discussed in the next chapter, judging in Nigeria is an act of precedent.[445] Therefore, in exercising discretion, the judge should not think randomly but apply precedent with precise legality. The judge's revered duty in dispensing

---

441 *Etokhana v. Progress Bank of Nigeria Plc (1997) LPELR-6258 (CA).*

442 *Okon Bassey Ebe v. Commissioner of Police (2008) LPELR-984 (SC).*

443 See *Osakwe v. FGN (2004) 14 NWLR (Pt.893) 305, Likita v. C.O.P. (2002) 11 NWLR (Pt. 777) 145, Atiku v. The State (2002) 4 NWLR (Pt. 757) 265.*

444 *Okon Bassey Ebe v. Commissioner of Police (supra).*

445 See full discussion on judicial precedent in chapter 5.

justice should be confined to the dictates of the law.[446] In *Onovo & Ors v. Mba & Ors*,[447] the court said discretion must be governed by rule, not by humor, and not arbitrary, vague, and fanciful but legal and regular. The court in *Alhaji Isiyaku Yakubu Ent Ltd v. Tarfa & Anor*[448] stated that an arbitrary exercise of discretion by a court, which is both a court of law and of justice as the court below, cannot be allowed to stand. However, there are instances where judges must deviate from precedent because applying precedent disrupts achieving justice in the case. Such instances would be under the doctrine of distinguishing the case, that is, when the circumstances of the case can be distinguished from the precedential case.[449] In *Alhaji Karimu Adisa v. Emmanuel Oyinwola & 4 Ors.*,[450] regarding a dispute about land title/ownership, where the Supreme Court considered "whether the Court of Appeal was not in error in failing to hold that the trial court lacks jurisdiction over the claims of the respondents having regard to the provisions of Sections 39 and 41 of the Land Use Act, 1978," the Court reinforced the doctrine of distinguishing the case as follows:

> A previous decision is not to be departed from, or even followed, where the facts or the law applicable in that previous case are distinguishable from those in the latter case. Where relevant statute laws have changed since the previous decision, what is called for is "distinguishing" rather than "departure." In the instant case, a significant difference between the present case and the case of Sadikwu v. Dalori (1996) 5 NWLR (Pt.447) 151 is that the scope of the jurisdiction of the High Court of the states has changed since the action in the latter was instituted.... The doctrine of stare decisis is based, first and foremost on the relevant likeness between the cases—the previous case and the one before the court. Where there is no relevant likeness between the two, it is an idle exercise to consider whether the previous one should be followed or departed from. In the instant case, the laws applicable for the determination of the jurisdiction of the High Court in the case of Sadikwu v. Dalori (1996) 5 NWLR (Pt.447) 151 are not the same ones applicable in the instant case. There is therefore nothing in the ratio decidendi in the Sadikwu's case which is a binding authority on which to determine the jurisdictional issue that has arisen for decision in the present case.[451]

---

446 Opcit: guidelines 2, 7, 9, and 10.
447 *Supra.*
448 *Alhaji Isiyaku Yakubu Ent Ltd v. Tarfa & Anor (2014) LPELR-24223 (CA).*
449 See a detailed discussion on precedent in Chapter 5.
450 *Adisa v. Oyinwola (2000) 10 NWLR (Pt. 674) 116 at P.168.*
451 Ibid.

Furthermore, the Supreme Court is entitled to depart from or overrule its previous decision in an appropriate situation when invited to do so. In other words, the Supreme Court as the final appellate court in Nigeria has the power and jurisdiction to depart from and overrule its previous decision whether or not by a full court.[452] According to Zonay, judges should take time to think over any decision; they should not unnecessarily look back at precedent; judges should not decide just because they can; they should apply the correct law.

3.4 Discretion must be Confined to the Facts and Circumstances of the Case

A judge's discretion, in any case, must relate to the material and relevant considerations of the particular case and not to extraneous considerations.[453] Discretion depends on the nature or type of case; therefore, the exercise of a court's discretion depends upon each case's peculiar facts and circumstances.[454] Hence, the court exercising its discretion, which depends upon the particular circumstances of the case before it, can limit the exercise of that discretion.[455] Again, this reiterates Judge Zonay's principle—to consider doing nothing, to take time to think over any decision, and to clearly and logically explain your decision.[456]

In *Chief Nicholas Banna v. Telepower Nigeria Ltd*,[457] the court held that an appellate court could not substitute its discretion in the administration of justice for that of the trial court because discretionary power is exercised within the confines of the facts of the case. This is because the trial judge, who is the judge of facts, is in the best position to exercise such discretion.

---

452 Ibid: 170.

453 However, the exception to this rule is that where such extraneous considerations may lead to a just determination of the material issues, the judge may, within the dictates of the law so apply.

454 *See: ICAN v. Attorney Gen. Federation (2004) 3 NWLR (Pt. 859) 186; Odusote v. Odusote (1971) 1 All NLR 219; Udeze v. Onuniju (2001) 3 NWLR (pt. 700) 216; Oyekanmi v. NEPA (2000) 15 NWLR (pt. 690) 414; Nicon Hotel Inter. S. A. v. Nicon Hilton Hotels & Anor. (2007) 7 NWLR (pt. 1032) 86 at 113–114.*

455 Ibid.

456 Opcit: guidelines 4,7, and 8.

457 *Chief Nicholas Banna v. Telepower Nigeria Ltd (2006) 7 SCNJ 182.*

According to the court in *Obidiegwu Onyesoh v. Nze Christopher Nnebedun & Ors*,[458] when a trial court exercises its discretion in a matter before it, an appellate court, be it the Court of Appeal or the Supreme Court, which has the power to review the exercise of the case on appeal, must approach the issue from the viewpoint that the discretion is that of the court of trial and not that of the appellate court and ought not, except in certain circumstances, interfere with the trial courts discretion. In the above case, the appeal raises the issue of the extent of an appellate court to override the exercise of discretion by a trial court, and the Supreme Court held that an appellate tribunal is not at liberty merely to substitute its exercise of discretion for the discretion already exercised by the trial Judge.[459] The rationale is that the trial court has first-hand information on the facts of the case and the appellate court's inference could be outside the facts and circumstances that are outside the appellate court's knowledge.

3.5 Discretion must be "Judicially and Judiciously" Exercised

The twin important words in applying discretion in Nigerian courts are "judicially" and "judiciously." These twin words have become compound words in Nigeria's judicial parlance. They rule the discretionary "world" of Nigerian judges. According to Tobi, JCA, "it has now become almost an axiom or an aphorism in our judicial system to say that a discretionary power must be exercised not only judicially but also judiciously."[460]

In *Nigeria-Ara Bank Ltd v. Nze A.U. Ogueru*,[461] an appeal from the lower court challenged the trial court's discretion in ordering an injunction restraining the defendants (Appellants) by themselves or through their agents from allowing water from any source whatsoever seeping through the man-made water runway into the plaintiff's (Respondent's) premises. The trial Judge relied on affidavit evidence and the submissions of the learned counsel for the parties without calling oral evidence to resolve the conflict in the affidavit evidence. Also, without any reference to the second prayer of the applicant, the trial court granted the first prayer

---

458 *Obidiegwu Onyesoh v. Nze Christopher Nnebedun & Ors (supra).*

459 Ibid.

460 *A.C.B. Ltd. v. Nnamani (1991) 4 NWLR (Pt. 186) 486.*

461 *Nigeria-Ara Bank Ltd v. Nze A.U. Ogueru (1990) 6 NWLR (Pt. 159) 751.*

of the plaintiff's application. In its judgment, the appeal court said that the Judge has an unfettered right in the exercise of judicial discretion which must be exercised judicially and judiciously, bona fide, uninfluenced by irrelevant considerations and based on sufficient materials placed before it.[462]

However, in the instant case, since the discretion of the trial court is exercised on contentious and unproved facts as to the existence or non-existence of a man-made water runway, it cannot be said that the trial Judge exercised his discretion judicially and judiciously. Consequently, the appeal court interfered and added that the trial judge's purported exercise of discretion was arbitrary and to some extent reckless.[463] Accordingly, the appeal was granted, and the Appeal Court ordered an accelerated retrial before another trial judge.[464] Also, in *Amos Motors Nigeria Limited & Anor v. Agboola*,[465] the court held that judges should act judiciously and judicially in all discretionary powers and consider the particular facts of a case.[466]

In the application of discretion, controversies often arise since different judges' unique personalities impact their exercise of discretion. Discretion is inconsistent and based on the peculiarity of individual judges. Also, judges differ in characterizing judicious and judicial discretion because of the imprecise definition of the concepts of judicial and judicious discretion. Different judges adopt different approaches in describing these terms. In the case of *Eronini v. Iheuko*,[467] the Supreme Court defined the phrases "judicial" and "judicious" as follows:

> Acting judicially imports a consideration of the interest of both sides and weighing them in order to arrive at a just or fair decision … Judicious means: a) proceeding from or showing sound judgment; b) having or exercising sound judgment; c) marked by discretion, wisdom and good sense….

---

462 Ibid: 763.

463 Ibid.

464 Ibid: 762.

465 *Amos Motors Nigeria Limited & Anor v. Agboola (2012) LPELR-8011 (CA).*

466 See *Etokhana v. Progress Bank of Nigeria Plc. (1997) LPELR-6258 (CA).*

467 *Eronini v. Iheuko (1989) 2 NWLR (101) 46 at 60 and 61, Hon. Justice GARBA, JCA (pp. 64–65, paras. B-D).*

Also, in *Enakhimion v. Edo Trans Services*,[468] the court stated that

> ...discretion is said to have been exercised well and judicially and judiciously when it is based only on the materials placed before the court and not extraneous or whimsical considerations. Every exercise of a discretionary power must aim at the attainment of substantial justice.[469]

Further, in *A.C.B. Ltd. v. Nnamani*,[470] the court distinguished judicial and judicious discretion as follows:

> The exercise of the court's discretion is said to be judicial if the Judge invokes the power in his capacity as Judge qua law. In other words, an exercise of a discretionary power will be said to be judicial, if the power is exercised in accordance with the enabling statute. On the other hand, an exercise of a discretionary power is said to be judicious if it carries or conveys the intellectual wisdom or prudent intellectual capacity of the Judge as judex. In this second situation, the exercise of the discretion must be replete with such wisdom and tenacity of mind and purpose. The exercise must be based on a sound and sensible judgment with a view to doing justice to the parties.[471]

In the first case above, the judge distinguished judicial and judicious discretion based on the parties' interest, fair decision, and sound judgment. The second judge lumped these words and simply said discretion is exercised judicially and judiciously when it is based on the material before the court and to attain sound judgment. Then, the third judge gave a more elaborate analysis of the terms. He said that judicial discretion is when the judge invokes the power in accordance with an enabling statute and judicious discretion is when the exercise of power conveys the judge's intellectual wisdom. All definitions or perspectives give divergent views of the concepts, but they mean and imply the same, as Tobi said, "but, discretion is discretion, whether it wears any of the two qualifying expressions mentioned above."

Judicial and judicious discretion is the court's or judge's power directed by sound judgment in determining the right of litigation where such right is not absolute. It reflects the judge's will as the will of the law through the judge's understanding. It is the judge's liberty to decide and act according to what he/she understands as fair and equitable under the peculiar circumstances

468 *Enakhimion v. Edo Trans Services (2006) All FWLR (pt. 391) 1683 at 1696.*

469 This research poses the question: what amounts to "substantial justice," (as this term is as generic as it is semantic?)

470 Supra.

471 Hon. Justice Tobi, supra at p. 494–495.

of the case, guided by the spirit of the law.[472] These terms also mean the employment of good judgment, restraint, and caution in applying judicial powers.[473] A more simplified definition is in *Enemuo & Anor v. Ezeonyeka & Ors,*[474] that when discretion is exercised judicially, it means it is according to the law. When discretion is exercised judiciously, it is based on a case's peculiar facts and circumstances.[475]

In *Tell Communications Limited v. Colonel Mohammed Buba Marwa,*[476] the courts held that any application for injunction calls for the discretion of the judge seized with the matter, and the judge must exercise such discretion judiciously and judicially. Judicial discretion must be exercised according to justice, common sense, the law, and clear proof that a tort/misdemeanor has been committed. A court exercising judicial discretion in addition to the peculiarities of each case as the facts and evidence disclosed should consider some of the factors or principles before its discretion can be judicial and judicious.[477]

Therefore, the court in *Akinyemi v. Odu'a Inv. Co. Ltd,*[478] said that for discretion to be judicial and judicious, it must be based on prudence, rationality, wisdom, consideration, and reasonableness. Thus, judicial discretion should consider peculiar facts and evidence in a case, the interests of both parties, established principles of relevant rules and the law, showing wisdom and good sense in deciding one way or the other.[479] The terms judicial and judicious seem to delineate the otherwise unfettered discretion of judges in exercising their powers. Also, the court in *Okon Bassey Ebe v. Commissioner of Police*[480] added that for judicial discretion to be properly exercised, it must be founded upon the facts and circumstances presented to the court from which the court must draw a conclusion governed by law, and nothing else.

---

472 *Mercantile Bank (Nig) Plc v. IMESCO Enterprises Ltd (supra).*

473 *Akpughunum v. Akpughunum (2007) ALL FWLR (Pt. 376) 746 at 758 Paras. B-D (CA).*

474 *Enemuo & Anor v. Ezeonyeka & Ors (2016) LPELR-40171 (CA).*

475 See Judge Zonay's guides to establish the record; to apply the correct law also fits in here (at p. 65).

476 *Supra.*

477 Ibid.

478 *Akinyemi v. Odu'a Inv. Co. Ltd (supra).*

479 This book adds to the list that the court in deserving circumstances should also consider the interest of society.

480 *Supra.*

The Supreme Court in *Obidiegwu Onyesoh v. Nze Christopher Nnebedun & Ors.*[481] aptly summarized the above five principles as follows:

> It is settled that when a judge of trial exercises his discretion in a matter before him, an appellate court which has the power to review the exercise of it on appeal, ought to approach the issue from the viewpoint that the discretion is that of the court of trial and not that of the appellate court. Once it is clear that the trial court exercised its discretion bona fide and judicially, that is not arbitrarily or illegally or by reference to extraneous considerations or by failing to take any material and relevant consideration into account, the appellate court cannot interfere.

The court in *Chief Nicholas Banna v. Telepower Nigeria Ltd*[482] stated the rationale for this principle: "an appellate court cannot substitute its discretion in the administration of justice for that of the trial court and because discretionary power is exercised within the confines of the facts of the case, the trial judge—the judge of facts, is in the best position to exercise the discretion."[483] However, where discretion is not properly exercised it amounts to an improper exercise of discretion or an abuse of discretion. An improper exercise of discretion is when discretion is not exercised judicially and judiciously or one that is characterized by arbitrariness.[484] According to the court in *Rida National Plastics Ltd v. Artee (Ind.) Ltd,*[485] the appellate court will only review a lower court's discretion where there is glaring evidence of the improper exercise of discretion leading to the obvious failure of justice.[486] Also, in *Williams v. Hope Rising Voluntary Funds Society,*[487] where the exercise of discretion is manifestly wrong, arbitrary, and injudicious, as in the instant case, the Court of Appeal is bound to interfere and set it aside.[488] This appeal to the Supreme Court, from trespass to land case, contends that the "Court of Appeal erred in law in failing to interfere with the exercise of the discretion of the trial

---

481 *Obidiegwu Onyesoh v. Nze Christopher Nnebedun & Ors (1992) LPELR-2742 (SC), Hon. Justice Karibi-Whyte, JSC.*

482 *Chief Nicholas Banna v. Telepower Nigeria Ltd (2006) 7 SCNJ 182.*

483 Also, the extent of the fettered-ness of the Court's discretion is from the standard of review of abuse of discretion appellate courts render.

484 *Nwaukoni v. Bielonwu & Ors. (2008) LPELR-4648 (CA).*

485 *Rida National Plastics Ltd v. Artee (Ind.) Ltd (2017) LPELR-43132 (CA).*

486 See also *The Resident Ibadan Province v. Olagunju (1954) 14 WACA 552* and *Enekebe v. Enekebe (1964) 1 ALL NLR 102.*

487 *Williams v. Hope Rising Voluntary Funds Society (1982) 2 SC 145.*

488 Such order to set aside may even lead to a mistrial or retrial, as the case may be.

Judge's discretion to set aside his own judgment when it was apparent that he has taken into consideration matters which he ought not to have taken into consideration thereby acting on wrong principles."[489] Hence, the Supreme Court ruled that the Court of Appeal should have interfered with the trial court's wrong exercise of discretion, as the trial court should have applied its discretion to overturn its judgment on realizing that it considered the wrong principles in arriving at his decision.

Therefore, the standard of review when the court abuses its discretion is quite stern in Nigeria. Where it is clear on the record that the court did not exercise its power judicially and judiciously, an appellate court may interfere.[490] Thus, a judge who exceeds their discretion may obtain the wrath of the appellate court.[491] In *Emueze & Ors v. Governor of Delta State & Ors,*[492] the appellant instituted an action at the trial court against the respondent, claiming several reliefs against the unlawful and unconstitutional demolishing of their building. the court stated:

> I would want to reiterate the trite principle, that the exercise of discretion (discretionary power) by courts or Judges, is an inherent aspect of judicial independence under the well cherished immutable doctrine of the separation of powers. Contrariwise, an abuse of discretion denotes a failure to take into proper consideration of the facts and relevant laws relating to a particular matter and arbitrary or unreasonable departure from precedent and well settled judicial tradition or custom.

In recapping the controversial connotations of these twin words, the court in *Nwobodo v. Nwobodo*[493] cautions judges as follows:

> When one exercises his discretion judicially he will be expected to act critically. So also, when a discretion is required to be judiciously exercised one expects the person so acting to do so with high degree of prudence and good judgment. Thus, when a judge is called upon to exercise his discretion judicially and judiciously, it follows that in reaching his decision on the subject matter in which his discretion is called into play, he must be involved in the judicial balancing of the pros and cons or the strength and weakness of the parties case as placed before him. In other words, the judge must be impartial and prudent in reaching a correct decision and with reference only and reasons connected with the case.

---

489 See *Williams v. Hope Rising Voluntary Funds Society (supra).*

490 See *Obidiegwu Onyesoh v. Nze Christopher Nnebedun & Ors. (supra).*

491 See the reprimanding remark of *Katsina Alu, JSC in Dalhatu v. Turaki*, Chapter 1.

492 *Emueze & Ors v. Governor of Delta State & Ors (2014) LPELR-23201 (CA).*

493 *Nwobodo v. Nwobodo (1995) 1 NWLR (Pt. 370) 203 at pp. 214–215.*

4 Constraints to Judicial Discretion[494]

As broad and liberal as the judge's discretion can be, it has constraints, which range from private/personal to public/social. The private/personal constraints are the external factors that influence the judge's discretion. They include the judge's idiosyncrasies, ideologies, views, and implicit biases. The public/social constraints are the external factors that impact the judge's discretion. They include the law, judicial policies, and society's influence on judges or the public's expectations. Some private constraints associated with judicial discretion are inconsistency and uncertainty, the use of instinct and intuition instead of reasoned decisions, the perpetuation of injustice, breach of fair hearing, miscarriage of justice, and bias.[495] Some public constraints include strict adherence to precedent or stipulated principles, corruption, abuse or disregard for judicial process or powers, and arbitrariness.[496]

Although discretion is individualistic, judges do not exercise it in a vacuum, since judges' idiosyncrasies, personal views, ideologies, philosophies, and experiences influence their choices. As human beings, judges are prone to natural weaknesses, so whenever courts exercise judicial discretion over matters before them, the outcome of such actions cannot be free from the judge's personal prejudices, whims, and caprices. Therefore, the exercise of law is completely a product of the judge's judicial discretion.[497] Hence, judges differ in their application of discretion, which is susceptible to error too, as no human being, including judges are infallible.

According to Tobi, the judge is just one human being with human reactions, but he reacts calmly within the private recess of his mind.[498] Within that private recess are words that carry diverse meanings of a statute. And amidst the choice of verbs and tenses in the statutes, judges face the challenge of interpreting ambiguous statutes with more than one grammatical principle that potentially applies to a word. These words may mean different interpretations, leaving courts to choose which principles apply most aptly.[499]

494 An elaborate discussion on this is the focus of my dissertation.
495 Abhulimhen-Iyoha, A. (2015). Judicial Discretion of Judges in Criminal Cases in Nigeria: Prospects and Challenges, opcit: 2.
496 Ibid.
497 Ibid: 3.
498 Tobi, ibid: 42.
499 Eig, ibid: 13.

Smithburn agrees and argues that the range of judicial discretion is not fully understood, as judges do not know the extent of discretion available to them.[500] As true as this is in Nigeria, some judges know the extent of their discretion and abuse it.

Bunker puts it rightly that one does not have to be a lawyer to recognize that even the clearest verbal formula can be manipulated.[501] Grammatically, words may carry different meanings from the legal context it is used and thus such words assume different meanings in law. Words also change with time and their interpretations determine the judge's discretion at a particular time. For example, over time in the Nigerian judiciary, the word "may" has fluctuated in interpretation. Grammatically the word "may" connote a likelihood or possibility. Accordingly, in the 1976 case of *Mokelu v. Fed. Comm. Works & Housing*,[502] Madarikan, JSC, held that "may" is an enabling or permissive word, in that sense, it imposes or gives a discretionary or enabling power.[503] In *Busari & Ors v. Oseni & Ors*,[504] Tobi, JCA, reinforces that it is an established canon of statutory interpretation that the word "may" is generally permissive and not mandatory. It does not foist on a party a legal duty which must be performed.

Over time, Nigerian courts have expanded on the meaning of the word "may." For example, the Supreme Court in *Nigerian Navy & Ors v. Labinjo*,[505] while acknowledging that the word "may" generally carries a permissive meaning, went on to say that in exceptional circumstances it may mean mandatory or compulsory action. In fact, depending on the circumstance, permissive words can have mandatory interpretation and vice versa.[506] Similarly, Nnaemeka Agu, JSC, stated, "I believe that it is now the invariable practice of the courts to interpret 'may' as mandatory whenever it is used to impose a duty upon a public functionary, the benefit of which enures to a private

500 Smithburn, J.E, (2006) Judicial Discretion opcit: 8.
501 Bunker, M. D. (1997). Justice and the Media, opcit: 124.
502 *Mokelu v. Fed. Comm. Works & Housing (1976) NSCC 187.*
503 See *British American Tobacco (Investments) Ltd v. A.G. Of Lagos State & Ors (2014) LPELR-23200 (CA).*
504 *Busari & Ors v. Oseni & Ors (1992) LPELR-14981 (CA) Paras B-C.*
505 *Nigerian Navy & Ors v. Labinjo (2012) LPELR-7868 (SC).*
506 See *Fidelity Bank Plc. v. Monye & Ors. (2012) 3 SC. (Pt. 73).*

citizen."[507] This was reiterated in *PDP v. Sherrif & Ors,*[508] where Rhodes-Vivour, JSC, stated that "The law is long settled that 'may' is not always 'may.' It may sometimes be equivalent to 'shall.'"

Similarly, in the United States, some words have shifting meanings from the literal to the figurative and the changing meanings of these words impact American law and culture.[509] According to Prestidge, one of the principal tendencies of semantic change is for the meaning of a word to often shift to what the speaker believes it to mean. Individual circumstances and schema, or broader social and cultural forces may influence semantics.[510] Accordingly, Prestidge observed, the words "liberty" and "privacy" have metamorphosed from their literal meaning in American legal jurisprudence.[511] Hence, in *Griswold v. Connecticut,*[512] the word "liberty" (which grammatically simply means freedom from something) and "privacy" (which grammatically conveys the simple meaning of secrecy, solitude, and seclusion) were given complimentary interpretation by the Supreme Court. Even though the court did not define the word "liberty," it established that the right to liberty protected a right to privacy within a marriage.[513] In other words, it appeared that courts defined *liberty* and *privacy* as conjunctive or coherent rights. Years later, in *Planned Parenthood of Southeastern PA. v. Casey,*[514] the court redefined *liberty* thus: "At the heart of liberty is the right to define one's own concept of existence, of meaning, of the universe, and of the mystery of human life."[515] In this case, *liberty* and *privacy* are cited together as seemingly complementary rights.[516]

Therefore, in the absence of a concise and precise legislative/grammatical definition of the word(s) in a statute, judges give a legal/judicial definition that is often not far from the grammatical meaning. Moreover, sometimes, even

---

507 *See Ude v. Nwara & Anor. (1993) LPELR-3289 (SC) P. 24, Paras. B-C.*

508 *PDP v. Sherrif & Ors (2017) LPELR-42736 (SC) P. 54, Paras. A-B.*

509 Prestidge, A. (2010). "Semantic Change in Supreme Context: Semantics in the Privacy Line and Originalist Interpretation," *Brigham Young University Prelaw Review, 24* (26), opcit: 119.

510 Ibid: 120–122.

511 Ibid.

512 *Griswold v. Connecticut 381 U.S. 479 (1965).*

513 *Ibid.* See also *Roe v. Wade, 410 U.S. 113 (1973),* where the principle was restated.

514 *Southeastern PA. v. Casey 505 U.S. 833 (1992).*

515 Ibid: 851.

516 Prestidge, A (2010), opcit: 130.

when the choice of the word in a rule (statute) is reasonably clear, situations also inevitably occur that the rule maker (drafter) simply never contemplated at the time of enactment.[517] In such a situation, the judge is constrained in attempting to interpret the words within their scope of understanding and discretion. What is even more constraining is that the judge's discretion changes with times and circumstances. Thus, statutory interpretation changes with times and circumstances of each case. For example, the judge's discretion in a case today may change in similar circumstances years later. The *Roe v. Wade*[518] and *Dobbs v. Jackson*[519] decisions in the United States are examples of how circumstances' and times' impact judicial discretion.[520] In some cases, simple words metamorphose in terms of semantics.[521]

Furthermore, another aspect where judges face the most constraint in exercising discretion is regarding a balancing factor—where judges weigh one person's interests or rights against another's; when judges decide on two equally desirable views/arguments, or when judges attempt to balance social interest with legal/judicial requirements. In other words, where does the justice of the matter lie or to what side does the scale of justice tilt? An overriding principle in the exercise of judicial discretion is to balance justice between parties, considering their rights. However, since the exercise of such discretion is not absolute, the party that feels the judge's discretion was unfair, can challenge it on appeal. The party can also challenge such exercise of discretion if it affects the parties right to freedom, showing that the court did not exercise its discretion judiciously.[522]

Judges interpret laws all the time even when the lawmakers lay no clear guidelines/parameters or procedures of interpretation. In such situations, the court finds itself in a state of absolute and unfettered discretion; where the judge must make findings and decisions even when the statute connecting

---

517 Bunker M.D. (1997) Justice and the Media, opcit: 139.

518 Supra.

519 *Dobbs v. Jackson Women's Health Organization, 597 U.S.215 (2022).*

520 See *Griswold v. Connecticut (supra); Planned Parenthood of Southeastern PA. v. Casey (supra).*

521 In all of these cases, the words/phrases on right to privacy, right to life, freedom of choice with respect to abortion, the viability of the fetus, etc., changed over time with different judicial opinions and dissents.

522 See *Abacha v. The State (2002) 11 NWLR (pt779) 437 at 484.*

the law is absurd vis-à-vis the question for determination or facts before the court.[523] However, in certain cases or at certain stages of the trial (depending on the motion or application before the court), where no precedent exists, the judge applies unfettered discretion judiciously and judicially to arrive at a just determination of the case.[524]

5 Significance of Judicial Discretion

Judicial decision-making can never be reduced to geometric precision, as legal formulations are subject to judicial discretion and interpretation. Nonetheless, the scrutiny structure, as the law articulates leaves wide latitude for lower courts to reach almost any result with substantive guidance from higher courts.[525] Hence, every judge, especially trial court judges, exercises a level of fettered or unfettered discretion with guidance from superior courts where necessary. Therefore, judicial discretion is unavoidable where the law does not anticipate how to decide facts based on unforeseen situations.[526]

Judicial discretion is indispensable in Nigeria's complex society, with a range of inequalities, and diverse people with different tribes/races, like the American society. So, judicial discretion is highly necessary for courts to embrace inclusion and diversity in every case. Judicial discretion shapes the jurisprudence of the court's interpretation of statutes and gives the law a human face. Thus, and very importantly, such discretion only makes sense when the parties/society understands, appreciates, and acknowledges it as fair and just.

Another value of discretion is that it operates/evolves with changing times and depicts reliance to society. It states or underscores the relevance of the judiciary to social justice and democratic development, which is a fundamental tool in this era of somewhat "unrestricted" liberties, diverse social interests, and technoscience advancements.[527] Judges' discretionary powers

---

523 Kana, A. A. "Perspectives and Limits of Judicial Discretion in Nigerian Courts, opcit: 157.

524 See *Total Engineering Services Team Inc. v. Chevron Nigeria Ltd. (2010) LPELR-5032 (CA).*

525 Bunker, opcit: 124.

526 Abhulimhen-Iyoha, A. (2015) Judicial Discretion of Judges in Criminal Cases in Nigeria: Prospects and Challenges, opcit.

527 Where people have freedom to exercise their rights in such a way that it infringes on the rights of another. An example is the freedom of the press.

arise in the final analysis to fill the gaps that ensue from legislative omissions. There are social issues that existing legislation does not fully cover.[528] Thus, judicial discretion through proper interpretation becomes necessary, and in the absence of precedent, judges apply unfettered discretion that eventually forms the basis for precedent or establishes precedent.[529]

Therefore, judicial discretion helps to advance the law and develop legal jurisprudence. No judge can boast of complete mastery of the law. Discretion creates the beauty of increased knowledge and diverse experiences from different judges because it is individualistic and subjective. Different discretions with idiosyncratic judging define philosophies and ideologies that eventually develops law and society.

Judicial discretion also saves judicial and legislative time. In the absence of precedent or guidance on how to interpret the law, applying judicial discretion can save valuable time in courts as well as the long procedure it will take to enact a new law or to amend an existing law. A ready example is a case this author presided as a magistrate in Lagos State Judiciary, Nigeria—*Commissioner of Police v. Jelilie Lawal & Kehinde Oyelara*,[530] where she relied on her judicial discretion. This case involved a threat to life of a journalist/editor. The threat was sent via a text message, but the cellphone that contained the alleged threat text messages could not come on when the plaintiff tendered it as evidence during the trial. Hence, in the absence of a provision in the Evidence Act or any other law guiding the Court on what to do (at that time), the presiding magistrate (this author) exercised discretion and asked the Court's registrar to recharge the said phone before both parties in open court and try powering it on again. Unfortunately, the phone could not come on even after several attempts in open court. Since this hindered the Court's ability to review the only incriminating evidence to the case (alleged threat text messages), this author gave a discretionary ruling on a no-case submission, for lack of evidence to support the subsisting charge and alleged

528 See discussions on canons and principles of interpretation in Chapter 3.

529 See discussion on judicial precedent in Chapter 5.

530 *Commissioner of Police v. Jelilie Lawal & Kehinde Oyelara (Unreported), Charge No. L/8/2009. Igbosere Magistrate Court, Lagos State, Nigeria.*

offense.[531] Accordingly, the defendants/accused persons were discharged for lack of evidence to prove their guilt.[532]

Judicial discretion is not an absolute power. It has limitations. Sometimes judges exercise unfettered discretion within broad legal and social context as the judge determines, according to the law and the case. When judges exercise their discretion, they have a level of autonomy that is free from strict legal rules, so they can exercise discretion without technicalities, to ensure justice.

6 Fettered and Unfettered Discretion

There are two arguments about judicial discretion. The first is that judge's discretion is absolute; the second is that judges do not and cannot exercise absolute discretion. Over the years, judicial discretion in Nigeria has developed around both arguments. While some judges believe judicial discretion in Nigeria is fettered, others believe discretion is unfettered.[533] According to Tobi, the moment a trial court is called upon to exercise its discretionary power by the enabling law, judiciously and judicially, it will not be correct to say that the court has unfettered discretion in the matter.[534] In *Mohammed v. FRN & Ors*,[535] the court held that the judge's discretion is not absolute when the judge is required to do or omit to do anything.[536] However, in *Awani v. Erejuwa*,[537] the court held *inter alia* that discretion conferred upon trial courts is generally unfettered and an appellate court cannot ordinarily interfere with the exercise of the discretion unless the party shows that the court wrongly exercised discretion. Similarly, according *Aso Motel Kaduna Ltd. v. Deyemo*,[538] all courts in Nigeria have unfettered discretionary power to adjourn any proceedings pending before them to do justice in the suit. The

531 See Vanguard Newspaper (September 1, 2009), opcit.

532 Usually in practice, it is the parties, either directly or their lawyers, that make a submission of no case to answer, which means that in the absence of any evidence to prove the guilt of the defendant, the said defendant has no case to answer, so the court must discharge them.

533 See cases below.

534 Tobi, opcit: 129.

535 *Mohammed v. FRN & Ors (2009) LPELR-8364 (CA).*

536 Ibid.

537 *Awani v. Erejuwa 11 (1976) H SC 307.*

538 *Aso Motel Kaduna Ltd. v. Deyemo (2006) LPELR-11596 (CA).*

guiding principle is that discretion must always be exercised judicially and judiciously on the material before the court in the peculiar circumstances of the case.[539]

In addition, the court stated in *Nwannewuihe v. Nwannewuihe*[540] that it has unfettered discretion to grant or refuse, as the case may be, an order of interlocutory injunction. Albeit, and as in all other discretions, the court should exercise such discretion not only judicially but also judiciously.[541] Also in *Stabilini Visinoni Ltd v. Mallinson & Partners Ltd,*[542] the court emphasized that courts have an absolute and unfettered discretion to award costs or not to award them; what is paramount is to consider all circumstances of the case.[543] Further, from *Plateau State Health Services Management Board & Anor. v. Goshwe,*[544] a court has an unfettered discretion to sort the pending issues for determination in the case.[545] In *Honey Crown Products Ltd v. Shell Electric Manufacturing,*[546] the court held that a judge is vested with unfettered discretion, but when such discretion is exercised erratically, it then restraints the parties before it.[547]

In summing up the above argument, it appears that whether a judge's discretion is fettered or unfettered varies, depending on the nature or type of case. This is how it appears in the United States, discretion swings depending on the case or court. Smithburn opines that sometimes discretion is fettered sometimes it is not fettered.[548] In family law or child custody cases,

539 See *Flour Mill of Nigeria Ltd v. Ogunbayo (2014) LPELR-24264 (CA).*

540 *Nwannewuihe v. Nwannewuihe (2007) LPELR-8247 (CA).*

541 See *Falomo v. Banigbe (Supra) at 695, paras. C-G.*

542 *Stabilini Visinoni Ltd v. Mallinson & Partners Ltd (2014) LPELR-23090 (CA).*

543 See *Total Engineering Services Team Inc. v. Chevron Nigeria Ltd. (supra).* I further restate the trite law that a court has an absolute and unfettered discretion to award or refuse costs in any particular case but that the discretion must be exercised judicially and judiciously.

544 *Plateau State Health Services Management Board & Anor. v. Goshwe (2012) LPELR-9830 (SC).*

545 *See Awojugbagbe Light Industries Ltd. v. P. N. Chinukwe & Anor (1995) 4 NWLR (Part 390) 379; (1995) 4 SCNJ 1; Latinde & Anor. v. Bella Lajunfin (1989) 5 SC 59; (1989) 5 SCNJ 59; Unity Bank & Anor. v. Edward Bonari (2008) 2 SCM 193 At 240.*

546 *Honey Crown Products Ltd v. Shell Electric Manufacturing (2013) Lpelr-20077 (CA).*

547 See *Okoh & Ors. v. University of Lagos & Anor. (2010) LPELR-4719 (CA).*

548 See Smithburn, opcit.

for example, discretion is unfettered as the best interest of the child is what determines the level of discretion a court should apply.[549]

Furthermore, in sentencing persons convicted of crimes, American courts had unfettered discretion as judges considered various mitigating factors. However, with the Federal Sentencing Guidelines, and the mandatory minimum sentencing legislation, federal courts in the U.S no longer have the broad latitude or discretion to make sentences to fit crimes and the defendant as before.[550] In Nigeria, judges appear somewhat to have unfettered discretion in sentencing. For example, the sentencing guidelines of the Federal Capital Territory of Nigeria[551] and Lagos State of Nigeria[552] give judges options to sentence convicted felons in the absence of statutory punishment.[553] These guidelines widen the judge's discretion.[554] For example, the Administration of Criminal Justice Law, which provides for custodial and non-custodial sentences, requires the court to consider concepts such as probation, parole, community service, rehabilitation, etc. Unfortunately, the absence or insufficient parole and probation facilities in Nigeria's criminal justice system, enables courts with unfettered discretion to give offenders alternative sentencing.

Therefore, the legal framework in both Nigeria and the United States gives judges huge discretion, depending on the type of case.[555] Courts in the United States have great discretion in rulings concerning the examination of witnesses, the way witnesses testify as well as the actual testimony,[556] but it must be with reason.[557] Ultimately, though not precise, Nigerian courts seem to have more unfettered discretion than fettered. Judges have the liberty to exercise their

---

549 Burns, B. D. (2024). "Lessons From Family Court on Parenting: What Your Children Tell the Judge They Need From Their Parents." Self-Published. U.S.A.

550 Kana, opcit: 160.

551 The Federal Capital Territory Courts (Sentencing Guidelines) Practice Direction, 2016.

552 Lagos State Judiciary (Sentencing Guidelines) Practice Directives, 2018.

553 See footnotes 109 and 110, ibid.

554 See sections 3, 12, 21, 30, 39, 48, and 57 of the FCT Sentencing Guidelines, ibid, and sections 4, 14, 24, 34, 44, 54, and 64 of the LSJ Sentencing Guidelines, ibid, which both provides for discretionary and non-discretionary punishments.

555 Refer to family law cases.

556 See *Louisiana v. Hayes, 806 So.2d 816 (La. App. 2001).*

557 *Montana v. Nelson, 48 P.2d 739 (Mont.2002); Willard v. State, 244 Ga. App. 469, 535 S.E.2d 820 (2000).*

discretions because of the leverage that section 6 of the 1999 Constitution grants. Also, based on the argument on the dangers of this "latitude" of discretion, Nigerian courts apply a concept/principle to regulate the extent of discretion—that judges should exercise discretion (somewhat fettered), "judiciously and judicially."[558] Hence, Tobi's argument that it is wrong to say a judge has unfettered discretion in all matters, would be appropriate.[559] Yet what is equally appropriate is the submission of Georgewill, JCA, that an exercise of discretion, though not subject to so much hard and fast rules or fettering, loses its salt of being a discretion and thus it is best served unfettered.[560]

Conclusively on fettered or unfettered discretion, it is important to note that the type of court,[561] the proceedings,[562] the nature of the case,[563] the stage of the hearing,[564] all determine whether a court has fettered or unfettered discretion. Also, the environment or society should determine the court's discretion. With our developing societies, technological and scientific advancements, a court's discretion could be fettered in a more developed environment or society (with available established legal framework) than in a developing or under-developed society or environment, like Nigeria with little or no established procedure or legal framework. For example, due to the COVID-19 pandemic, judges' unfettered discretion took the front burner. Also, with AI technology, the court's fettered discretion takes the backburner. Courts now improvise to obtain justice in the cases before them.

---

558 Kana, opcit: 161.

559 See footnote 377.

560 *Adelaja v. C.M.S. Grammar School Bariga & Ors (2017) LPELR-42729 (CA) at 11.*

561 See *Mobil Producing (Nig) Unltd v. Ajanaku & Ors (2007) LPELR-8758 (CA)*: "it has become trite law that all superior courts of record have unfettered discretion in the exercise of their equitable jurisdiction to stay their proceedings. The same unfettered discretion avails the appellate courts to stay not only their own proceedings but the proceedings of the courts from which the appeals pending in the appellate courts arose. This discretion must however be exercised judicially and judiciously."

562 See *Awure & Anor. v. Iledu (2007) LPELR-3719 (CA)*: "trial courts are allowed free hand to exercise their discretion to amend any pleading any time before judgment provided no issues have been introduced."

563 See *Iche v. State (2013) LPELR-22035 (CA)*: "a judge of the High Court trying an accused person has unfettered discretion to review the bail."

564 In *IPCO Nigeria Ltd. v. NNPC (2013) LPELR-22083 (CA)*, the court has an unfettered discretion to allow an amendment of the Notice of Appeal at any time before the hearing of the appeal.

7 Technology and Judicial Discretion

Our societies—the developed and developing, have experienced diverse levels of technological and technoscientific advancements, which have impacted not only the sociological framework of society but also the legal framework, thereby causing socio-legal dilemmas that create the vacuum for judges to apply unfettered discretion. These advancements go to the crux of our democratic mandate and question the essence of constitutional rights. Therefore, now more than ever, the courts' unfettered discretion plays a more impactful democratic role in benefiting society to ensure social change.

On the eve of the year 2020, through to 2021, the COVID pandemic came like a tsunami, sweeping people like fish into the sea and leaving families in pain of losing loved ones who died abruptly with little or no medical support because even the doctors struggled to understand the ailment, diagnosis, treatment, or cure. Therefore, to avoid contamination and the spread of this villainous airborne virus, and to curtail the mass deaths and the spread of the virus, in-person court attendance was suspended. According to Sule et al., the outbreak of COVID-19 brought about the hitherto uncommon practice of e-filing and virtual court proceedings in Nigerian courts to dispense with extremely urgent, essential, or time-bound matters.[565] Hence, the pandemic brought virtual court proceedings into the limelight.[566]

Therefore, following the CJN's directives, the Chief Judge of Lagos State signed the Lagos State Judiciary Remote Hearing of Cases (COVID-19 Pandemic Period) Practice Direction.[567] Under the Practice Direction,[568] and to comply with the social distancing requirements, the Lagos State High Court's first virtual sittings via Zoom was a criminal case of one Olalekan

565 Sule, I., Olurunyemi, F., Ajah, J., & Usman, A. (2024). "Virtual Court Proceedings in Nigeria: Some Legal Matters Arising," *European Journal of Law and Political Science*, *3* (3), 17–22.

566 Ibid. Also available at CNN. Adebayo, B. (May 7, 2020). <https://www.cnn.com/2020/05/07/africa/nigeria-zoom-death-sentence-intl/index.html>

567 Ibid: 19.

568 The essence of the Practice Direction is to ensure the hearing and determination of urgent and time-bound cases through digital platforms like Zoom, Skype, Microsoft Teams, or any other video and audio-conferencing tool.

Hameed. The Court found him guilty of the murder of a woman and sentenced him to death by hanging.[569]

Arguments ensued on the constitutionality of virtual hearings based on the decision in *Simon Edibo v. The State*,[570] where the Supreme Court set aside the appellant's conviction and sentence for culpable homicide punishable with death on the contested ground that his plea was taken in the trial judge's chambers. This old Supreme Court precedent was based on the provisions of sections 33 (1) and (3) of the 1979 Constitution, which is *impari material* with sections 36 (1) and (3) of the 1999 Constitution (as amended).[571] Hence, in setting aside the decisions of both the trial and appeal courts, the Supreme Court held that taking the appellant's plea in the judge's chambers, which was not a public place by the constitutional provision, was irregular, fundamentally defective, and unconstitutional. Similarly, Sule et al., submitted that any Practice Directions that seek to create and regulate virtual courtroom proceedings in a judge's chambers or any other forum where there is no right of ingress and egress by the public, conflicts with the provision of sections 36 (3) and (4) of the 1999 Constitution.[572]

However, despite the controversies on virtual hearings, courts improvised procedures to ensure that justice was done in the same way as in-person public hearings. These hearings gave judges the latitude to redefine the constitutional requirement of in-person evidential hearings. Thus, to ensure compliance with the constitutional requirements, all courts live-streamed proceedings through the web or social media channels and courts also published the details of the virtual court sittings in the same way they published regular sittings.[573]

Furthermore, digitization is taking root in Nigerian courts. While the courts are struggling with the new reality of digitizing documents and court processes and procedures, AI technology is looming from the corner. As Nigerian courts struggle to catch up with the digitized technology, they are not ready for the technoscience of AI, because of the lack of facilities

569 Ibid.
570 *Simon Edibo v. The State (2007), 13 NWLR (Pt. 1051) 306.*
571 These fair hearing sections require hearings to be done in public.
572 Sule et al., opcit: 21.
573 Ogbuagu, U. & Takuru, K. (n.d). Innovations for the development of remote justice in Nigeria.

and proper legal framework. Agbakoba says, "one of the most significant regulatory threats to AI adoption in Nigeria is the lack of an appropriate legal framework for its emerging technology. Following several scientists' concerns about the possibility of a technological singularity, which could pose an existential threat to humans."[574]

In her presentation at a conference of court administrators, this author argued that judicial discretion plays a fundamental and indispensable role in checking AI's excesses and "judges should let AI know who is in charge."[575] Although AI cannot replace judicial discretion, judges must be cautious. The Honorable Chief Justice Menon of Singapore stated as follows:

> The prospect of "Al judges" replacing human judges is a distant, even a remote one. But in this age of Al, the role of the human judge will itself need to evolve … So, beyond cultivating technological expertise in relation to the use of AI tools, judges must also renew their commitment to their professional duties and their ethical responsibilities to exercise judgment, fully and fairly, in managing both the process and the outcomes of judging in each case.[576]

The Honorable Chief Justice Kudirat Kekere-Ekun of Nigeria reinforced as follows:

> As we embark on this transformative journey, we must remain aware of the delicate balance between leveraging AI's capabilities and maintaining the integrity and independence of the judiciary….AI is a tool to augment, not replace judicial wisdom. The deployment of AI must be approached with caution. Ethical oversight, data privacy and algorithmic bias must be carefully considered to avoid unintended injustice.[577]

---

574 Agbakoba, O. The Threats of Artificial Intelligence (AI) On The Legal And Regulatory Systems – All You Need To Know. Mondaq. (7 August 2024) <https://www. mondaq. com/nigeria/new-technology/1501938/the-threats-of-artificial-intelligenceai-on-the-legal-and-regulatory-systems-all-you-need-to-know>

575 Niki-Tobi, A. (2024, November 12). AI and Courts: A Socio-Judicial Dilemma. International Association of Court Administrators Conference, Singapore State Courts, Singapore.

576 Chief Justice Sundaresh Menon, Keynote Speech, Inaugural Singapore-India Conference on Technology. SG Courts. <https://www.judiciary.gov.sg/news-and-resources/news/news-details/media-release--supreme-court-of-singapore-and-supreme-court-of-india-hold-inaugural-singapore-india-conference-on technology-#:~:text=In%20his%20speech%2C%20Chief%20Justice,will%20affect%20our%20justice%20systems>

577 Punch Newspaper. Let AI assist and not replace you, CJN warns judges. 19th June 2025. Available at https://punchng.com/let-ai-assist-not-replace-you-cjn-warns-judges/

It is a combination of the judge's discretion with the law that determines the reasonable weight on the scale of justice. Judges cannot quantify the level or dose of judicial discretion to apply in a case. Hence, the determinant factor is that the exercise of judicial discretion must be founded on justice, fairness, and law and not on the judge's whims and caprice with scanty or no regard to the facts of the case and the rule of law.[578] In reiterating this point, the court in *Ozigbu Engr Co Ltd v. Iwuamadi*[579] held that while deciding on the circumstances of a case, courts are endowed with unfettered discretion to keep up with the times and economic trends in the country and most especially with prevailing fluctuating and a rather obvious decline of purchasing power of the Nigerian currency—the Naira.[580]

In conclusion, the bottom line is that the judges' discretionary powers are indispensable in the act of judging. Judges are neither machines nor equipment. They are humans who must assess, review, and decide on the best justice in each case, based on diverse extenuating circumstances that evolve with times in a constantly evolving society. As diagram six above outlines, the discretion of a judge is significant to society—sociological, scientific, technological, and technoscientific advancements. It is the judges' role to use the law for its true purpose in society—social change and to gain public confidence on the merits of substantial justice. This author argues that AI is a threat to public confidence in courts, as the unhindered speed and digitized expertise that AI offers is likely to replace the public's confidence in courts, with trust for AI's efficient delivery of justice.[581] Hence the necessity for judge's discretion to focus on building public confidence through putting AI in its place and leading the judicial process.[582] According to Abiru, JCA, in *Mbas Motel Ltd. V. Wema Bank Plc:*[583]

---

578 See *University of Lagos v. Aigoro (1985) 1 NWLR (Pt.1) 143*. See also *Aboseldehyde Lab. Plc. v. U.M.B. Ltd. (2013) 13 NWLR (Pt.1370) 91 @ pp. 97–98; Aroh v. PDP (2013) 13 NWLR (Pt.1371) 235; Thimnu v. UBN Plc. & Ors. (2013) LPELR 22127 (CA) @ pp. 20–21; Abiodun v. CJ. Kwara State (2007) 18 NWLR (Pt.1065) 109 @ p.152; Adeniji v. Adeniji (2013) 15 NWLR (Pt.1376) 102 @ p. 125. In E.F.P.C. Ltd. v. NDIC. (2007) All FWLR (pt. 367) 793 @pp. 825–826.*

579 *Ozigbu Engr Co Ltd v. Iwuamadi (2009) 16 NWLR (PT.1116) 44 @ 79.*

580 *Anyah v. African Newspaper of Nig. Ltd (1992) LPELR-511 (SC).*

581 Niki-Tobi, opcit.

582 Ibid.

583 *Mbas Motel Ltd. v. Wema Bank Plc (2013) LPELR-20736(CA) at P. 26, Paras. E-G.*

> We must never lose sight of the fact that justice is rooted in public confidence, and it is essential to social order and security. It is the bond of society and the cornerstone of human togetherness. Justice is the condition in which the individual is able to identify with society, feel at one with it and accept its rulings. The moment members of the society lose confidence in the system of administration of justice, a descent to anarchy begins.

Accordingly, the concept of judicial discretion in Nigeria creates opportunities for courts to build or restore public confidence in the courts. And judges can build public confidence on the platform of creating precedent, especially in emerging societal changes and technological advancements.

Chapter 5
Judicial Precedents/Stare Decisis

> The principle of stare decisis allows a lower court to depart from the decision of a higher court if the case is distinguishable. And here lies the problem. It is a known fact that there are instances when a lower court strains the ratio decidendi and facts of the decision of the higher court to justify his departure from the decision. There are known instances where the lower court makes a distinction where none exist ... While there are known instances where decision of a higher court may seem wrong, the principles of stare decisis seem to say that the lower court is not knowledgeable enough to come to that conclusion. And so, the lower court is bound to follow the apparently wrong decision, to put it mildly.[584]
>
> — Hon. Justice Niki Tobi, J, as he then was.

1 Introduction

This chapter reviews the doctrine of judicial precedent and its impact on judging in Nigeria. It will define judicial precedent/stare decisis and outline the hierarchy of courts in Nigeria and explain the challenges that courts encounter in adhering to precedent. We will also discuss the concept of distinguishing factors and how it has caused confusion and impending threats to respect and sustaining precedent in Nigeria's judicial system. By the end of this chapter, readers will appreciate how judicial precedent influences judging in Nigeria, how undue adherence to precedent endangers judging in Nigeria, and the exception that allows deviating from precedent.

584 Tobi, The Nigerian Judge: opcit.

2 Judicial Precedents/Stare Decisis[585]

Judicial precedent or stare decisis is an established principle of law on which judges base their judicial decisions.[586] The doctrine of judicial precedent is the foundation that erects the Common Law system in Nigeria. The Common Law doctrine of stare decisis states that once a court has decided a legal issue, subsequent cases presenting similar facts should be decided in conformity with the earlier decision.[587] The general principle in Common Law systems, like Nigeria and the United States, is that similar cases should be decided to give similar and predictable outcomes. The principle of precedent is the mechanism by which that goal is attained. So, courts are generally required to abide by precedent and not counter the status quo. In *National Electric Power Authority v. Onah,*[588] the Supreme Court of Nigeria defined stare decisis as standing by your decision and the decisions of your predecessors, however wrong they are and whatever injustice they inflict.[589] The doctrine of stare decisis was also explained in the case of *Osakwe v. Federal College of Education (Technical) Asaba*[590] as abiding by former precedent where the same or similar points came up again for litigation.[591]

Judicial precedent was not part of Nigeria's traditional legal system; however, it is one of the oldest legal principles that Nigeria inherited from the English legal system. Thus, the British Common Law principle of *stare decisis* or judicial precedent influences the act of judging in Nigeria. The doctrine of judicial precedent is dependent on settled judicial hierarchy, as decisions of higher courts are generally binding on lower courts in the hierarchy. By the general principle of stare decisis,

---

585 Although these terms are slightly different, for the purpose of this book, we will use them as one and the same; to mean the dependence of a court on the decision of a superior court.

586 Olong, A. M. (2007). The Nigerian Legal System, An Introduction, Malthouse Press Limited, Nigeria. P 21.

587 See *People v. Bing, 76 N.Y.2d 331, 337–338 (1990).*

588 *National Electric Power Authority v. Onah (1997) 1 NWLR (Pt. 484), Page 680 at 688.*

589 *Supra.*

590 *Osakwe v. Federal College of Education (Technical) Asaba (2010) NWLR (pt.1201) at 34.*

591 See also *Moghalu v. Ngige (2005) 4 NWLR (pt. 914).*

a lower court is bound by the decisions of a higher court.[592] The hierarchy of Nigerian courts, from the highest court of record to the lower courts, is as follows:

1. The Supreme Court of Nigeria[593]
2. The Court of Appeal[594]
3. The Federal High Courts[595]
4. The High Court of Federal Capital Territory, Abuja[596]
5. The Sharia Court of Appeal of Federal Capital Territory, Abuja[597]
6. The Customary Court of Appeal of Federal Capital Territory, Abuja[598]
7. State High Courts[599]
8. The Sharia Court of Appeal of a state[600]
9. The Customary Court of Appeal of a state[601]
10. The Magistrate Courts
11. Area Courts or District Courts of various grades, Customary and Native Courts

The National Industrial Court, Investment and Securities Tribunal, and Court Martials are special courts.

592 *Idris v. A.N.P.P. (2008) 8 NWLR (Pt.1088) 1 at 75, paras. E-H.*

593 Section 230 (1) of the Constitution established this court as the highest court of record in Nigeria, and its decisions binds the court of Appeal and all other courts in Nigeria, as affirmed in the case of *Dairo v. UBN Plc (2007) 16 NWLR (pt. 1059) 99 at 159.*

594 See section 237 of the Constitution.

595 See section 249 of the Constitution.

596 See section 255 of the Constitution.

597 See section 260 of the Constitution.

598 See section 265 of the Constitution.

599 See section 270 of the Constitution.

600 See section 275 of the Constitution.

601 See section 280 of the Constitution.

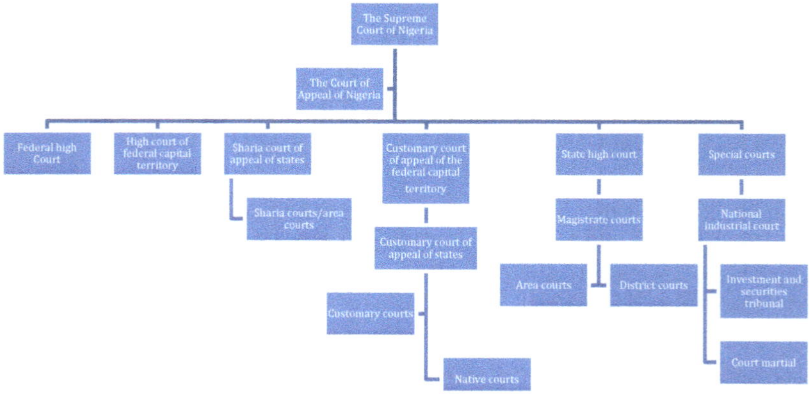

Figure 5.1: Hierarchy of Courts in Nigeria

This hierarchy of courts stipulates that lower courts are bound by the decision of the Supreme Court of Nigeria. This means that the law requires lower courts to pursue justice through the eyes and views of higher courts' decisions.

Judicial precedent can be binding or persuasive. According to Murgan, Kwagyang, and Bello,[602] the doctrine of *stare decisis* makes higher courts' decisions binding on lower courts, and persuasive between one high court and another high court or between courts of coordinate jurisdictions.[603] In other words, binding precedent is one that lower courts must follow, while persuasive precedent may bind court of coordinate jurisdiction. A case's *ratio decidendi*, also known as the reason for the court's decision, is what establishes a binding precedent.[604] Any other reasonings that do not "necessarily" relate to the facts in issue before the court are known as *obiter dictum*, or the persuasive precedent.[605] Thus, the Supreme Court admonished that even though an *obiter dictum* is not regarded as the binding precedent, an *obiter dicta* of the Supreme Court should not be disregarded as they are strong pointers to the probable direction of the law.[606]

602 Murgan, M. G., Kwagyand, G. U., Bello, H. (2015). "Judicial Precedent, and the Prevention of Contradictory Judgments," *IOSR Journal of Humanities and Social Science, 20* (2), *65–75.*

603 Ibid: 71.

604 *Amobi v. Nzegwu & Ors (2013) vol. 12 MJSC Pt. 1 at page 1.*

605 Ibid.

606 *Ifediora v. Umeh (1988) 2 NWLR page 5 at 13* and *Buhari v. Obasanjo (No.3) (2004) 1 W.R.N. Page 1 at 46.*

3 The Impact of Precedent on the Nigerian Judicial System

This doctrine of *stare decisis* has both positive and negative impacts on the judicial system and society. According to Abiru, JCA, "if progress be desirable, if the growth of the nation, in the perfect development of constitutional government, as well as in the stability of its institutions, be a desideratum, these objects can certainly not be attained by a disregard of the principle of stare decisis."[607] The Supreme Court also said precedent ensures equal treatment of litigants before the courts and spares the judges the stress and drudgery of re-examining rules and principles of law, since they can afford some degree of predictability and stability from already existing legal order.[608] Similarly, in the American case of *Payne v. Tennessee*,[609] the court said that "stare decisis is the preferred course because it promotes the even-handed, predictable, and consistent development of legal principles, fosters reliance on judicial decisions, and contributes to the actual and perceived integrity of the judicial process." Also, in *Hilton v. SC Pub. Rys. Comm'n*,[610] "adherence to precedent promotes stability, predictability, and respect for judicial authority."

Additionally, the Court of Appeal gave a balanced view in *Ojukwu v. Agupusi & Anor*[611] that precedent enhances consistency and coherence as well as presents continuity and manifest respect for the past decisions in our legal order, but it also obviates stability.[612] Also, Justice Agim, JSC submits that judicial precedent strengthens the rule of law in Nigeria.[613]

---

607 See *Adeyemi & Ors. v. O. Achimu/Ndic/Assurance Bank Ltd & Ors (2015) LPELR-24379 (CA) pp.43–47.*

608 See also *APC & Ors. v. In Re: CPC & Ors (2014) LPELR-24036(SC), Adegoke Motors Ltd v. Adesanya (1989) 3 NWLR (pt109) at 266.*

609 See the American case of *Payne v. Tennessee,501 U.S. 808, 827 (1991).*

610 *Hilton v. SC Pub. Rys. Comm'n 502 U.S. 197, 202 (1991).*

611 *Ojukwu v. Agupusi & Anor (2014) LPELR-22683 (CA) Hon. Justice Agube, JCA, at pp 41–41, paras F-A.*

612 Ibid.

613 Agim, E. "The Impact of Judicial Precedent in Societal Development." (2022, September 1) *The Impact of Judicial Education on Developing Law and Society* (Courts & Society Webinar Series, 3rd Edition) A.T. Socio-Judicial Consulting. <https://atsjconsulting.com/>

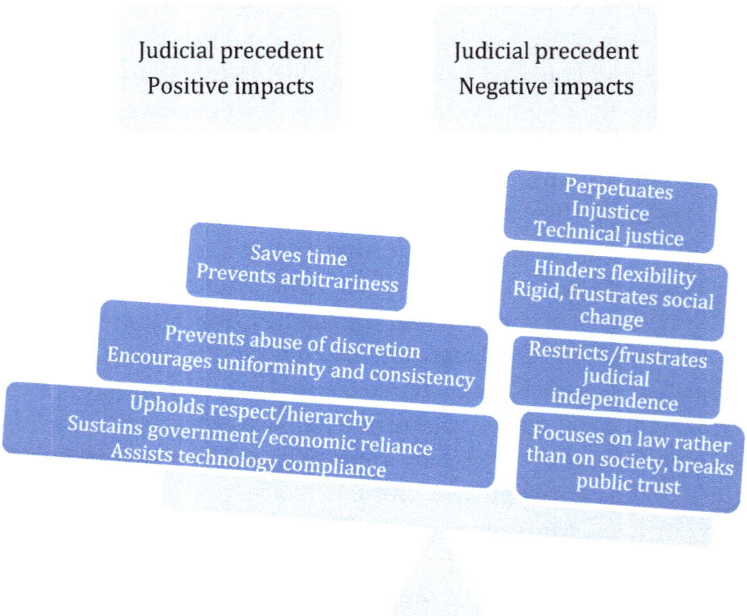

Figure 5.2: The Scale of Judicial Precedent in Nigeria

3.1 Positive Impacts of Judicial Precedents

This author gleaned the below positive impacts from the above cited cases, and presentations from A.T.Socio-Judicial Consulting's Courts and Society Webinar Series.[614] They are as follows:

- Precedents save judicial time and prevent arbitrariness in judicial decisions.
- Precedents enhance consistency and coherence as well as present continuity.
- Precedents check against abuse of discretion.
- Precedents strengthen the rule of law and increase respect for the Constitution, the sovereignty of the people.

614 See Niki-Tobi, A. (2022, April 25) "The Impact of Judicial Precedent on Societal Development." (Courts & Society Webinar Series, 1st Edition) A.T. Socio-Judicial Consulting. <https://youtu.be/KfQytGfFexE>

- Precedents assist lawyers predict the decision of courts in similar cases.[615]
- Precedents somewhat encourage uniformity in judicial decisions.
- Precedents predict the relevant and applicable laws to the case.
- Precedents uphold respect, hierarchy, and compliance to the status quo.
- Precedents create economic reliance where businesses and individuals rely on the court for interest.
- Precedents are established as guides to future conduct.
- Precedents create government reliance as they provide guidance to government officials on appropriate actions to take about a given statute.
- Precedents enable easy algorithms for AI-powered proceedings.

3.2 Negative Impacts of Judicial Precedents

Conversely, the negative impacts also gleaned from case law, are as follows:

- Precedents hinder flexibility in judicial decisions and frustrate social change and development.
- Precedents are rigid and do not allow for easy transition or easy transformation in interpretation.
- Precedents focus more on technical justice rather than substantial justice that impacts law and society.
- Precedents center on the impact of the precedent on the law, rather than on the impact of law on the society, as laws are created for the benefit of society.
- Precedents' stereotypical structure, weaken or restrict the power of judicial independence and judicial discretion.
- Wrong precedents would impact the entire algorithm and would cost more time, money, and resources to reprogram.

Figure 5.2, above shows that the negative impact of precedent outweighs the positive impact, as the negative impacts are weighing down the scale of justice, which makes justice unstable and anecdotal with the judicial system's agenda. Figure 5.2 also shows that over-reliance on judicial precedent tilts the scale

615 This could be good and bad for the judge, as no two cases are similar, and some lawyers have the habit of taking advantage of the slightest opportunity to accuse judges of corruption or ignorance of the law.

of justice unfairly against societal justice. Thus, adhering to precedent can be challenging for the judge, society, and eventually democratic governance, which will create judicial dilemmas.[616]

4 Challenges to Adhering to Precedents

There are three pragmatic challenges that adherence to precedent creates in contemporary Nigeria.

The first is that precedent loses its relevance to prevailing social views, culture, values, and interests. Often precedent becomes stale and undeveloped regarding some areas of law, compared to the pace of advancement in the socio-legal society. The court's adherence to precedent restricts the advancement of the judicial/legal system when society develops or when there are unforeseen changes in society. For example, with the arrival of the COVID pandemic, the courts were divided in applying discretion to deviate from the traditional in-person trial, as the established precedent in *Simon Edibo v. The State*,[617] that hearing outside the courtroom was unconstitutional, held some judges back from doing the unconventionally needful. Thus, creating a vacuum in the law that judges cover through applying their discretion in statutory interpretation. The inevitable risk is that following precedent may lead to stereotyped procedures that frustrate justice and restrict progress.[618] Olong states that precedent perpetuates injustice; encourages rigidity in the judicial process; and prevents progress and the spirit of experiment.[619]

The second challenge that strict adherence to precedent creates is that sometimes precedent (i.e., the judicial philosophy of the higher court judge or the precedent establishing judgment) conflicts with the lower court judge's judging philosophy or discretion, and this puts the lower court judge in a dilemma to either apply discretionary powers and follow his/her philosophy to ensure justice in the case, or to abide by precedent and maintain stability in the law, but interpret injustice.[620] If the judge applies the former option

---

616 A more elaborate discussion on judicial dilemmas is in the second volume of this author's research on courts and society.

617 Supra.

618 Olong, Nigerian Legal System, opcit: 26.

619 Ibid: 30.

620 Murrill, B. J. (2018). Modes of Constitutional Interpretation, opcit: 22–23.

of exercising discretion, the lower court stands the risk of facing the wrath of the high court. A vivid example is the case of *Dalhatu v. Turaki*,[621],where Katsina Alu, JSC, in strong terms condemned a trial judge who departed from the decision of the Supreme Court:

> The conduct of the learned trial judge I.U. Bello is to say the least most unfortunate. This is the highest and final court of appeal in Nigeria. Its decisions bind every court, authority or person in Nigeria. By the doctrine of state decisis, the courts below are bound to follow the decision of the Supreme Court. The doctrine is sine qua non for certainty to the practice and application of law. A refusal therefore by a judge of the court below to be bound by this court's decision, is gross insubordination (and I dare say such a judicial officer is a misfit for the judiciary).[622]

The above case was an election appeal from the High Court of the Federal Capital Territory, Abuja, where the presiding judge deviated from precedent to determine the appellant's writ of summons against the respondents, claiming a declaration that the purported return of the first respondent as the A.N.P.P. gubernatorial candidate for the 2003 election in Jigawa State was unconstitutional and void and that the return was a violation of the appellant's right to fair hearing and right to be elected for any elective office.[623] The trial court dismissed a preliminary objection challenging its jurisdiction. The appellants appealed the ruling to the Court of Appeal, and filed a motion for stay of execution pending appeal, but the trial court denied that motion, even when appellant referred the trial court to the Supreme Court's decision in *Onuoha v. Okafor*,[624] which had similar facts with the present case, and the court ignored the decision.

The Supreme Court in Onuoha's case established that the right to sponsor a candidate by a party is not a legal right but a domestic right of the party which cannot be questioned in a court of law.[625] This means that a political party or organization has an unfettered discretion to choose their candidates and no court of law has jurisdiction to question such discretion. If a court goes into such a domestic affair of the party, it has involved itself in nominating a particular candidate, a jurisdiction which a court cannot, and should

621 *Dalhatu v. Turaki (supra).*

622 *Osakwe v. Federal College of Education Asaba (supra).*

623 *Dalhatu v. Taraski (supra).*

624 *Onuoha v. Okafor* (1983) *2 SCNLR 244.*

625 See Dalhatu's case: opcit.

never exercise.[626] Unfortunately for the trial judge, he failed to apply this precedential reasoning. Consequently, he attracted a barrage of reprimands from the panel of Supreme Court justices. Thus, in addition to Katsina Alu's quote above, Justice Ogundare commented as follows:

> I entirely agree with my learned brother, Katsina Alu that *Onuoha v. Okafor & Ors (1983) 2 SCNLR 244; (1983) 14 NSCC 494* was rightly applied to the facts of the case on hand by the Court of Appeal. This case was cited to the trial Judge. He failed, rather he refused, to apply it. He thought the Supreme Court was wrong in its decision in that case and arrogantly closed his judgment in these words: "I also with great respect call on the Supreme Court to re-amend its position on the internal affairs of political parties." This to my mind is the height of judicial impertinence ever exhibited by a Judge of a court lower than the Supreme Court. The doctrine of stare decisis is fully entrenched in our jurisprudence to ensure certainty of the law. Had the learned trial Judge in this case cared to read that case and the various dicta of their Lordships of this court he would not have exhibited such crass ignorance that ran through his judgment.[627]

Also, Justice Tobi added the following:

> The learned trial Judge refused to follow Onuoha, That was not all. He asked this court to re-amend its position in Onuoha. In his words: "I also with the great respect call on the Supreme Court to re-amend its position on the internal affairs of political parties." The word "re-amend" gives the impression that this court had earlier amended its position in Onuoha, whatever that means. I cannot remember the case in which this court amended its position in Onuoha. But that is not very important. The important thing is that a trial Judge would have the courage and the strength not to follow a decision of the Supreme Court merely because he feels that the decision is wrong. As if that is not bad enough, the Judge has called upon this court to "re-amend its position" to fall in line with his. This is an extremely unfortunate situation. Apart from the fact that it attempts to destroy the well settled principle of stare decisis, this court is invited to abandon its own correct decision to follow a wrong decision of a trial Judge. This is very serious. On my part, I will not obey him. He is wrong in his judgment and this court is correct in Onuoha.

A trial judge's error in disregarding precedent is a judicial sin that every lower court must resist. Assuming the lower court had justified reasons about changes in society, from when the Onuoha court's precedent was established, he could, based on the distinguishing the case principle deviate from the

---

[626] Ibid. The court went on to say that while a court of law has the jurisdiction to declare a particular candidate as the winner of an election, a court of law cannot be involved in the domestic affair of nomination of a candidate or candidates in primaries.

[627] *Hon. Justice Ogundare, JSC, Dalhatu's case, supra at page 340, paras. A-D.*

upper court's decision. Unfortunately, that was not the case, and Oh! the justices did not spare him.

Third, precedent also creates a pragmatic challenge among superior court judges. For instance, there are conflicting precedents from the Supreme Court and sometimes the Courts of appeal, which confuses lower courts. In other words, there are varied opinions that do not give the lower courts clear precedent to follow. For instance, one opinion states that where precedents conflict, the lower courts are bound to follow the more recent precedent even if the older one is more relevant to the interests of justice.[628] In *Osakwe v. Federal College of Education Asaba*,[629] the Supreme Court held that where there are two conflicting decisions of the same high court, the lower court is bound to comply with the latter or latest decision even if it was reached *per in curium*. Then, in *Bronik Motors Ltd & Anor v. Wema Bank*,[630] the Supreme Court enumerated that it could deviate from its previous decision where there is a breach of justice, on ground of Public policy, and where the retention of the decision will amount to a perpetuation of injustice. The apex court further stated in *Abdulkarim v. INCAR Nigeria Ltd*[631] that although it will respect its previous decisions as a court of last resort (not bound by precedent), it will not hesitate to overrule its previous decisions, which was reached on wrong principles, as that is the only way to keep the streams of justice pure.[632]

The above conflicting views of Nigeria's Supreme Court clearly creates judicial dilemma that lower court judges must solve to ensure justice in applying precedent to a case. Nevertheless, judges have learned to solve this quagmire with different strategies by inadvertently considering several factors that impact applying precedent. Sanni (2016), gave a detailed account of these factors as follows:

> (i) Age: Generally, the greater the age of a precedent, the greater would be the reluctance of the court to disregard it even where the reasoning in it is not sustainable or convincing.

628 Osipitan, opcit.
629 *Supra.*
630 *Bronik Motors Ltd & Anor v. Wema Bank (supra).*
631 *Abdulkarim v. INCAR Nigeria Ltd (1992) 7 SCNJ P.366.*
632 Ibid.

> (ii) The status of the court and its composition are also of essence as to the value of the case as a precedent. In Nigeria, the decisions of Supreme Court Justice (sic) are accorded great weight.
> (iii) The adequacy of law report is another factor that affects the weight of precedents. Early cases are often inadequately reported due to lack of modern standards of law reporting. In fact, some law reports concentrate on reporting judgments of certain specific courts thereby indirectly causing greater weight to be attached to such judgments. Example of this can be found in Nigeria where emphasis is concentrated on reporting judgments of only the Court of Appeal and the Supreme Court thereby deliberately omitting reporting sound judgments of the High Courts (State or Federal).
> (iv) The history of a precedent is also very significant in determining its weight. First, the extent to which such precedent has been applied in later cases and approval of such precedent by jurists will definitely affect the weight attached to it. Second, whether the case was fully argued on the particular point taken or relevant authority cited also affect the weight attached to such precedent. Judgment given on merit of the case is likely to have more weight than judgment devoid of pleading or strict principle of law. Third, subsequent courts are responsive to argument based on the unjust or absurd consequences resulting from a previous case. This factor is often linked with a change in social condition which renders the earlier decision obsolete.
> (v) Where the court is unanimous in a given judgment, more weight is likely to be given to such judgment than where there is a dissenting judgment. The situation becomes complex where circumstances change, making the precedent inappropriate to modern condition.[633]

The above factors often aid judges in applying precedent, but judges differ in their choices—some judges apply precedent based on how old the precedent has been or its history with the facts of the case (i.e., the latter or latest decision). SJT advocates for the "latest decision" precedent, as society changes and old law/caselaw becomes irrelevant with diverse socio-technological advancements.

Judges should not underestimate the value or impact of society in the act of judging because society forms the bedrock of the court's existence.[634] The Appeal Court in *Dasofunjo v. Ajiboye*[635] stated that the court's function is to do justice between parties by settling their disputes, and anything short of

633 Sanni (2016) "Introduction to Nigerian Legal Method, Ile Ife OAU Press Limited: 187–188, from Idahosa, Doctrine of "Stare – Decisis" and Judicial Precedent: The Need for Lower Courts to Be Bound by Decisions of The Superior Courts of Record, opcit.

634 This highlights the hypothesis of this writer's research discussed in chapter 6—how judging impacts society.

635 *Dasofunjo v. Ajiboye (2017) LPELR-42354 (CA)*; see also *Engineering Enterprise Contractor Co. of Nigeria v. Attorney- General of Kaduna State (1987) 1 NSCC 601.*

that defeats the spirit of the law and the Constitution.[636] Accordingly, where litigants/the public do not understand or appreciate the justice that the courts render as just, the Constitution's essence is defeated, making a caricature of Nigeria's democracy. Sanni's last point on dissenting judgments offers leeway for judges to deviate from the status quo precedent—it enables change and gives room to develop precedent. Where circumstances change under modern conditions, the case becomes complex, and this challenges judges to "reconcile" the law with the complex cases and modern conditions in society.[637]

Therefore, where conflicts arise in applying precedent, it is fundamental that judges distinguish the cases to permit departure from precedent. When a lower court is unable to justify its departure from the rule based on distinguishable facts, Tobi states that it is judicial rascality, as it will be tantamount to distinctions of the facts where no distinction exists.[638] So, the judge has no other option where the decision of the higher court seems inappropriate or unjust under the circumstances of a given case, as the only deviation from this fundamental doctrine of order in the judicial hierarchy is the concept of distinguishing the case.[639] This means the court can only deviate from a superior court's decision if the cases' material facts are different.[640] Thus, where judges face such "similar" yet different cases, they must point out essential differences between the present case and an existing precedent, and use such difference as justification for departing from precedent.[641]

Accordingly, judges must emphasize such distinction(s) and give reasons why they are unable to abide by the subsisting precedent.[642] They should support their opinion rather than make bare declarations that the facts of the case are different.[643] Nonetheless, amidst the concept of distinguishing cases, issues arise due to obstacles—the possibility that no facts or situations in two cases are identical. Also, there are numerous cases with identical facts

636 Ibid.

637 This creates a dilemma for the judge, one that eventually affects the act of judging.

638 Tobi, opcit: 79.

639 This is an exception to the general rule of precedent.

640 See *Janus v. Am. Fed of State County*, from Murrill, ibid: 11.

641 Ibid.

642 This may either be on the ground that facts of the earlier case are different from the facts of the pending case, or that the decision is too wide, considering the issues before that court.

643 Ibid.

yet minor differences, and judges are required to resolve these cases in similar ways with seemingly similar precedents. Tobi, JSC, observed in *Oladeji (Nig.) LTD v. Nigeria Breweries Plc*[644] that "factual distinctions or differences in cases can only avail a party when they are germane or material to the stare decisis of the case ... This means that the facts that give rise to the principle of stare decisis are the material facts, devoid of or without the unimportant details. This also means that the facts need not be on all fours in the sense of exactness or exactitude."

The rule on precedent in Nigeria is somewhat like the United States', but in the United States, adherence to precedent is more flexible. In *Citizens United v. FEC*,[645] the American court confirmed that abiding by its prior decision supports the legitimacy of the judicial process and fosters the rule of law. The significance of precedent was emphasized in *Vasquez v. Hillery*[646] as follows:

> "The important doctrine of stare decisis is the means by which we ensure that the law will not merely change erratically but will develop in a principled and intelligible fashion. That doctrine permits society to presume that bedrock principles are founded in the law, rather than in the proclivities of individuals, and thereby contributes to the integrity of our constitutional system of government, both in appearance and in fact."

Furthermore, in the United States, overruling incorrect precedents may occasionally be necessary to rectify egregiously wrong decisions or to account for changes in society.[647] Where adherence to precedent affects the justice of a case or society, the U.S. courts overrule precedent. A ready example is the case of *Brown v. Board of Education*,[648] where the court held that the segregation of public schools by race violated the equal protection clauses of the Fourteenth Amendment. In addition, the Supreme Court of the United States stated that the decision to overrule precedent must be based on strong grounds that extend beyond the court's mere disagreement with the merits of the prior decisions' reasoning.[649]

---

644 *Oladeji (Nig.) LTD v. Nigeria Breweries Plc (2007) 5 NWLR (Pt. 1027) P. 415 at P. 436.*
645 *Citizens United v. FEC, 558, U.S 310, 378 (2010).*
646 *Vasquez v. Hillery, 474 U.S. 254, 265–66 (1986).*
647 Murrill, B.J (2018) The Supreme Courts Overruling of Constitutional Precedent, opcit:7.
648 *Brown v. Board of Education 347 U.S. 483.*
649 Murrill, (2018) opcit: 11.

Also, by a 2018 decision in *Janus v. American Federation of State, County and Municipal Employees*,[650] the U.S. Supreme Court outlined factors to be considered when the court decides to overrule (constitutional) precedent. These factors include the quality of the precedent's reasoning, the workability of the rule the precedent establishes, its consistency with other related decisions, developments since the decision was handed down, and reliance on the decision/interest at stake. In other words, the court's reasoning was whether the precedent had been abandoned by subsequent legal developments and whether overturning the precedent would threaten the legitimacy of the judiciary.[651]

The U.S. courts expressed concern that if precedent is overruled on grounds of mere disagreements with prior decisions' reasoning, the court's legitimacy may suffer. Similarly, the Nigerian Supreme Court states that where it is necessary, proper, and just to depart from previous decisions, courts should not hesitate to overrule its previous decisions.[652] In *Board of Customs and Excise v. Bolarinwa*,[653] the court held as follows:

> It is not sufficient to say that the facts are different. A Magistrate who does not intend to apply a decision of the High Court must state:
> (1) The ratio decidendi of that decision;
> (2) The facts proved in that decision; and
> (3) Show by judicial reasoning in the body of the judgment, in what manner the High Court decision is different from the case before him.

In addition, the Supreme Court can overrule its own decisions where its previous decision was given wrongly or reached *per incuriam*.[654] Courts balance a lot of "non-dispositive factors" in deviating from precedent.[655] Therefore, any court, even the high court, can deviate from precedent, if the interest of justice warrants and if the principle of distinguishing the case gives reasons for their opinions, rather than making bare declarations that the facts of

650 *Janus v. American Federation of State, County and Municipal Employees 585, U.S (2018), No.16, 1466, slip opt at 43–35.*

651 Walker, J.M (2016) The Role of Precedent in United States: How do Precedent lose Their Binding Effects?, opcit.

652 *Johnson v. Lawanson (1971) 1 All NLR P. 56; Maclean v. Inlaks (1980) 8–11 SC 1.*

653 *Board of Customs and Excise v. Bolarinwa (1968) NMLR 350 at 352, Hon. Justice Thompson J.*

654 Ibid.

655 Walker, opcit.

the case are different. The latter can resort to abuse of judicial discretion.[656] So, what determines the right "justice" principle or criteria upon which the Supreme Court would overrule itself?[657]

Also, a lawyer can petition the court to overturn its precedent, but as Tobi, JCA (as he was then) said in *Awuse v. Odili*,[658] "counsel who calls on a court to overrule its earlier decision has an herculean task to satisfy the court that the decision is wrong." He must show that the decision has caused or perpetuated injustice through the doctrine of stare decisis or it has impeded the development of the law or is in fact against public policy, or the decision was given per incuriam."

Based on several factors, Nigerian courts have experienced inconsistencies in adhering to precedent. Unfortunately, the lack of uniformity, inconsistencies, and conflicts among different courts affects the reputation of the judiciary and the legal profession, and has ripple effects on society. These conflicting decisions of the apex court create confusion among lower court judges and eventually trickle down to society. This frustrates the judge's discretion, as lower courts cannot afford to overrule precedent. So, where old precedent outweighs the new and at the same time challenges the justice of the case, the lower court judges get trapped in a cage of frustration. This is one delicate quagmire the Nigerian judiciary cannot afford to ignore amidst Nigeria's chaotic democracy,[659] as the consequences of such inconsistency, unfortunately, fall back on society and increases public distrust for the courts.[660]

Generally, despite its disadvantages, *stare decisis* is firmly rooted in Nigeria's legal system and in other Common Law jurisdictions. Precedent is a fundamental doctrine of order that judges must comply with to avoid arbitrary abuse of discretion. Therefore, judges of lower courts must abide by the previous decisions of higher courts, as superior court's decisions are binding on

---

656 See discussion in Chapter 4.

657 A detailed discussion of this dilemma is discussed in the second phase of this research.

658 *Awuse v. Odili (2003) 18 NWLR (Pt. 851) 116 at 179, C.*

659 The recent conflicts and abuse of rule of law that has been incessant in the country for the past couple of years, that is, the disregard and disrespect for courts and court orders, the arrest and prosecution of senior justices without due process, the suspension of a former Chief Justice of Nigeria, etc.

660 As the proverbial African phrase goes, when the elephants (courts) fight (disagree), it is the grasses (society) that suffers.

all inferior courts, and the inferior courts have no option than to follow the decision of the superior court. It is immaterial even if the inferior court thinks otherwise.[661] Also in the American case of *Alleyne v. United States*,[662] Associate Justice Sotomayor[663] stated, "we generally adhere to our prior decisions, even if we question their soundness, because doing so promotes the evenhanded, predictable, and consistent development of legal principles, fosters reliance on judicial decisions, and contributes to the actual and perceived integrity of the judicial process."[664] Although this principle is a bedrock principle in the American legal system, it is not an "inexplorable command."[665] According to Judge Walker,[666] "the doctrine is a principle of policy and not a mechanical formula of adherence to the latest decision."[667]

Previously, during Chief Justice Marshall's tenure, American courts strictly adhered to precedent, but now the courts strike a balance in maintaining a stable body of consistent jurisprudence while at the same time preserving some "mechanism for error correction."[668] Thus, courts consider the *stare decisis* principle as a discretionary "principle of policy" that weighs and balances the court's views about the merits of the prior decision and several pragmatic considerations.[669]

Precedent has come a long way in Nigeria's judicial system, and it is here to stay. It is a fundamental requirement in the judicial process. Hence, Justice Tobi's introductory quote above says even if the precedent is wrong, the lower court judge is bound to apply it blindly.[670] Although precedent frustrates

---

661 See *Ola Animashaun v. A.G Lagos State & 5 Ors, (supra)*.

662 *Alleyne v. United States* 570 U.S. 99, 118 (2013).

663 Justice of the Supreme Court of the United States of America.

664 Also, in *Vasquez v. Hillery*, 474 U.S. 254, 265–66 (1986), "the important doctrine of stare decisis [is] the means by which we ensure that the law will not merely change erratically but will develop in a principled and intelligible fashion. That doctrine permits society to presume that bedrock principles are founded in the law, rather than in the proclivities of individuals, and thereby contributes to the integrity of our constitutional system of government, both in appearance and in fact."

665 Walker, J.M (2016), opcit.

666 Senior circuit judge, U.S Court of Appeals for the Second Circuit.

667 Walker, opcit.

668 Murrill, opcit: 5.

669 Ibid: 6.

670 See the quote introducing this chapter.

judges' discretion, it is indispensable to the act of judging in Nigeria.[671] However, like every aspect of human life, when a rule is excessive, non-compliance is inevitable. Rules are made to ensure compliance and a safe society, just like precedents are meant to ensure compliance and a just society.

Therefore, judicial precedent should be relevant to the specific society's needs and interests. Applying precedent that is irrelevant to the circumstances of a case, ridicules the court's mandate to achieve justice. In other words, when courts unfairly adhere to precedent without regard to relevant contemporary facts and the circumstances surrounding each case, the court's impact and relevance/value in society declines. Unfortunately, the reality in Nigerian society, as is in many other democracies, is that some precedents are outdated and accordingly irrelevant to recent cases, but the lower courts still apply them to avoid being called or tagged judicial rascals. This is a dilemma, and a threat to judicial independence, democracy, and the development of law and society.

---

671 This author discussed the dilemma of adhering to precedent in her dissertation, the second volume of this research.

Chapter 6
The Impact of Judging on Society

> Rules of Court are meant to be obeyed. Of course, that is why they are made. There should be no argument about that. But there is an important qualification or caveat, and it is that their obedience cannot or should not be slavish to the point that the justice in the case is destroyed or thrown overboard. The greatest barometer, as far as the public is concerned, is whether, at the end of the litigation process, justice has been done to the parties. Therefore, if in the course of doing justice, some harm is done to some procedural rule which hurts the rule, ..., the court should be happy that it took that line of action in pursuance of justice. This court cannot myopically or blindly follow the Practice Directions and fall into a mirage and get physically and mentally absorbed or lost. Let that day not come ... Full opportunity should be given to parties in the interest of justice without due regard to technicalities. Gone are the days when courts of law were only concerned with doing technical and abstract justice based on arid legalism. We are now in days when courts of law do substantial justice in the light of the prevailing circumstances of the case. it is my hope that the days of the courts doing technical justice will not surface again.
>
> —Hon. Justice Niki Tobi, JSC (as he then was)[672]

1 Introduction

This chapter examines the relationship between courts and society, emphasizing society's relevance to the act of judging, which involves interpreting statutes and applying judicial discretion to create social change. This chapter summarizes the court's role in society and states how procedural and substantial justice impacts the act of judging. It further defines society's relevance to the judge's decision-making process and highlights the interplay between judges and society. Specifically, while reinforcing her socio-judicialism theory, the author introduces twelve stages of judging that she applied as a magistrate-judge. In conclusion, by reiterating the above quote, this chapter attempts to define what justice means and explains the fundamental place

---

672 *Abubakar & Ors. v. Yar'Adua & Ors. (2008) LPELR-51 (SC).*

of justice in the act of judging. At the end of this chapter, readers will also understand what the act of judging means in Nigerian courts, and how the act of judging interprets (or should interpret) the judges' main assignment– executing real justice and not a caricature of justice.

2 Courts and Society

Courts are connected to the society, as the society is connected to the courts, and judges are part of the society. Judges and the law are the connecting cords between courts and society. While the law is designed for social compliance and maintaining order in society, judges are responsible for administering justice by exercising judicial discretion to interpret the law and maintain social order. So, judges are intermediaries between society and the law/ lawmakers (legislature). Statutes are sometimes ambiguous, and the judge's unfettered discretion clarifies the ambiguity.[673] Lord Denning opines that it is not within human power to foresee the manifold sets of facts that may arise. Even if it were, it is impossible to provide laws free from all ambiguity to tackle these facts.[674] Thus, the court's "judicial and judicious" discretion in interpreting these laws is invaluable to society's best interest

The judge's perception in interpreting a statute or the judge's idiosyncrasy/ personality in exercising discretion affects the relationship between the courts and society. Often, such a relationship determines the judge's discretion and wherever the pendulum of justice sways. As Tobi stated in the above introductory quote: "the greatest barometer, as far as the public is concerned, is whether, at the end of the litigation process, justice has been done to the parties." However, the dilemma is who determines what justice means, or the criteria to apply in interpreting justice in any case.

The social perception of justice sometimes differs from the court's perception. The public perceives judges/courts as divine and above error, as their judicial office elevates judges to the high pedestal—the bench. They often forget that judges are also infallible members of society. As drafters are not above errors, judges are also not above errors. The diverse forms or principles of interpretation and the liberal exercise of judicial discretion indicate judges'

---

673 Hine, opcit: 1770.
674 *Seaford Estate Ltd v. Asher (1949)2 K.B 481.*

humanness. The court's discretion in interpreting contemporary statutes may differ when interpreting old statutes. In interpreting contemporary statutes, judges should feel society's pulse, that is, social values, interests, perspectives, and social changes. This embrace of society ensures a more realistic interpretation of statutes in contemporary society. Whether the statute is contemporary or medieval, the judge's personality influences its interpretation.

The legislative branch enacts law according to relevant social realities[675] at a given time, making such realities lawful. Then, eventually, the law loses its relevance due to inevitable social changes that occur from time to time, making these realities that were legal at one time illegal. Also, on the flip side, some realities in our society make unlawful practices or unlawful laws eventually lawful, thereby creating diverse interpretations of the law that appeal to the judge's discretion. An example is the law against euthanasia or assisted suicide.[676] By Nigerian law, both the criminal code[677] and penal codes[678] assumably criminalize euthanasia, as both laws *mutatis mutandis*[679] prohibit the taking of life directly or indirectly by anyone. Accordingly, except as set forth, any person who causes the death of another directly or indirectly, by any means whatsoever is deemed to have killed that other person.[680] The person's consent to his/her death does not decriminalize the offense. In other words, consent by a person to the causing of his own death does not affect the criminal responsibility of any person by whom such death is caused.[681]

675 The phenomenological level is created through social interactions that transcend individual motives and actions. Examples are social norms or practices like cultural diversities, health and scientific developments and discoveries, medical and pharmacological research, media rights, such as free press versus fair trial, social media advancement, LGBTQ movements, women empowerment, such as the Me Too Movement, global business networking, election campaigns, etc.

676 Also known as mercy killing or assisted suicide.

677 See sections 306, 326 (3) of the Criminal Code Act Cap 41 Laws of Federation of Nigeria 2004.

678 See sections 221, 222, 227, and 228 of the Penal Code, Cap 89, Laws of Federation of Nigeria 2004.

679 A Latin maxim that means that the respective differences have been considered.

680 See section 308 of the criminal code, opcit.

681 Oniha, B. (n.d.). Legality of Euthanasia and The Right to Die in Nigeria. P.12. <https://edojudiciary.gov.ng/wp-content/uploads/2017/07/LEGALITY-OF-EUTHANASIA-AND-THE-RIGHT-TO-DIE-IN-NIGERIA-BY-BRIGHT-E.-ONIHA-CORRECTED.pdf>

The Nigerian Supreme Court stated the above point in the celebrated case of *Medical and Dental Practitioners Disciplinary Tribunal v. Dr. John Emewulu Okonkwo*,[682] when it upheld the right of a patient to consent to medical intervention/treatment in pursuit of her exercise of the right to freedom of thought, conscience and religion under the constitution.[683] In this case the patient, developed post-delivery complications after having a baby. She was admitted to the hospital for nine days and was diagnosed with a serious condition that required blood transfusion. She declined the transfusion on religious grounds as, she, her husband, and one Dr. Okonkwo are all members of the Jehovah's Witness Christian religious sect, which passionately believes that blood transfusion is contrary to God's injunctions for Christians not to "eat blood." Thus, she was on this ground discharged from that hospital with a note that she refused transfusion and that she might die.

Hence, she was taken to another hospital where the respondent, Dr. Okonkwo, practices. Here, she presented the doctor with a card directing that in accordance with her rights as a patient and her beliefs as a Jehovah's Witness, no blood transfusion should be carried out on her. She also absolved the medical personnel of the hospital from responsibility. Her husband also executed a similar document. Hence, the doctor treated her without a blood transfusion per her directive. She subsequently died. Consequently, the doctor in charge, Dr. Okonkwo was later charged before the medical and Dental Practitioner's disciplinary tribunal for acting contrary to his oath of practice and negligence. The tribunal found him guilty of the counts and suspended his practice for six months. Upon appeal to the Court of Appeal, his appeal succeeded. The Tribunal further appealed to the Supreme Court, with a unanimous decision, the Apex Court dismissed the appeal with the reasoning that the patient was well within her legal and constitutional rights to decline medical treatment which included blood transfusion, and the doctor could not have done anything infringing this right.

Ayoola, JSC, stated as follows:

> The patient's constitutional right to object to medical treatment or particularly, as in this case, to blood transfusion on religious grounds is founded on fundamental

---

682 *Medical and Dental Practitioners Disciplinary Tribunal v. Dr John EmewuluOkonkwo.58 (2001) 3 SC 76.*

683 Oniha, opcit.

> rights protected by the 1979 constitution .... preserved in section 37 and 38 of the 1999 Constitution respectively. The right to privacy implies a right to protect one's thought, conscience or religious beliefs' and practice from coercive and unjustified intrusion and one's body from unauthorized invasion. The right to freedom of thought, conscience and religion implies a right not to be prevented, without lawful justification from choosing the course of one's life ... if a competent adult patient exercising his right to reject lifesaving treatment on religious grounds thereby chooses a path that may ultimately lead to his death, in the absence of judicial intervention overriding the patient's decision, what meaningful option is the practitioner left with other than perhaps to give the patient's comfort. More so against the backdrop of the fact that prevailing medical ethical practice does not without exceptional demand that all efforts towards life prolongation be made in all circumstance but seems to recognize that the dying are often in need of comfort than treatment.

According to Oniha, the Supreme Court's decision effectively endorsed passive voluntary euthanasia by way of the exercise of a patient's right to self-determination expressed in her refusal of medical intervention even where it will surely lead to her death, where such intervention runs contrary to her constitutionally guaranteed right.[684]

Another example is the landmark decision of the Supreme Court of the United States (SCOTUS) in *Dobbs v. Jackson Women's Health Organization*,[685] overturning the agelong *Roe v. Wade* precedent.[686] The Dobbs' decision that the U.S. Constitution does not grant the right to abortion, impacts the courts' role as agents of social change. Thus, in a Courts & Society Webinar Series titled "Courts as Agents of Social Change," Makoba posits that from the Dobbs case, the American society influenced the SCOTUS to change the law from the *Roe v. Wade* status quo.[687]

The controversies on the courts as agents of social change inevitably impact the act of judging, which evolves with time (or should evolve as society changes).[688] It is pertinent to note that diverse judicial interpretations of similar laws often affect public understanding of such laws, the implications of such laws to their social issues, and/or public perception of social values

684 Oniha, opcit: 17.

685 *Dobbs, State Health Officer of the Mississippi Department of Health et al. v. Jackson Women's Health Organization et al., 597 U.S. (2002).*

686 See *Roe v. Wade, supra.*

687 See Makoba, J. (2002). Courts as Agents of Social Change, opcit.

688 Part of this book's argument is that the act of judging in Nigeria has remained static in some cases.

underpinning those laws.[689] Thus, where conflicts emanate from such social realities or diverse interpretations of law (based on judges' idiosyncrasies, knowledge, or judicial experiences), judges, as well as society, get caught up in controversial interpretations that further complicate issues. An example is the controversy in precedents.[690]

Society does not understand the basic principles of law because judicial interpretations are often abstract, and some judges use legal terminologies/jargons that confuse litigants. When a concept is not understood, the abuse of the concept is often inevitable. So, if society does not understand the law as the court interprets it, the public will abuse or violate the law. Accordingly, since the public does not understand the justice that judges interpret in court, they get "smothered" by vague abstract interpretations, which defeats the aim of justice. Thus, there is a disconnect in social perception of the law, which causes a disconnection between courts and society or judges and social reality.

Courts can connect law to society when they understand what justice means to society, how the public perceives justice and the real purpose of interpreting statute which is explaining the legislature's thoughts and applying it to relevant contemporary social realities.[691] Although the intent of legislatures is fundamental and should be the first step in interpreting statutes, the legislatures' old thoughts are not valuable or relevant to the needs of contemporary society. Thus, courts should not limit interpreting laws to legislative intent but rather focus on social interests. If statutes are relevant to social interest, judicial interpretation will impact societal development and social change. In *A.G. Lagos State v. A.G. Federation*,[692] the Supreme Court held "that the interpretation of the provision of any statute should mirror the social accentuation of the society and also meet the needs of the society."[693]

Therefore, if legislators could review the laws they made with the contemporary changes in society, they are likely to amend the law to align with

---

689 See comment on precedent in Chapter 1.

690 See discussion on judicial precedent in Chapter 5.

691 See Tobi-Aiyemo, A. (2021) The Role of the Nigerian Judiciary in a Democracy: The Judge's Dilemma, opcit.

692 *A.G. Lagos State v, A.G. Federation (2013)16 NWLR (pt. 1380) 383, Para D-E.*

693 See also the case of *Oketie-Eboh v. Manager (2004) 18 NWLR (pt. 905) 246* and *A.G. Ogun State v. Aberuagba (1985) 1 NWLR (pt. 3) 395.*

relevant social circumstances and interests. According to Galinje, JSC, in *Abiodun v. FRN*,[694] the court is more interested in substance than in form as justice can only be done if the judge examines the substance of the case. Therefore, it is the court's duty to align or realign laws with social realities to achieve the aim of justice. Courts achieve substantial justice when the rules of law accommodate social views, values, and interests. Thus, the act of judging is not just to settle disputes between parties; judges also have the important role to uphold the essence of democracy by interpreting statutes fairly and exercising discretion justly.

The court's mandate to do justice should inspire creativity through judicial discretion.[695] Consequently, courts should uphold the law and not get caught between interpreting the law (as is)[696] and ensuring justice (as should be).[697] The court's role of interpreting law and upholding justice,[698]reveals a competing interest between law and society, both contending for the courts' attention, intervention, and favor. These competing interests create judicial dilemmas and question the court's obligation or role in society—whether the court's obligation is to the law or to society. In other words, does the scale of justice tilt toward the side of the law or the side of society, or is the courts' role to support the law or to support society?

3 The Courts' Roles in Society

Barack aptly summarizes the judge's role as follows:

> The role of the judge is to understand the purpose of law in society and to help the law achieve its purpose. But the law of a society is a living organism. it is based on a factual and social reality that is constantly changing. … Law's connection to this fluid reality implies that it too is always changing. Sometimes change in the law precedes societal change and is even intended to stimulate it. In most cases, however, a change in the law is the result of a change in social reality. Indeed, when social reality changes, the

694 *Abiodun v. FRN (2018) LPELR-43838(SC) Pp. 18–19, Paras. C-A.*
695 Oshio, ibid: 24.
696 From the literal meaning of the statute, the intention of the drafters as it was or the legislative history.
697 A guarantee that both parties have had a fair and just trial.
698 The focus of another research series on Courts & Society.

law must change too. Just as change in social reality is the law of life, responsiveness to the change in social reality is the life of the law.[699]

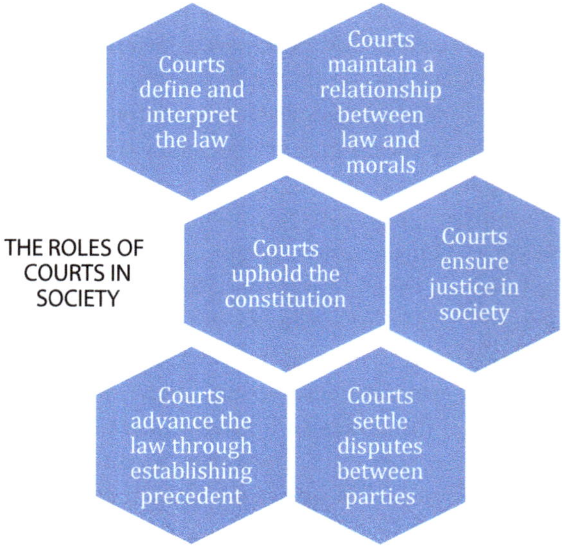

Figure 6.1: Courts and Society

The court's first role is **to define the law.** In stating what the law is, the court has to help the law achieve its purpose. The purpose of law is to ensure compliance and order in society. The courts are agents that direct compliance with the law. The law is like an island and can only be connected to the rest of society with the court's help. Law is created for the benefit of social order but is sometimes vague to the society that is supposed to benefit from it. However, judges can only state what the law is if they understand the law.[700] Judges are supposed "masters" of the law who perform their role in society through judicial pronouncements to determine the law. This was the court's position in *AC & Anor v. INEC*,[701] that the judge's main function is to declare

---

699 Barack, A. (2006). The Judge in a Democracy, opcit:3.
700 Ibid.
701 *AC & Anor v. INEC (2007) LPELR-66 (SC).*

what the law is and not to decide what it ought to be. Nothing is law until the courts declare it as law.[702]

Secondly, the judge's role within the statutory limits of his judicial discretion is to **maintain a relation between law and morals,** between the precepts of jurisprudence and those of reason and good conscience.[703] In performing this duty, the judge straightens the wrinkles or ambiguities in the law. These wrinkles are the vague, ambiguous, or unjust aspects of the law that are unclear to the public. Lord Denning said, "a judge should ask himself the question: if the makers of the Act has themselves come across this ruck in the texture of it, how would they have straightened it out? He must then do as they would have done. A judge must not alter the material of which it is woven, but he can and should iron out the creases."[704]

Thirdly, the courts have the primary role **to uphold the Constitution**, as custodians of the Constitution. The Court of Appeal held in *Olusanya v. UBA Plc*[705] that courts of record established as custodians of the Constitution have the primary judicial obligation and duty to comply and ensure compliance with the clear and plain provision of the Constitution in the discharge of their adjudicating functions. The Constitution is the mentor of all other laws of the land so judges should safeguard it jealously.[706] It is unnecessary for courts to misconstrue or frustrate the Constitution's clear provisions, which judges should comply with and uphold. The court in *Nafiu Rabiu v. The State*[707] aptly captured this argument below:

> My lords, in my opinion, it is the duty of this court to bear constantly in mind the fact that the present Constitution has been proclaimed the supreme law of the land, that it is a written organic instrument meant to serve not only the present generation but also several generations yet unborn … that the function of the Constitution is to establish a framework and principles of government broad and general in terms intended to apply to the varying conditions which the development of our several communities must involve, ours being a plural, dynamic society, and therefore, mere technical rules of interpretation of statutes are to some extent inadmissible in a way

---

702 Duxbury, N. (2001) Patterns of American Jurisprudence, opcit: 51.

703 Cardozo, B. N. (1921). The Nature of the Judicial Process, opcit: 135.

704 *Seaford Estates Ltd v. Asher (supra).*

705 *Olusanya v. UBA Plc (2017) LPELR-42348(CA).*

706 See *Dingyadi v. INEC (2011) 10 NWLR (1255) 347.*

707 *Nafiu Rabiu v. The State (supra).*

> so as to defeat the principles of government enshrined in the Constitution....I do not conceive it to be so to construe any of the provisions of the Constitution as to defeat the obvious ends the Constitution was designed to serve, where another Constitution equally in accord and consistent with the words and sense of such provisions will serve to enforce and protect such ends.

Fourthly, courts also have the important but demanding and somewhat controversial role **to interpret the law.**[708] In interpreting statutes, most judges rely on the drafter's intent; some rely on the text's original meaning, while others rely on legislative history. These factors align the court's obligation as a go-between the law and society.[709] According to the courts in *PDP v. CPC. & Ors,*[710] a judge is hired to interpret the laws of the country which includes the Constitution and other statutes. In *I.G.P. v. A.N.P.P,*[711] the Court held that its duty is to simply interpret the law or Constitution as made by the legislators or framers of the Constitution. Cardozo states that the power of interpretation must be lodged somewhere, and the custom of the Constitution has lodged it in the judges.[712] The court determines the original meaning of a statute when the judge interprets the statute in its original context—its historical, literary, and political context from the framer's perspective. According to Hon. Justice Fatayi-Williams, CJN:

> it is our view that in most countries with Common Law jurisdictions such as Nigeria, it is generally accepted that it is the function of the judiciary to interpret the law with the minimum of direction from the legislature as to how thy should set about the task. Thus, nearly all the principles, precepts and maxims of statutory interpretation are judge-made. Here are some examples. A statute should always be looked at as such a whole; words used in a statute are to be read according to their meanings as popularly understood at the time the statute became law; a statute is presumed not to alter law beyond that necessarily required by the statute.[713]

Fifthly, courts have a role **to advance the law through creating precedent.** Law is an evolving concept, as what was considered law in the nineteenth century is not necessarily law today in the twenty-first century. For example, the law

708 This duty has been challenged as making law and usurping the duty of legislature.
709 Tobi-Aiyemo. (2017). "The Intermediate Obligation of a Judge Vis A Vis Law and Society: A Matter of Interpretation," opcit: 1.
710 *PDP v. CPC. & Ors (unreported) SC.272/2011.*
711 *I.G.P. v. A.N.P.P (2007) 18 NWLR (Pt. 1066) 457 at 496–497, paras. G-E (CA).*
712 Cardozo, B.N. (1921), The Nature of the Judicial Process, opcit.
713 *Awolowo v. Shagari & Ors (supra).*

of retribution was a prominent mode of punishment at one time but now, as per certain crimes, it is no longer law to give an eye for an eye punishment.[714] The judges who created the Common Law did it to provide a solution to the social needs of their time. As these social needs change, judges must consider developing the judicial precedent by expanding or restricting the existing case law or overturning old precedents. Sometimes the new social reality necessitates creating new case law to resolve problems that did not arise at all in the past, where the goal of the new case law is to bridge the gap between law and new social realities.[715] According to the Court in *Dapianlong & Ors v. Dariye & Anor,*[716] though judicial precedent or *stare decisis* is an indispensable foundation to decide the law, there may be times when a departure from the precedent in the interest of justice, would stimulate appropriate development of the law.

Sixthly, the most prominent role of the court as the layman in society understands, is **to settle disputes between parties** and protect the rights of citizens. Different sectors of people make up society, so conflicts are inevitable, and when these conflicts ensue, it is the courts' role to settle them. Courts guarantee the rights of citizens/society. A judge is the cynosure of the litigating public as well as the entire populace.[717] The court in *Oguneyehun & Ors. v. The Governor Ondo State & Ors*[718] reinforced this point.

The seventh and most important role of the court is **to do justice in society**, for the benefit of the parties and the public. Judges must understand that their decisions exceed the immediate parties before them. Judicial decisions are also for prospective parties, eventually impacting the development of the law and society.[719]According to *Davies & Ors v. Odofin & Ors,*[720] the court's duty is to render undiluted justice to the citizenry, and it must do this scrupulously without any fear or favor, ill will or affection.

In explaining the courts' roles, Oputa said:

---

714 Campaigns to abolish the death penalty is an example of changes in the criminal justice law.

715 Barak. A. (2006) The Judge in a Democracy. opcit: 10.

716 *Dapianlong & Ors v. Dariye & Anor (2007) LPELR-928 (SC).*

717 Tobi, opcit: 42.

718 *Oguneyehun & Ors. v. The Governor Ondo State & Ors (2007) LPELR-4239 (CA).*

719 See *Irepodun-Ifelodun Local Government v. Balemo (2007) LPELR-8439 (CA).*

720 *Davies & Ors v. Odofin & Ors (2017) LPELR-41871 (CA).*

> The Judge should appreciate that in the final analysis, the end of law is justice. He should therefore endeavor to see that the law and the justice of the individual case he is trying go hand in hand. To this end he should be advised that the spirit of justice does not reside in formalities, nor in words, nor is the triumph of the administration of justice to be found in successfully picking a way between pitfalls of technicalities. He should know that all said, the law is, and ought to be, the hand maid of justice, and inflexibility which is the most becoming robe of law, often serves to render justice grotesque.[721]

4 Justice in Judging

Justice is a concept of semantics.[722] Different people interpret justice as they perceive and understand it. Society assumes justice to be what the courts say justice is, and the courts presumably define justice as the law portrays it. However, social perceptions and circumstances also define justice as society changes. Justice has several components and means different things to diverse people/groups in society. While adjudicating, judges should consider their intentions as per society-based versus law-based interpretations. Justice gets strangled if judges interpret the law according to statutory stipulations and such interpretation contradicts social interests. Hence, this author's research questions whether courts apply social criteria or legal criteria to define justice. It is pertinent that courts define justice with social and human criteria, that is, the reasonable man's perspective of justice.

Justice is for the parties and not for the court, so courts should interpret justice according to social standards and interests. Hence, Nigerian courts reiterate the aphorism that justice must not only be done but must manifestly be seen to be done.[723] When the public "sees" or perceives that justice is done to litigants, as they understand and interpret it (the reasonable man's view), then they will believe the court has done justice, as the saying goes—justice for one is justice for all. In *Okpalaeke v. NEPA*,[724] the Court of Appeal held that "a court owes a duty to do justice to all parties. A court is a court of

721 Oshio, opcit.

722 This author examined details on the scale of justice and its impact on judicial roles in her dissertation, which is the follow-up research and second volume of this book.

723 See *The Admin. & Exec. Of The Estate Of Abacha v. Eke-Spiff & Ors. (2009) LPELR-3152(SC)* and *PDP v. INEC & Ors. (2012) LPELR-9724 (SC)*, conveniently adopted from the holding of Hewart CJ in the English case of *R v. Susses Justices Ex Parte Marcathy (1924) 1 K.B, 256.*

724 *Okpalaeke v. NEPA (2003) 14 NWLR (pt.840) 383 at p. 403.*

justice and to be properly so called, justice must be seen to be done to all parties. It is therefore expected to take all the necessary pains to go into the depth of each case for the purpose of a just determination of the case, no matter how cumbersome it may be."

The courts' roles are (or should be) focused on society. Society, as the recipients and beneficiaries of judicial decisions, should be at the center in the act of judging. Society is the key factor that inspires justice in any case. Society is the reason for the law, and judges should ensure that the public's experiences with the law/courts are concrete, and not abstract. According to Judge Simac,[725] "judges are public servants ... The parties are the most important people in the courtroom but in reality, it is the judges and lawyers that are considered the most important, while parties are lost in legal laboring."[726] Also Hon. Justice Oguntade, JSC, states that all courts in Nigeria have a duty that flows from a power the Constitution grants to ensure Nigerians obtain the justice they deserve.[727] We cannot overstate the court's duty to fulfill the object and true intent of the Constitution. The court's duty however exercised, should not be detrimental to social justice. Thus, courts must always construe the Constitution to protect the society it sets out to protect, and to guide the law it should guide.[728] The preamble of the Constitution of any country and other statutes set to protect the Constitution's focus—"WE the people."[729]

As an intermediary between law and society, courts/judges are obligated to understand the law's function in society and interpret it to achieve its purpose according to society's perception of justice.[730] Thus, judges may give a statute a new or dynamic meaning that seeks to bridge the gap between law and society/life's changing reality, without changing the statute itself.

---

725 Judge Srdan Simac is a judge of the High Commercial Court of the Republic of Croatia.

726 Niki-Tobi, A. (2024, December 12) *The Court's Role in Implementing Human Rights* (Courts & Society Webinar Series, 10th Special Edition) A.T. Socio-Judicial Consulting. <https://atsjconsulting.com/>

727 See *Ameach v. INEC (supra).*

728 See *Adeleke v. Oyo State House of Assembly (2006) 6 NWLR (Pt 1006) 608.*

729 "We the people of the United States, in order to form a more perfect union, establish justice, ensure domestic tranquility, provide for the common defense, promote the general welfare, and secure the blessings of liberty to ourselves and our posterity, do ordain and establish this Constitution for the United States of America."

730 Ibid: 2.

Although statutes may remain as they were enacted, their meanings could change as courts give statutes new meaning that suits contemporary social issues/needs.[731] On the other hand, courts can also transform the law through their roles in society, and such transformation cannot happen without society.

The courts' essence in society will be valueless if there is a gap between how society understands and interprets justice and the statutory/legal definition of justice.[732] Often, it appears judicial interpretation of justice is more by the books/statutes (that only lawyers and judges understand), rather than for the parties/society. This book somewhat poses the question of how the act of judging adequately interprets justice along with lawmakers' intentions to accommodate the interests of a complex and changing society. As different predominant individual views, interests, and needs conflict with incessant changes and development in society, some statutes appear outdated, vague, irrelevant, and inadequate; making the public view of such statutes, and the impact of judicial decisions on society ineffective. The courts' interpretation eventually influences legislative amendment, which trickles to impact society. Hence, this author posits that judges are agents of social change.

Furthermore, complex social realities often confront judges, yet the public expects them to interpret the law in its "original context" and uphold justice amidst complex societal changes. Although, there is nothing wrong with interpreting law in its "original context," if the words are clear and consistent. However, the words' meaning evolves with time, and the context in which words are used often changes.[733] Hence, a rigid approach makes such interpretation stale, making the law/statute irrelevant or ineffective to society. In *Attorney General Bendel State v. A.G Federation*,[734] Obaseki, JSC, rightly observed that where the Constitution's language does not change, the changing circumstances of a progressive society for which it was designed can generate a new meaning. Adhering strictly to literal interpretation can lead

---

731 Barak, opcit: 4–5.

732 Again, this gap has been bridged by judicial or equitable discretion including both law and equity.

733 Brannon, opcit: 9.

734 *Attorney General Bendel State v. A.G Federation (supra).*

to illogical conclusions.[735] Even scholars of the textual form of interpretation have adopted realist perspectives where necessary.[736]

Therefore, courts should interpret and define justice with changing socio-legal contexts and consider social interests, social empathy, and changing social circumstances to decide cases. Thus, to embrace social changes, judges should embrace the full range of equitable discretion and its influence on the law in decision-making. Judges should remember that the public does not understand court procedures and modus operandi. The public sees the court as their "savior," a justice custodian, and the last hope for the common man.[737] Thus, the court's value dwindles when judges settle on procedural justice or judicial technicalities, rather than on substantial justice.

Throughout history, equity emerged in the administration of justice to ensure justice. Law without justice does not make sense. A judge must adhere to the historic inclinations of equity and give justice to the laws/statutes that lack social empathy. Judges are humans, not robots or computers that reproduce the evidence they receive.[738] Judges digest and analyze the evidence along with the established law during and after trial. In the act of judging, judges summarize the facts of a case in a nutshell, review the evidence before the court, analyze the facts with evidence, and align it with stipulated law, which the judge interprets with judicial and judicious discretion.

Judges play a key role in molding the law and society to the public's benefit, which can eventually bridge the gap between courts/law and society. In Britain, it was the judge's perceptions that molded, changed, and developed the law that created the Common Law—the English legal culture. These judges who formed the English Common Law, decades ago realized how society impacts the act of judging, and they gave decisions for

---

[735] Lessig L. Scalia, The Legal Sociologist. *Harvard Journal of Law & Public Policy per Curiam. No. 4 Winter 2023.*

[736] Coplan. K. S., Legal Realism, Innate Morality, and the Structural Role of the Supreme Court in the U.S. Constitutional Democracy, 86 Tulane L. Rev. 181 (2011), <http://digitalcommons.pace.edu/lawfaculty/809/> at 211–209.

[737] Is the Judiciary Still the Last Hope of the Common Man? (16 August 2021). <https://www.google.com/url?sa=t&rct=j&q=&esrc=s&source=web&cd=&ved=2ahUKEwi-Y7t7Cu9n8AhV7AjQIHYigC2EQFnoECCgQAQ&url=https%3A%2F%2Fwww.thehopenewspaper.com%2Fis-the-judiciary-still-the-last-hope-of-the-common-man%2F&usg=AOvVaw0zx4wjLKoo-3O67bS1d8Ck>

[738] It is not a garbage-in, garbage-out situation.

common public interest that eventually established the Common Law from the English culture. Even though the British Common Law did not emanate from a written Constitution like the Constitution of the Federal Republic of Nigeria, the judges still enforced a Common Law that Great Britain and other Commonwealth countries codified into written Constitutions.

Therefore, judges should regard Nigeria's customary laws and not replace them with the British Common Law. Nigerian judges should glean how their decisions impact social change within the Nigerian context or society, to create a Nigerian Common Law that connects with different Nigerian cultural practices, traditions, laws, and beliefs. Thus, as judges exercise their discretion to apply foreign decisions in interpreting statutes, they should not adopt foreign decisions to the detriment of Nigerian culture and practices.[739] When judges base such interpretations on Nigerian Common Law and practice, it discourages the strict adherence to legalities that may affect society adversely and reinforces their roles to do justice. Aguda quoted Lord Denning's popular words as follows:

> My root belief is that the proper role of a judge is to do justice between the parties before him. If there is any rule of law which impairs the doing of justice, then it is the province of the judge to do all he legitimately can: to avoid that rule—or even to change it-so as to do justice in the instant case before him. He need not wait for the legislature to intervene because that can never be of any help in the instant case, I would emphasize however, the word "legitimately": judge is himself subject to the law and must abide by it.

The Nigerian courts have long-established principles that advocate for substantial rather than technical justice. The Court in *Saleh v. Abah & Ors*[740] stated that the current trend is where substantial justice takes pride of place, and very little time is given to matters pertaining to technical justice in our judicial administration.[741]

739 See Tobi's quote in Chapter 2.

740 *Saleh v. Abah & Or (2017) LPELR-41914 (SC).*

741 See *Egbo v. Agbara (1997) 1 NWLR (Pt. 481) 293 at 321; Uwazuruike v. A.G. Federation (2013) 10 NWLR (Pt. 1361) 105; Omoju v. FRN (2008) 7 NWLR (Pt. 1085) 38 at 57; Ukiri v. Geco – Prakla (Nig.).*

5 Procedural or Substantial Justice

The impact of judging on society is wrapped around two words—Procedural and substantive justice. How these words influence the act of judging viz interpreting and applying discretion can directly or indirectly impact society. Justice is a relative term, and as stated previously, society may not understand justice as the court interprets it. What justice means to the court may not be justice for some people. Also, judges understand substantial and technical justice from different perspectives based on individual judges' perspectives. Thus, this book reviews the courts' struggles with interpreting substantial or technical justice in cases that eventually affect society.

Substantial justice is justice fairly administered according to the rules of substantive law, regardless of any procedural errors affecting the litigant's (substantive) rights.[742] It is justice according to the peculiar circumstances of the case, and justice based on the equity or fairness of the case. According to Tobi, JSC, "substantial justice, which is actual and concrete justice is justice personified. It is secreted in the elbows of cordial and fair jurisprudence with a human face and understanding. It is excellent to follow it in our law. It pays to follow it as it brings invaluable dividends in any legal system anchored or predicted on the rule of law, the life blood of democracy."[743] Tobi further explained technical justice as follows:

> A technicality in a matter could arise if a party is relying on abstract or inordinate legalism to becloud or drown the merits of a case. A technicality arises if a party quickly takes an immediately available opportunity, however infinitesimal it may be, to work against the merits of the opponent's case. In other words, he holds and relies tenaciously unto the rules of court with little or no regard to the justice of the matter. As far as he is concerned, the rules must be followed to the last sentences, the last words and the last letters without much ado, and with little or no regard to the injustice that will be caused the opponent.[744]

Nigerian courts have made consistent attempts to distinguish between procedural/technical justice and substantive/substantial justice. Substantial justice is based more on the substance of the case rather than the law's letters, while procedural justice is justice based on stipulated procedures. It is based on

---

742 See *Bassey v. A.G Akwa Ibom State & Ors (2016) LPELR-41244 (CA).*

743 See *Samuel Ayo Omoju v. The Federal Republic of Nigeria (2008) LPELR-2647 (SC).*

744 *Yusuf v. Adegoke & Anor (2007) LPELR – 3534 (SC).* See also *Adedeji v. The State (1992) 4 NWLR (Pt. 234) 248 at 265.*

the laid down laws or letters of the law, while technical justice is procedural justice based on the strict application of the principles of law and the procedures of law. Technical or procedural justice is the court's attempt to solve the pending issues for determination through the strict application of required legal/judicial procedure without due consideration of the case's merits or the parties' adverse interests. According to *Monye v. Abdullahi*,[745]

> Courts of law have long moved away from the domain or terrain of doing technical justice to doing substantial justice. This is because technical justice, in reality is not justice but a pretentious caricature. It is justice with a question mark and not justice which is synonymous with the principles of equity and fair play. Caricatures by whatever template are not the best presentations or representations of the real entity.[746]

Sometimes courts pursue procedural justice under the guise of ensuring substantial justice, which adversely affects the public/ society. In other words, judging impacts society directly when the court's decision affects social issues, views, interests, principles, and customs. For example, the court's decision in the Nigerian case of *Mojekwu v. Mojekwu*,[747] impacted Nigerian traditional customary practices/beliefs that women do not have a right to inheritance, as the Court pronounced the *Oli Ikpe* native law and custom of the Nnewi tribe as sexually discriminatory and unconstitutional.[748] The brief facts of the Mojekwu case is necessary to understand the impact of judicial decisions on culture and society. In this case, the appellant was the plaintiff in the High Court where she commenced an action against the respondent who sought a declaration that he is entitled to the property in dispute. The case of the appellant was that her father's name was Charles Nwofor Mojekwu, who died in 1963. Nwofor had an only brother, Okechukwu Mojekwu, who

---

745 *Monye v. Abdullahi (2012) LPELR-20103(CA)*

746 See also *State v. Gwonto (1983) 1 SCNLR 142; Union Bank of Nigeria Plc. v. Ikwen (2000) 3 NWLR (Pt. 648) 223) Sha v. Kwan (2000) 8 NWLR (Pt. 670) 685; Adebayo v. Okonkwo (2002) 8 NWLR (pt. 768) 1; Asims (Nig) Limited v. Lower Benue River Basin (2002) 8 NWLR (Pt. 769) 349; Afro-Continental (Nigeria) Ltd. v. Co. Operative Association of Professionals Inc. (2003) 5 NWLR (Pt. 813) 303.*

747 *Supra.*

748 Although this case was overturned by the Supreme Court, subsequently, its principles were adopted by the same Supreme Court in cases like *Motoh v. Motoh (2010) LPELR-8643 (CA)*, where the court declared that customary law which discriminates against female children in terms of inheritance is repugnant to natural justice, equity, and good conscience.

predeceased him. Okechukwu died in 1944. The property in dispute was owned by Okechukwu, who married two wives, Janet and Caroline, the respondent. Janet had two daughters while Caroline had a son. His name was Patrick Adina. He died during the Nigerian civil war. Patrick was neither married nor had a surviving child. Okechukwu, the appellant's uncle, bought the property in dispute from the Mgbelekeke family of Onitsha under Kola tenancy land tenure system. The Court reversed the patriarchal culture and ruled that a female child had the right to inherit her late father's estate.[749]

Similarly, the American Court in *Dobbs v. Jackson Women's Health Organization*[750] created change in American society, as the Supreme Court established the Dobbs standard that disabused constitutional abortion rights, and permits individual states the liberty to regulate abortion rights.[751] In addition, this controversial decision continues to stimulate severe debates across American society, because it alters the landscape of reproductive healthcare and the freedom of expression and choice.[752] This decision has created mixed reactions that believe the SCOTUS has not just overturned the *Roe v. Wade* status quo, but has changed the liberty which the American society strongly thrives on, by overturning the constitutional "freedom of liberty" of women to decide an abortion as free choice.

Over the years, Nigerian courts have maintained that courts should never interpret Court Rules in a manner that will prevent the court from doing substantial justice between the parties in the dispute for adjudication.[753] The court in *Ekwere v. The State*[754] reiterated this principle and stated that procedural irregularity should not overcome substantial justice. This position is based on the firm understanding that the court's primary purpose is to do substantial justice between the parties before it and not to adhere to technical issues that becloud the justice of the case.[755] Since reliance on technicalities

749 See Mojekwu's case (supra).

750 *Dobbs v. Jackson Women's Health Organization (supra).*

751 <https://www.supremecourt.gov/opinions/21pdf/19-1392_6j37.pdf>

752 The *Dobb v. Jackson* case is a historic case in the United States that overturned an age-old status quo of the case of *Roe v. Wade* and held that the Constitution does not confer the right to abortion.

753 *Adeyemi & Ors. v. O. Achimu/Ndic/Assurance Bank Ltd & Ors, supra, at p.17 Abiru, JCA.*

754 *Ekwere v. The State (1981) LPELR-1103 (SC).*

755 Ibid.

leads to injustice, courts should adopt a broad and liberal spirit in interpreting statutes.[756] Although in the process, judges should constantly consider the statutes' objective; as social circumstances and changes at a particular time may overtake the statutes' intention. The Court restated this in *Orhiunu v. FRN*[757] as follows: "A broad and liberal approach should prevail in interpreting the Constitution, undue regard must not be paid to mere technical rules; otherwise, the objects of the provisions, as well as the intention of framers of the Constitution, would be frustrated."[758]

The dichotomy between substantial and procedural justice is where judges decide discretionarily that, despite all, they will apply the law for its true purpose. In *Akeredolu v. Abraham & Ors.*,[759] the Supreme Court said, "technicality in the administration of justice shuts out justice. A man denied justice on any ground, much less a technical ground, grudges the administration of justice; it is, therefore, better to have a case heard and determined on merit than to leave the Court with a shield of 'victory' obtained on mere technicalities." It is trite law that courts have the duty to do substantial justice rather than procedural justice.[760] In *Alioke v. Oye & Ors*,[761] the Supreme Court stated thus: "As a court of law and justice, our duty must be to look beyond procedural technicalities to do substantial justice, particularly where fair-hearing is in issue." In *T.M. Lewin (Nig) Ltd v. Smartmark Ltd*,[762] the court also stressed that strict adherence to technical justice may still have its adherents and apostles, but the era of technical justice riding over and above substantial justice is long gone, as substantial justice is now king.[763] Accordingly, over time, courts

---

756 *NEPA v. Atukpor (2000) LPELR-5931 (CA)*; it is trite that a liberal approach be given by the courts in the interpretation of statutes.

757 *Orhiunu v. FRN (2005) 1 NWLR (Pt.906) pg. 55 paras B-D.*

758 Ibid, Galadima, JCA.

759 *Akeredolu v. Abraham & Ors (2018) LPELR- 44067 (SC).*

760 Subsequently, this book will argue that in some cases, this principle is more theoretical than practical.

761 *Alioke v. Oye & Ors (2018) LPELR-45153(SC) Hon. Justice Bage, JSC (P. 24, Paras. A-B).*

762 *T.M. Lewin (Nig) Ltd v. Smartmark Ltd (2017) LPELR-43136 (CA).*

763 See also *Oruobu v. Anekwe (1997) 5 NWLR (Pt. 506) 618; Sarakatu v. Nigerian Housing Development Society Ltd (1984) 4 SC 26; Odi v. Osafile (1987) 2 NWLR (PT. 57) 510; Deen Mark Constr. Co Ltd v. Abiola (2002) 3 NWLR (PT. 754) 418 @ PP. 449 – 450; Dyeris v. Mobil Oil Nigeria Limited (2010) 1 NWLR (PT. 1175) 309; Agu v. Nicon Ins Plc. (2009) 11 NWLR (PT. 677) 187 @ P. 194; Registered Trustees Of The Airline Operators Of Nigeria v. Nigerian Air Space Management Agency (2014) 8 NWLR (PT. 1408) 1 @ PP. 30–31.*

have gravitated from the regime of condoning technical justice to the arena of doing substantial justice. This is in coalition with the jurisprudence of the wider world and its universal legal system.[764] Indeed, the need for courts of law to do substantial justice becomes more imperative when courts consider the Constitution, which is democracy's origin.[765]

Nonetheless, it appears that in some cases, the consensus to do substantial justice rather than technical justice appears more theoretical than practical. This is because, in Nigerian courts, undue reliance on precedent often conflicts with substantial justice.[766] Strict adherence to rules or principles of interpretation can lead to injustice as the framers' intentions and motives often change with the changing times. According to Bunkers, rules in a constantly changing world, are sometimes guaranteed to produce such dysfunctional results.[767] According to the American case of *Buckley v. City of New York*,[768] adherence to precedent "should depend upon its continuing practicality and the demands of justice." Hence, judicial discretion has evolved to include equity in some jurisdictions like the United States.[769] In *Matter of Kasabian v. Chichester*,[770] the Family Court stated that imputing a party's income from the United States Department of Labor statistics was a proper application of the support Magistrate's discretion in a child support case. Thus, a judge's proper application of discretion in a case interprets justice in society.

6 Judges and Justice in Society

Judges apply discretion in determining the applicable law to any case.[771] As human beings who are part of the same society, judges should apply discretions according to relevant social interests to determine justice for society. Most of the time, the exercise of judicial discretion is not immutable; it is

764 See *Inakoju v. Adeleke (Ladoja's case) (2007) 4 NWLR (Pt. 1025) 423.*

765 Ibid.

766 This is a major dilemma that judges face—a point this writer discussed in detail in the second volume of this research.

767 Bunker, opcit: 139.

768 *Buckley v. City of New York 56 N.Y.2d 300, 305 (1982).*

769 Smithburn, opcit.

770 *Kasabian v. Chichester, 72 A.D.3d 1141; 898 N.Y.S.2d 293 (3rd Dept., 2010).*

771 Larsen, J. H. (2018). opcit: 74.

governed by several factors which change with the changing circumstances or times.[772] Bunker stated that as culture and technology change, rules may lock in anachronisms that could be avoided by using adaptive standards.[773] The practices or procedures obtained in the era of paper records, file cabinets, type-writing machines, photocopy machines, fax machines, and duplicate papers have changed with the introduction of laptops, tablets, iPhones, computers, and hard drives. In addition, we are now in an AI era where we do not need to use our hands or fingers to type, as there are AI-enabled softwares that type what we dictate. Technology advances by the day as the clock ticks. It is not waiting for the courts to catch up. Technology is one of the greatest challenges to judging in Nigeria. So, as technological advancements could impede the court's role in ensuring justice, judges can only achieve justice by exercising judicial discretion appropriately.

However, changing circumstance also affects judicial discretion, so courts should not lose touch with this reality in deciding cases. Otherwise, injustice will prevail, that is, sacrificing substantial justice for technical justice and calling it equity. Judicial discretion influences judicial decisions, and judicial decisions determine the parties' rights to an action that eventually becomes the public's right at a certain time in history.[774] So, judicial discretion is not static opinions that govern the conduct of mankind, neither is it designed for the ages, such as the Ten Commandments.[775]

Even though judicial discretion follows the required law, the judge's discretion should comply with changing circumstances to remain relevant to society. According to Roscoe Pound, the law must be stable, but it cannot stand still.[776] Stability without change is degeneration and change without stability is anarchy. Judges should bridge the gap between society's needs and the law without allowing the legal system to degenerate or collapse into anarchy. Judges must ensure stability with change and change with stability.[777]

---

772 *D.Y.S. Trocca Valsesia & Co. v. Osaghae (2008) ALL FWLR (Pt.413)1313 at P. 1335, paras C – E* A.

773 Bunker, opcit: 138.

774 Courts have more discretion in such cases because the law provides less guidance in areas where technology changes. Hence, discretion is less fettered.

775 Newman, T. R. & Ahnuty, J. S. (2015). *New York Law Journal*, opcit.

776 Barak, opcit: 11.

777 Ibid.

The law is not just logic or experience, but renewal based on experience and logic, which adapts law to the new social reality, as there are always changes in law caused by changes in society.[778] According to Professor Hart, "the time has come when it is understood again, inside the (legal) profession, as well as outside that reason is the life of the law and not just votes for your side."[779]

However, situations often arise where judges resign to procedural rather than substantial justice, especially in the absence of precedent. Some judges rely on the procedure to avoid judicial or social criticisms, and others stick to the procedure because that is the only available option. Therefore, these judges are helplessly stuck with the procedural option and use a phrase like "the court's hands are tied."[780] One is often tempted to ask—who or what tied their hands? Such expression connotes that there is no precedent or law to back up the court's action, and the judge would not take the chance to adopt judicial discretion and apply substantial justice to the case. Hence, even when the required law is clearly unjust, the judge must apply it; otherwise, the judge will act outside the required law and incur the appellate court's wrath as a "judicial rascal."[781]

Therefore, such helplessness makes some judges resort to foreign cases. As stated in Chapter 2, the application of foreign decisions in Nigerian courts is a pending controversy. In *Araka v. Egbue*,[782] the court opined that foreign authorities of the greatest learning cannot supplant Nigerian case law rightly decided on any issue. If Nigerian judges apply foreign case law to guarantee justice, it cannot be wrong if the court exercises such discretion for society's benefit. Though foreign decisions and legal principles should

---

778 Opcit.

779 From Miller, A. S. & Howell, R. F., The Myth of Neutrality in constitutional Adjudication, opcit: 662.

780 *Awosika v. State (2018) LPELR-44351 (SC)*: "Ordinarily, this is a clear example of a case in which this Court would have reversed the sentence passed on the appellant by the Court below and restore the correct sentence of death earlier passed on the appellant by trial Court. However, this Court's hands are tied for the simple reason that there is no cross appeal against the sentence of 21 years passed by the Lower Court filed by the Respondent herein. I will therefore stop at that and say no more except to say that the appellant is just lucky to have narrowly escaped the hang-man's noose." *Hon. Justice Sanusi, JSC (P. 44, Paras. B-D).*

781 See Justice Katsina Alu's statement in Chapter 1.

782 *Araka v. Egbue (2003) 3 WRN 20.*

not be applied at the expense of available local decisions, justice for society and the judge's discretion should be the determining factor under such circumstances. Also, the Nigerian Constitution supports resorting to foreign cases. The preamble to the Constitution states, "we the people of the Federal Republic of Nigeria…, dedicated to the *promotion of inter-African unity, world peace, international cooperation, and understanding*."[783] According to the above underlined phrase, Nigeria is dedicated to international collaboration, which means that all Nigerian institutions, including the courts, should cooperate with international law to serve the Constitution's aim. Thus, judges can resort to international law, case/treaties law and authorities in the absence of precedent to ensure justice in the case.

The Nigerian judicial process was created to serve Nigerian society and since society is not static but ever-changing, the act of judging should equally change with society to respond progressively to social values, views, and interests. So, with the borderless implications of socio-economic relationships worldwide, applying foreign law/caselaw is inevitable and quite appropriate in connecting law and society. Thus, bridging the gap between law and society means aligning law with social expectations through caselaw.

7 The *Daudu* Case Law and Nigerian Society

The Nigerian Supreme Court in *Daudu v. FRN*[784] substantially altered a fundamental principle in Nigeria's criminal justice system, which generated debates and divergent opinions/interpretations.[785] In this case, the apex court interpreted section 35(5) of the Constitution, which states that every person who is charged with a criminal offense shall be presumed innocent until proven guilty, with an addendum to fit the then/present sociopolitical climate of constant corrupt practices in Nigeria.[786] The court decided as follows:

---

783 Emphasis mine.

784 *Daudu v. FRN (2018) 10 NWLR (Pt.1626) 169, 183 E -F (2018) LPELR-43637 (SC).*

785 While some lawyers and politicians appear to believe that it has substantially changed the coloration and established position of our criminal justice system, others believe it has merely reinforced and restated the position of the law and did not upstage or overturn it.

786 UN News (2016), opcit.

> Proving Money Laundering cases is a herculean task because it requires a prior establishment of the predicate offence before the money laundering aspect can be established. To obviate this problem a remedy was introduced by statutorily inferring money laundering from not only the conduct of the defendant but his lifestyle which is similar to the Proceeds of Crime Act 2002 of the UK. Even though Section 36(5) of the 1999 Constitution provides that every person charged with a criminal offence shall be presumed to be innocent until he is proven guilty, the proviso allows for shifting the burden of proof on the defendant ... By Section 19(3) of the Money Laundering Act, if an accused person is in possession of pecuniary resources or property which is disproportionate to his known source of income, or he obtained an accretion to his pecuniary resources or property, the burden of giving a satisfactory account of how he made the money or obtained the accretion shifts to him. The prosecution is relieved of the burden of having to prove that the money so found in his account or in his possession is proceeds from illicit traffic in narcotic drugs or psychotropic substances or of any illegal act. To explain the point further, where A is a fixed salary earner and suddenly his account is credited with an amount beyond his income or has property which his legitimate income cannot afford, the burden shifts to him to explain how he got the money with which he bought the property or the legitimate transaction he was engaged in for which the account was credited.[787]

The above decision implies that any person who exhibits a lifestyle beyond his known means of livelihood assumes the burden for how he/she obtained such wealth. The argument as to whether the judgment in *Dauda v. FRN*[788] overturned section 35 (5) of the Constitution is not one for this discussion. However, the point this book stresses is that the sociopolitical cultural views, interests, and perspectives of the Nigerian society, influenced the Court's discretion in interpreting section 35(5) of the Constitution together with Section 19(3) of the Money Laundering Act.[789] Daudu's case is an example of an Appellate Court establishing a guideline for the exercise of discretion.[790]The Supreme Court's exception to the presumption of innocence principle in this case shows a social perspective of judging with the predominant needs, circumstances, and culture (positive or negative), in the Nigerian society, at that time. This case shows the Court's "socio-judicious"[791] approach in applying discretion and creating precedent, as the justices applied their

---

787 *Daudu v. FRN (supra).*

788 Ibid.

789 See Chapter 3 on the basic principles of interpretation of statutes in Nigeria.

790 Smithburn, J. Eric. Judicial Discretion. (2006).

791 The term socio-judicious is formed from this author's hypothesis, from where she created her theory—socio-judicialism.

judicial discretion from both legal and social perspectives, to arrive at a fair decision for the parties and society. Aguda's admonition supports the Court's discretion in Daudu's case. He said: "our system of criminal justice firmly entrenched the principle that a person is presumed innocent until he is proven guilty. This is as it should be, except that we have to be very careful not to bring this principle to a pedestal whereby it is used for the unnecessary protection from the hands of justice of some evil members of society."[792]

However, preceding Daudu's case, the Supreme Court maintained the status quo in *Chibuike Amaechi v. INEC*,[793] where Oguntade, JSC, declared that the burden to prove guilt beyond a reasonable doubt is on the accuser. The court added that it is a subversion of the law and an unconcealed attempt to politicize the investigation and prosecution of criminal offenses, to hold otherwise. Nevertheless, the Daudu Court considered extenuating circumstances in making an exception to the general rule. Similarly, in the American case of *Bowers v. Hardwick*,[794] the U.S. Supreme Court held that a statute criminalizing consensual homosexual relations between adults was constitutional. Then seventeen years later in *Lawrence v. Texas*,[795] the court overturned its prior holding and stated that the Constitution bars legislation criminalizing consensual sexual relations between adults.[796] In other words, gay relationships are now legal. There is no telling what the future holds on gay relationships in the U.S.A., as society and laws change.

The fundamental point here is that as society changes judicial discretion changes (should change) to enable justice for the parties and ultimately

---

792 Aguda, opcit: 17.

793 *Chibuike Amaechi v. INEC (2008) 5 NWLR (Pt 1080).*

794 *Bowers v. Hardwick 478 U.S. 186 (1986).*

795 *Lawrence v. Texas 123 SC 2472 (2003).*

796 See also the celebrated English cases of *Rylands v. Fletcher (1868) L.R.3 H.L.330*, which established a new area of English tort law ("If a person brings, or accumulates, on his land anything which, if it should escape, may cause damage to his neighbor, he does so at his peril. If it does escape, and cause damage, he is responsible, however careful he may have been, and whatever precautions he may have taken to prevent the damage") and *Transco Plc (formerly BG plc and BG Transco plc) v. Stockport Borough Council (2004) 1 All E.R. 589 at 29*, which has considerably narrowed down the scope of liability established in *Rylands v. Fletcher*, about 150 years ago (the claimant was denied the right to recover damages caused by a seriously leaking water pipe because the use of water pipes is ubiquitous and of 'daily usage).

for society because the parties/litigants are a tiny fraction of society and the court's decision which is a potential precedent will eventually impact the larger society. This is evident from three factors that connect Daudu's case with the cases cited above in this book.[797] The first is that the case law changed from the status quo over time. Secondly, societal changes eventually influenced the court's decisions. The third is that these changes emanated from society's interests, views, and cultures. In other words, it was not the law per se that influenced the Court's discretion to decide as they did in the cases cited above. Rather, it was the change in society and relevant social realities(challenges) of the changing times. For example, there are arguments that the prevailing interests of the American public influenced the overturning of the *Roe v. Wade* status quo.[798] So, amidst the lingering values, and interests in society, judicial discretion connects the law with justice.

Accordingly, substantial justice transcends mere adherence to substantive law principles. It speaks more to the law's relevance and impact on the parties before the court and society. For example, social views, interests, and perspectives influenced the landmark decision of *Brown v. Board of Education of Topeka*,[799] where the U.S. Supreme Court ruled that American state laws establishing racial segregation in public schools are unconstitutional, even if the segregated schools are otherwise equal in quality.[800]Also the transformation in society influenced the decision in *Lawrence v. Texas*[801] that struck out the sodomy law in Texas.[802] These are examples of how equity and morality guided judicial discretion at the time.[803]

Furthermore, some antiquated legal principles are disconnected from social reality, yet some courts are hesitant to overrule them due to the

797 *Chibuike Amaechi v. INEC; Bowers v. Hardwick; Lawrence v. Texas.*

798 See Makoba, J. (2022, July 21) *The Courts as Agents of Social Change* (Courts & Society Webinar Series, 2nd Edition) A.T. Socio-Judicial Consulting. <https://atsjconsulting.com/>

799 *Brown v. Board of Education of Topeka 347 U.S. 483 (1954).*

800 See also the *Roe v. Wade (supra)* landmark decision where the U.S. Supreme Court ruled that a state law that banned abortions (except to save the life of the mother) was unconstitutional. The ruling made abortion legal in many circumstances.

801 *Lawrence v. Texas 539 U.S. 558 (supra).*

802 See also *United States v. Morrison 529 U.S. 598 (2000)* which held the Violence Against Women Act of 1994 unconstitutional.

803 Smithburn, opcit.

obstinate doctrine of *stare decisis*. Even when there are exceptions that courts can depart from precedent if the case is distinguishable, some courts still adhere to precedent to the detriment of justice because distinguishing cases is not a straightforward process.[804] There are times that the nature of the case may be the same, but the technology, the parties, scientific discovery, social perception, or perspectives, among other factors, may change. This raises a question of whether appellate courts consider such changes under the distinguishing the case standard,[805] in appraising lower courts' deviation from precedent.

Holmes opines, "we must be weary of petrifying the Common Law into a rigid system, utterly behind the times and totally at odds with the progress of technology, science and social change."[806] Accordingly, if a statute has become obsolete, a judge should not hesitate to state so and pronounce it as unconstitutional and then deviate from precedent. Barak suggested that the court may not repeal an obsolete statute, but it may repeal a Common Law holding that has become obsolete. He added that the court may change even a non-obsolete precedent if it does not suit today's social needs.[807] However, it does not mean that judges should completely ignore precedent. Hence, where the justice of the case is required, judges can exercise their discretion and uphold justice by analyzing the case and considering social interests. This was the court's finding in *People v. Bing*:[808] that a court should not hesitate to overrule its precedents when persuaded by the lessons of experience and the force of better reasoning. In his research, Judge Larsen captures this point as follows:

> Legal reasoning is more uncertain or indeterminate the less clear the law is. This is more often the case at the highest levels of appeal. At such levels, a judge's decision may be more formalistic or realistic, depending on the judge's willingness to infer, fill-in, or determine law not previously applied to a certain case ... However, in inferring the law, judges are not free to disregard logical connections to precedents, statutes, and other sources of material law. Judges have more discretion in how they decide and explain their reasoning.[809]

---

804 See Chapter 5.
805 See Chapter 5.
806 Duxbury, opcit: 48.
807 Barack, opcit: 10
808 *People v. Bing 76 N.Y.2d 331, 337–338 (1990).*
809 Larsen, opcit.

Law and equity have now merged into a jurisprudential paradigm of discretion that allows trial courts to exercise a range of equitable discretion corresponding to the guidance provided by statutes and appellate courts if any.[810] There appears to be a new paradigm of judicial discretion in Nigerian courts for implementing human rights. According to Falana,[811] the Nigerian courts, in enforcing the Fundamental Rights Procedure Rules (FRPR),[812] have taken a major stride in adopting the African Charter on Human and People's Rights, and also to implement the FRPR's requirement that the principle of locus standi should give way to public interest litigation.[813] In other words, although the primary principle of law is that for you to pursue or file a case, you must be a person directly affected by the case or the results of the case the FRPR has made an exception that in the interest of the public, anyone can institute a human rights action in the public interest. Hence, the 2009 Rule confers *locus standi* on every concerned person or institution.[814] A ready case where the judge applied discretion in implementing human rights is the Mojekwu case,[815] where the court explained the bone of contention as follows:

> Under the Nnewi native law and custom, if a man dies leaving a male issue, the property belongs to the male child. If on the other hand, the deceased has no male child, his brother will inherit his property. If the male issue who survives the father dies leaving no male issue, the father's brother will inherit the property. If, on the other hand, the deceased's brother dies leaving sons, the sons will inherit the property of the dead cousin. In particular, the "diokpala," that is the eldest son of the uncle, will inherit the property. If a man dies and subsequently his only son and brother dies, if the late brother has sons, the first son of the late brother will inherit all the property. The son of the late brother is called "Oli-ekpe" i.e. he inherited the property of his relation.

---

810 Smithburn, opcit: 49.

811 Femi Falana is a senior Advocate of Nigeria and human rights expert and activist who has constantly campaigned for the human rights enforcement for the common citizen. He has held the Nigerian government accountable for their various human rights abuses/violations.

812 The Fundamental Rights Procedure Rule 2009 empowers any high court in Nigeria to hear and determine human rights conflicts. The rules allow Nigerian courts to apply international instruments.

813 Niki-Tobi, A. (2024, December 12). *The Court's Role in Implementing Human Rights* (Courts & Society Webinar Series, 10th Special Edition) A.T. Socio-Judicial Consulting. <https://atsjconsulting.com/>

814 See Fundamental Rights (Enforcement Procedure) Rules, 2009. <https://www.refworld.org/legal/decreees/natlegbod/2009/en/104236>

815 Supra.

> The "Oli-ekpe" inherits the land, the wives of the deceased and if the deceased had daughters, he will give them in marriage. In other words, the "Oli-ekpe" inherits the assets and liabilities of the deceased. In the instant case, the appellant claims to be the "Oli-ekpe" entitled to the property of the deceased, to the exclusion of the respondent, who is the daughter of the deceased.

The above narrative clarifies the violation of the respondent's fundamental rights to her late father's estate because she is a woman and not so entitled under customary law. In applying judicious discretion and a socio-judicial interpretation into the case, Justice Tobi held as follows:

> Nigeria is an egalitarian society where the civilised sociology does not discriminate against women. However, there are customs all over which discriminate against the womenfolk which regard them as inferior to the menfolk. That should not be so as all human beings, male and female, are born into a free world and are expected to participate freely without any inhibition on grounds of sex. Thus, any form of societal discrimination on grounds of sex, apart from being unconstitutional, is antithesis to a society built on the tenets of democracy. The "Oli-ekpe" custom, which permits the son of the brother of a deceased person to inherit his property to the exclusion of his female child, is discriminatory and therefore inconsistent with the doctrine of equity.[816]

Similarly, the U.S. courts have applied new standards of discretion in combining law and equity.[817]Hine argued that the idea that laws, not individuals, govern American society is at the core of most citizens' understandings of the American Judicial system, so they elect legislatures to enact laws, rather than depend solely on judge-made Common Law.[818] So, to maintain equity within the court system, New York enacted the Field Code (a new code of civil procedure), which about half the states adopted, covering the majority of the country's population. Hence, law and equity forms the majority basis of the American judicial system.[819]

Subsequently, after the turn of the twentieth century, the American Bar Association led by Roscoe Pound began a push for procedural reform in the U.S. courts. Pound argued that the then-existing procedural rules hampered the judge's ability to search independently for truth and justice. This as well as the concern for public confusion caused by reliance on

816 *Mojekwu, (supra) at pp 304–305. paras. H-B) Hon. Justice Tobi JCA at Page 305, paras. B-C.*

817 Hine, opcit: 1774–1776.

818 Ibid: 1770.

819 Ibid: 1776.

technicalities led to the enactment of the Enabling Act in 1934. Four years later, the U.S promulgated the modern Federal Rules of Civil Procedure.[820] However, with the SCOTUS' overrule of the *Roe v. Wade* status quo, it appears that Hine's position, that the laws and not individuals govern American society, no longer stands.[821] The *Jackson v. Dobbs*[822] decision and the social mayhem around it show how majority of the American people influenced the court's decision and overturned the *Roe v. Wade* status quo.[823] Therefore it is not realistic to still argue that the law and not individuals govern the American society.

Nevertheless, merging law and equity seems to be the Nigerian judicial system's present position where judges review the law and rule by it. So, if a law is bad, it behooves judges to ensure that the judiciary remains the last hope of justice for the public—the type of justice that the reasonable man on the street recognizes as justice. The Nigerian Supreme Court upheld the Mojewkwu decision and established precedent in the case of *Ukeji v. Ukeji*[824] and reiterated that women are entitled to inherit their father's estate regardless of the gender or circumstances of their birth. Since this updated precedent, Nigerian courts have maintained the status quo on women's rights in Nigeria.

Ijaiye opines that a judge in his interpretative function can adjust the stated law to the applicable sociopolitical context, which shows that the judiciary and the judicial process is instrumental to the nation's sociopolitical development.[825] The judges' interpretative role should impact the public to give meaning and life to the law so that peace, justice, and equality will thrive in society.[826]

8 Society and the Act of Judging

It is unequivocal that society influences the act of judging in Nigeria and other societies worldwide. Judges are the conduits for such influence. So, judges are undoubtedly agents or instruments of social change in a democracy. Judges

820 Ibid: 1777.
821 See page 136.
822 Supra.
823 See Makoba: opcit.
824 *Ukeje v. Ukeje (2014)* 11 NWLR (PT. 1418) 384.
825 Ijaiye, opcit: 184.
826 Ibid: 186.

respond to society's needs by analyzing the law and how it justly and reasonably applies to facts/social conflicts before the court.[827] The actions or omissions of the courts influence statutory amendments, which is a good thing for society. Oshio argues that judges should be allowed to expound, refine, and develop the law for the good of society through sound dynamic, liberal, creative interpretations. He added that if judges are not ingenious or creative, the Nigerian society will suffer.[828] Aboki, JCA, reiterates this in the following words:

> A Judge that is confronted with a legal problem does not have to resign helplessly where the established laws are inadequate in resolving the problem. It is a cardinal maxim of law that where there is a wrong, there must be a remedy—Ubi Jus Ubi Remedium. Judges are, therefore, encouraged to formulate fresh rules of law or to extend the existing ones to deal with novel cases by so doing they add to the corpus of existing laws through their judicial pronouncements.[829]

Also, in *Ameachi v. INEC,*[830] the Supreme Court said:

> The primary duty of the court is to do justice to all manner of men who are in all matters before it ... when the courts set out to do justice so as to cover new conditions or situations placed before it there is always that temptation, compelling one, to have recourse to equitable principles....And judges who dispense justice in this court of law and equity must always be ready to address new problems and even create new doctrines where the justice of the matter so requires.[831]

Judges' creativity in interpreting statutes connects law to society and bridges the gap between courts and society, as the court's primary focus should be the statutes' impact on the predominant needs and changes in society. Although the drafter's intention is fundamental to interpreting statutes, the views and interests of society supersede the drafters' intentions, which may be obsolete with the changes in society. Hence, society should be paramount in judicial decision-making, as Judge Simac reiterated in the Courts and Society Webinar series,[832] and as the SCOTUS exemplified in Dobbs' case.[833]

---

827 Carter, L. & Burke, T. (2010). Reason in Law, opcit: 33.

828 Ibid: 23.

829 Idahosa, C.O. (2016) The Doctrine of Stare-Decisis and Judicial Precedent : The Need for Lower Courts to be Bound by Decisions of Superior Courts of Record, opcit: 4.

830 *Supra.*

831 Ibid.

832 See above.

833 Supra.

Through the act of judging the courts interpret the law for society by extending or adapting an old rule to a new situation to ensure substantial justice.[834] Some have interpreted this role as lawmaking. This book's position is clear that judges are not lawmakers. They do not make laws and should never make laws. It is too complicated, plus judges already have enough on their plates. In a dissenting view, in *Chief Emma Onuorah Emesim v. Hon. Calista Nwachukwu (Mrs.) & Ors,*[835] Ubaezonu, JCA, agreed that it is not the duty of the court to make law. It is the court's duty to interpret the law and the justice that courts administer is justice according to the law. In *Magor and St Mellons Rural District Council v. Newport Corporation,*[836] Denning rebuffed the argument that judges make laws when he said, "we sit here to find out the intention of parliament and ministers and carry it out, and we do this by filling in the gaps and making sense of the enactment than by opening it up to destructive analysis."

Law making involves legislating or enacting a law to pass a bill. Judges do not go through this legislative process. Judges only "attempt" to define what the law is from the circumstances of the social conflict presented in court and in appropriate circumstances, they explain the law. In this context, judges are like first aid kits with immediate necessities as an emergency team in an ambulance to take immediate actions to save a conflicting or chaotic situation in society. According to Oshio, judges expound and declare the law.[837] This act of expounding and declaring the law vis a vis the act of judging (i.e., judicial interpretation and judicial discretion), is not a legislative venture. The judiciary is the lawgiver while the legislature is the lawmaker.[838] However, from the past, there have been legislative restraints to judges making laws. Thus, where the courts exceed their limits, the legislature ignores the court's decision as contrary to the intention of the legislator. For example, in *Adegbenro v. Akintola,*[839] the Western Nigerian Constitution (Amendment) Law nullified the decision of the Privy Council, and

---

834 Oshio, ibid at 22.

835 *Chief Emma Onuorah Emesim v. Hon. Calista Nwachukwu (Mrs.) & Ors (1999) LPELR-6573(CA)PP.33–34, para-D-B.*

836 *Magor and St Mellons Rural District Council v. Newport Corporation (1951)2 All E.R 839.*

837 Ibid.

838 Ibid.

839 *Adegbenro v. Akintola (1963)3W.L. R 63.*

the Federal Government eventually ratified this action. There can also be judicial restraints—where judges can personally restrain themselves or by appellate review procedures.[840]

Further, unsatisfactory laws create conflicts in society for courts to settle one way or the other. Judges' idiosyncrasies as human beings and the principles of interpretation influence the judicial revision of the law.[841] In addition, the words of statutes are like beauty in the eyes of the beholder, they are interpreted from various perspectives and given varied interpretations. It is the perception of the writer/hearer(judge) on the one hand, and the view of the reader/speaker (public/parties), on the other hand. In other words, a cup may be half full or half empty, depending on the viewer's viewing angle or perception. It is common knowledge that words on their own can be misunderstood because of semantics. Thus, interpretation is all about the judge's view and perception of the law and society. Even lawyers often misunderstand and misinterpret judicial pronouncements—what the judge means and what lawyers or society understand can differ.

Furthermore, society would be in a state of anarchy if courts were to leave statutes as vague or ambiguous. Denning conveyed this in *Seaford Estates Ltd v. Asher*:[842]

> It would certainly save the judge trouble if Acts of Parliament were drafted with divine prescience and perfect clarity. In the absence of it, when defects appear in the Act, the judge cannot simply fold his arms and blame the draftsman. He must set to work on the constructive task of finding the intention of parliament and he must do this not only from the language of statute but also from a consideration of the social conditions which gave rise to it, and of the mischief it was passed to remedy, and then he must supplement the written words so as to give "force and life" to the intention of the legislature.

Thus, it does not make sense to give a statute or a word in the statute its literal meaning if such meaning is absurd or will manifest injustice to the parties or society. What society interprets and understands as justice is (should be) justice. So, courts should interpret these laws from society's perspective of justice, as the courts are public servants who should serve society and not the law. Laws are instruments to raise a platform for courts to serve the public.

---

840 This could be through practice procedures, etc.

841 However, this may be redundant, as dwelling on the old paradigm of realism and formalism, may be more reliable.

842 *Seaford Estates Ltd v. Asher (supra).*

The courts' relevance in society should be more than just interpreting the intent of drafters, it should also be to interpret the social perspectives of justice and act as intermediaries between the law and society.[843]

When a law is "bad" or socio-politically inadequate, the judge should ensure that the society/public sees courts as a clone of justice. When society recognizes, appreciates, and acknowledges the courts as reasonable and fair, they will trust the courts and have confidence in the court's ability to achieve justice.[844] As the Supreme Court in *Alioke v. Oye & Ors*[845] says:

> Our duty as an Apex Court is to do substantial, justice-stark justice, based on fairness which, to all intent and purposes, seeks to not only ensure fairness in dispensing justice but which is manifestly seen and duly acknowledged by all and sundry as justice both in content and context. We are not judicial technicians in the workshop of technical Justice. The jurisprudence or logic of our reasoning is and, as humanly possible, would be devoid of technicalities.... The need to do substantial justice and avoid delving into the error of technicalities is well settled. Even in cases where errors of omission or commission called blunders have been made, it is unjust to hold that because blunders have been committed, the party blundering is to incur the penalty of not having the dispute between him and his adversary determined upon the merits.[846]

Therefore, courts impact society through diverse forums—executing justice through applying discretion that changes the status quo or precedent.[847] In the process of executing justice, the courts develop the law, and the law advances society to create social change, affirming culture that emphasizes diversity to enforce human rights.

---

843 This author discussed details of the courts role in society in the second phase of this research, titled "The Role of the Nigerian Judiciary in Democracy."

844 Most of the above-cited cases show that, at different times in history, with different circumstances, diverse courts from separate jurisdictions, spoke about the relevance and impact of the law to society at the material time. The interests, views, cultures, and perspectives of society appear to have directed the court's discretions.

845 *Alioke v. Oye & Ors (2018) LPELR-45153 (SC).*

846 See also *Makeri Smelting Co. Ltd v. Access Bank (Nig.) Plc (2002) 7 NWLR (Pt.766) 411 at 476–417.*

847 See *Awuse v. Odili (supra).*

9 The Act of Judging in Nigeria[848]

Judging in Nigeria is an act of adjudication that develops over time, into an art of experience on the bench. Judging combines several factors—statutory stipulations, ethical requirements, judicial education, judicial experiences, societal influences, and judges' backgrounds and idiosyncrasies. It is not a week's or year's affair; it is a continuous process that produces mastery or an art over a devoted period. The act of judging is a life journey that started from when the judge was born and accumulated all her experiences, encounters and history into an ideology that guides her decision-making. It is a relay race where one stage hands over to another stage until the final judgment baton crosses the finished line. Meanwhile, the judges previous life encounters and experiences combine to inadvertently play a key role in the judge's final decision. Judging is a long-term affair where judges take their oaths of office to devote their lives to render justice to the individual and society.

Judging is an act involving stages that produce an art. This action is an undertaking, a commitment, and a lifestyle devoted to positive change and societal impact. Thus, the various actions that judges take from stage 1 to stage 10 of the stages of judging outlined in the next section, constitute the act of judging.[849] It is an art that requires levels of creativity—thinking outside the box in the absence of statutes or precedents. The act of judging is the function, the roles, and the procedure judges take in stating or constructing a well-considered decision backed by law. Judging is about settling disputes through interpreting law/statutes with the art of judicial and judicious discretion based on social perspective and social awareness. Judging is an avenue where judges make the law more impactful to society.

The act of judging is a hands-on, all-encompassing role that involves the entirety of the judge—the judges lifestyle, personality, history, experiences, ideologies, culture and beliefs. Marsh said, "judging is so terribly unique. It is so different than just about any other occupation. And for lots of reasons—an independent branch of government; the worlds that they serve; the decisions that they make; the life-type

---

[848] A major part of this section is from this writer's experience as a magistrate judge in three of Lagos State's busiest judicial districts (Igbosere, Tinubu, and Adeniran Ogunsanya) and information from my late father who mentored me in the act and art of judging. I was taking notes every time I visited him during vacations.

[849] See the next section on the stages in the act of judging.

existential decisions they make … This is extremely difficult work."[850] I repeat what Hon. Justice Amina Adamu Augie, a retired judge of the Nigerian Supreme Court,[851] said—"each judgment I write takes a part of my soul. Then I move to the next without ever looking back."[852] The act of judging takes a toll on judges.[853]

Consequently, despite the obvious facts of the case and the obvious provisions of the law/statutes/legislation that may require specific and clear verdicts, judges often observe obscure facts, laws, and evidence that create an enigma that requires abstract approaches to the case. This abstract approach is the wand of discretion, where the art of judging shows up. With the art of judging, judges design the best discretionary option available. Hence, the act or art of judging is never straightforward. Judges have to be creative at this time; this is where the act of judging turns into an art to think outside the box, especially as facts and evidence unfold. So, the public, and lawyers should desist from criticizing judges without in-depth knowledge of the full picture regarding the case, the respective parties, and their lawyers, the accompanying evidence, and the judge's unique unapologetic discretion, which is also connected to the judges' personal experiences, background, philosophy, psychology, biology, and environment.

Judging concentrates on two key acts/actions—interpretation and discretion, which are two key determinants in any court's judgment. The conceptual diagram below gives a synoptic view of the act of judging in Nigeria. The interpretation of statutes/law and application of judicial discretion embodies judging. In the act of interpreting the laws, facts, etc., judges aim (or should aim), for substantial rather than technical justice, which is more ardent in applying precedents. Substantial justice focuses on the court's role to impact society and create social change. This act attempts to override precedent set by the Common Law and English courts. The act of applying judicial discretion,

---

850 Marsh, S. (2022). The Impact of Judicial Education in Developing Law and Society. The Courts & Society Webinar Series. A.T. Socio-Judicial Consulting, LLC. <https://youtu.be/r8i3Q3Psp3g>

851 Opcit.

852 This statement was made during this author's interview of Justice Augie. Available at the Courts & Society Webinar Series, Sixth Edition.

853 The second volume of this author's research/(her dissertation) discusses judicial dilemmas that judges encounter in performing their roles. This author categorized about six dilemmas.

though fettered by the Common Law status quo and the principle of stare decisis, is also unfettered in certain respects. So, some judges use this leeway to (rightly or justly) enforce substantial justice.

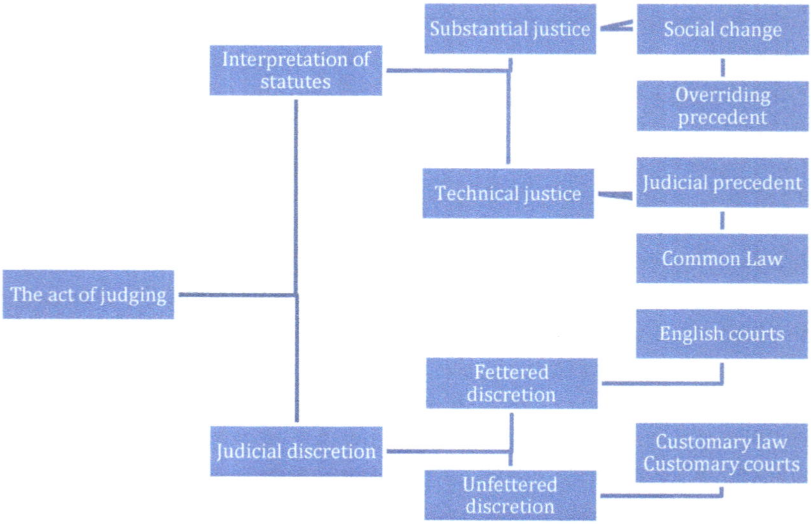

Figure 6.2: Judging in a Nutshell[854]

Since customary courts do not have strict evidential rules, the customary court judges have more unfettered discretion than the courts of record that rely on English Common Law. These customary courts are less technical and hinged on judicial precedent, which this author argues is a major hindrance to social change. Customary court judges apply customary law to achieve the justice of the case. Substantial justice ensures social change and creates an overriding precedent that focuses more on the long-lasting impact of the decision than the immediate outcome.[855]

When judges interpret statutes, the aim is to understand how the statute or law changes the status quo/ existing position of the case file to a solution that would

[854] I created this diagram to capture what I believe summarizes the act of judging in Nigeria.

[855] Please see discussions on substantial and technical justice.

satisfy the suing party or the opposing party and to determine which party's argument complies with interpreting the law and applying discretion, where necessary.[856]

The act of judging has various components and stages, which implicitly encompass the judge's private and public life.[857] It entails interpreting statutes and applying judicial discretion. Applying judicial discretion in judging is not just fundamental, it is necessary and most valuable to societal development as it invokes the humanity of law and the judge's humanness. Judging impacts a judge's public and private life in ways only judges can explain. Different judges encounter diverse tasks in their official capacity daily that often pull in, and challenge their private lives, safety, and well-being throughout their judicial careers. Therefore, at every stage of their decision-making process, judges should aim for substantial, rather than technical justice.

10 Ten Stages in the Act of Judging[858]

The act of judging starts when the judge/judges/justices receive the case file from the registry, and it "ends" (technically), after the judgment, if there is no motion for an appeal or post-judgment motion like a garnishee proceeding, execution of judgment motions etc. Even after the appeal records have been sent to the appellate court's registry, there is a possibility of a retrial order from the appellate courts. So, technically, the act of judging is not really over after judgment or even after a notice of appeal is filed. It is like a marathon, depending on the nature of the case, and sometimes, the type of attorney.[859]

---

856 In some rare circumstances, the judgment may satisfy both or neither party.

857 This author expounds this perspective in research that is currently awaiting publication.

858 These stages of judging are this writer's coinage and technique in over a decade in her practice as a magistrate judge. My categorizing these stages into ten made judging easier for me. I would recommend it to new judges who have not set down a procedure or a better procedure to adopt from a senior judge/justice.

859 Some lawyers who lack integrity have an unfortunate practice of deceiving their clients into flogging a dead horse by filing all sorts of frivolous applications in court to buy time and get more money, especially if they charge for transportation to and from court, or per document filed.

Therefore, the ten synoptic stages of judging, which this writer applied in judging, are as follows:[860]

1. Introductory stage. This is where the registry moves the case file to the assigned court, and the judge glances through the file. At this stage, some judges review the file and take mental notes. This writer had a notebook and took notes of each file with any special or complex issue that needed research in case there was the need for a bench ruling,[861] to prepare ahead.[862] At this stage, the judge decides if there are urgent matters that need to be heard immediately. For example, human rights cases should be fixed for hearing within seven days of filing.[863] Also, if the case is high-profile or time sensitive like a family matter, the judge could ask her registrar to fix it for the earliest date. These impromptu instances affect other cases in the docket and cause delays, which makes litigants, and some lawyers castigate judges and accuse them of laziness or corruption. The average judge is not lazy, just overwhelmed with lots of cases (or corrupt), especially frivolous cases.[864]
2. The thinking stage. This is a behind-the-scenes stage, where some judges ruminate on the facts of the case at any given opportunity. Some judges form an informal opinion at this stage, which may change at subsequent stages. This is the stage of preliminary prediction that was discussed earlier. This stage occurs through the trial and is not definite. Unfortunately, this stage follows the judge everywhere—from the office to their homes until the case is over. Some judges go to bed thinking about it (some even in their dreams).[865]
3. Preliminary stage. At this stage, the parties may file preliminary motions

---

860 These stages may differ among judges as some judges do not follow this hierarchy, but at one point of the process that leads to decision-making, all judges apply these stages.

861 A bench ruling is a decision given on the spot during a hearing/trial or after an application without an adjournment

862 This practice is important to check the abuse of the court process or the ploy for delay from some lawyers.

863 See Order IV, Rule 1 of the Fundamental Human Rights Procedure Enforcement Rules, 2009. <https://www.refworld.org/legal/decreees/natlegbod/2009/en/104236>

864 Sometimes, diligent registrars who have studied their judges would suggest dates to the judge for a specific case.

865 This is a true story. This author knows of a couple of judges who informed her of how they dream about a pending case. Believe it or not, some of these dreams eventually impact their decisions.

that attempt to stall, delay, or kill the case.[866] This is the stage where applications such as stay of execution, objection to jurisdiction, or locus standi, etc., are filed. At this stage, the court also regularizes the procedure to determine moving ahead with the trial. After taking care of the inhibitions, if necessary, the judge sets the case down for hearing.

4. The hearing stage. This is the stage where the judge spends hours, days, weeks, months, or years patiently listening to the parties testify and present evidence. The court takes evidence from all sides. After the testimonies and evidence, the judge calls the parties to file written addresses and exchange the addresses. Then, the judge invites parties to respond on points of law and then sets a date for parties or attorneys to adopt their written addresses. After written addresses are adopted, the judge adjourns the matter for a decision/judgment. However, if the hearing is not a trial but a motion or application, some judges give a bench ruling/bench verdict or instant ruling, which is why it is key to take notes and do some preliminary research when browsing through the case file at the first stage.
5. The research stage. At this stage, the judge recalls the mental note he/she took after receiving the case file in stage one. If it is noted in the notebook, the judge reviews the salient points from the notebook with the facts, and begins to research relevant laws, and available materials like books to answer vital questions from the closing remarks or briefs. This is the stage where the judge considers international law, foreign case law, treaties, and statutes that support the salient points and somewhat forms a first formal opinion that may substantiate or disagree with the informal opinion in stage 2.
6. The review stage. This is the stage where the judge juxtaposes all information gathered during research and analyzes the evidence, facts, and law to understand the litigants' cases. At this stage, the judge reviews her earlier opinions from stages 2 and 5 and questions the facts, evidence, motion, or submissions/addresses to ascertain how they align with her wavering opinions, if the opinions conflict, or if the case is not straightforward.[867]
7. The interpretation stage. This is also the stage where the judge's subsequent

866 Unfortunately, this happens a lot as litigants would take advantage of every leeway the law provides.

867 Not every case is as straightforward as it seems. There is more than meets the eyes for many cases that come before the court.

decision differs from her earlier prediction. This is the critical stage that eventually determines the judge's final decision. At this stage, the judge considers diverse factors, not just the obvious—the law or statutes, but also the facts, evidence and sometimes extrinsic social factors, especially if it is a high-profile, potentially social change case. This stage collates all that the judge understands and intends to apply in deciding the case.

8. Judicial discretion stage. This is the stage the judge thinks out of the box to see what makes more sense to determine justice in the case. At this stage, the judge applies intuition, philosophy, and (inadvertently) personal or sociocultural experience[868] and connects the facts to the law, to determine whether it makes sense to her intuition and previous thoughts when she was reviewing the facts, testimonies, written submissions, and the law. This is a dicey stage in the act of judging, and in some cases, a most powerful stage as it gives the judge latitude that is not often determined by law. Like a deep well, no one can discern the judge's discretion. It is also at this stage that the judge's mental note or observation of the witness or party's demeanor impacts his/her decision. The discretion of a judge though fettered, determines the entire case.[869] And further this is also the stage where 'judicial activism' takes front role and the judge dares precedent where the need arises in the interests of justice.
9. The delivery stage. This is the final stage where the judge gives a verdict or delivers judgment (and waits for all hell to break loose). The rules of courts require three months or ninety days to deliver judgment, otherwise the judgment becomes ineffective.[870] Therefore, judges endeavor to deliver their verdicts within this time frame. However, where that time elapses, the judge could ask the lawyers to re-adopt their written submissions, and the ninety days or three months start counting again from the date of re-adoption of writing addresses.[871]
10. House-keeping stage. This is not necessarily the last stage, but it is more convenient to list it as last because it is amenable. It sneaks up on the

868 There will be more discussion on the judicial decision-making process in the second volume of my research on courts and society.

869 See detailed discussion on discretion in Chapter 4.

870 See the Lagos High Court Rules.

871 This procedure saved this author a lot of time, especially when I encountered deadlock cases in which it was difficult to decide one way or the other, and there was no law or precedent to bell the cat. Hence, the extra time gives me more time to think and research. Plus, it alleviates a lot of judicial stress from a busy judge.

judge at any time before, during or after the hearing. It is the extempore stage that interferes with regular proceedings. The act of judging is not just about the case file, the hearing, and the court's decision. It also involves issues that transpire in court between parties, lawyers, and even the judge and their courts staff.[872] Some of these issues could be conflicts, fights, and rage. For example, this writer adjourned a trial after several unsuccessful attempts during the hearing to settle quarrels between two attorneys in court. First, I stood the matter down[873] to talk to them, but when the matter was recalled, they continued bickering and throwing tantrums. So, I adjourned the matter for another day to let them cool off. At that time, I had to reiterate notes from law school on the rules of professional conduct and explain to the confused litigants that such an embarrassing situation was unacceptable in any court of law. Two lawyers fighting over their clients' cases was embarrassing, to say the least.

This stage involves issues on ethics, courtroom decorum, constitutional requirements on the rights of parties, especially in criminal cases, or any impromptu action or reaction that requires the judges/justices' attention and an ad hoc decision. So, over the course of the hearing, the judge makes administrative, ethical comments. For example, a judge may correct a lawyer's appearance or use of language.

This is also the stage where the judge considers diversity, equity, and inclusion, or human rights. Judges assure everyone that their diversities are considered and that they will receive equal treatment. This is also the time to be candid with litigants that although their motions may not necessarily be granted, their interest is important to the court, and they will attain a fair trial.

---

872 Some court staff interfere with the proceedings because they are bribed by either or both parties and the judge gets to know this at any stage of the trial. The court has to deal with this before continuing with the business of the day.

873 Standing a matter down is a terminology in Nigerian courts that means setting the case aside for a few minutes or hours for important reasons to reconvene and continue with the hearing later in the same day.

> This is also the stage where the judge could comment on an amicus curiae brief,[874] or explain court procedures to prose litigants,[875] making them comfortable in the tensed courtroom atmosphere, and assuring them of their rights in court, and answering any questions. Another act that the judge performs in this stage is one of encouraging mediation or out-of-court settlements. Although it is not a typical practice, some Nigerian judges comply with procedures to encourage mediation and alternative means of litigation, especially if it is a family matter or conflict between family members. On a few occasions, this author applied this settlement technique in convincing two brothers in one case, and a mother and her two sons in another case to settle their long lingering family conflicts. Thankfully, all parties in both cases received the court's counsel and reported back to the court. Happy endings! Consequently, they asked this author to enter their settlement agreement as consent judgment.
>
> This stage is indeterminate as the judge could make any statement she deems fit, as the circumstances predict.

Hence, courts are the most important connection between law and society.[876] Although most Nigerian courts adopt the liberal approach to judging, it is pertinent that judges understand their full range of discretion and apply it appropriately and socio-judicially. Thus, if courts fail to apply socio-judicial discretion, a gap will ensue between the courts and society. Consequently, the vacuum created by this gap will make the public to question the courts' value or impact on society, and this eventually breaches the public's confidence and respect for the court system; creating a travesty of the justice that courts represent.

According to Figure 1.3 in chapter one, judging in Nigeria has two basic features. The first is to interpret statutes, which enables the courts to interpret

---

874 An amicus curiae brief is a free unsolicited representation of a party in court by a lawyer interested in the case or one just offering pro bono services to a litigant for various reasons (empathy, pity, passion, or a request from the judge); amicus curiae is a Latin phrase for a friend of the court.

875 A prose litigant is a self-represented person who has no lawyer and so has to defend herself/himself before the court.

876 The author is a convener of a unique Courts & Society Webinar Series (CSWS) that gathers judges, lawyers, and intellectuals from different countries to discuss the courts' roles in society. Details on these webinars are available at https://atsjconsulting.com/

substantial or technical justice. The second basic act of judging is to apply judicial discretion in each case to ensure justice is achieved. Therefore, judging is a combination of when the judge interprets statutes and applies (fettered or unfettered) discretion in arriving at a just decision.

Chapter 7
Conclusion

> In doing justice according to law in a situation where there is an enabling statute, a court of law should allow itself or pet itself to follow the course of a liberal interpretation of the statute to accommodate the tenets of justice, while at the same time not throwing overboard the intention of the draftsman … The day a court of law, which is also a court of justice, in the course of exercising its interpretative jurisdiction, yields or kotows to arid legalism and abandons its primary function of doing substantial justice, a crisis situation permeates the entire system of administration of justice or the enforcement of the judicial process. Democracy in its shapeless and amorphous content and its twin brother, the rule of law, will be threatened in such a situation which will definitely result in anarchy. That will be a very strange and most unhappy moment for the judiciary. I hope that day does not come. I can still add this bit. The day a party who has not committed a wrong is made to suffer a reverse or victimized in the judicial process by way of such sanction, the judicial system should receive a censor from the litigating public. How this will be carried out I am not prepared to theorize here. I leave that for a most appropriate situation.[877]
>
> — Hon. Justice Niki Tobi, JCA (as he then was)

Previous chapters of this book examined the act of judging in Nigeria, vis a vis interpretation of statutes and exercise of judicial discretion. Our journey started with a historical tour of Nigeria's legal/judicial system from precolonial to post-colonial. Since international law plays a vital role in the Nigerian legal system, Chapter 2 discussed the impact of international law in judging in Nigeria. Chapter two also explained how judges and culture influence the application of international law in Nigeria. Chapter 3 discussed judicial interpretation as the primary act of judging in Nigeria's modern democracy, and this author introduced her unique socio-judicial approach as a new canon for interpreting statutes. Chapter 4 examined judicial discretion as the second act of judging in Nigeria. Chapter 5 encapsulated judicial precedent and its impacts on judging.

877 *Chief Emma Onuorah Emesim v. Hon. Calista Nwachukwu (Mrs.) & Ors. (supra)*, emphasis mine.

Chapter 6 discussed the impact of judging on society and debates the dichotomy between technical justice and substantial justice. In this chapter, the author shares ten stages of judging she created and applied in her judicial career on the bench. This final chapter concludes with suggestions to the act of judging.

Based on several unconventional studies in different court systems within and outside Nigeria, this author concludes that courts are agents of social change, underscoring the importance of societal and public values in judicial decision-making. Therefore, I hypothesize that courts will have more impact on society if judicial discretion incorporates social views, interests, and culture in the act of judging. This does not mean that courts should make decisions upon the whims and caprices of individuals, groups, or races. Certainly not! It means the predominant culture, views, and public interest, not selfish political or sociopolitical inclinations should be considered by the court. An example will be what impacts the public majority and not a selected sect in society. For instance, in a recovery of premises case, the court's consideration of the predominant public view, culture, and interest would be to take judicial notice of the Nigerian culture of landlord and tenancy, which sometimes involves manipulative, dishonest tenants and complexities. The court should also consider the interest of both parties even if the laws appear biased against landlords, as some tenants have taken undue advantage of the law to oppress their landlords. Society is an aggregate of diverse political, social, economic, religious and cultural factors. Thus, it behooves courts to deeply consider this diversity and navigate the socio-judicial terrain. Judges should also attempt to connect the seeming divide between the law judges are called to uphold/interpret, and the society they are called to serve. In the words of Professor Nwanbueze:

> The judicial approach stands indeed in dire need of revitalization if the rule of law is to become or remain a really effective principle of government ... The maintenance of the rule of Law demands that they should look beyond the formal letters of the law and engage themselves in a purposeful effort to try to distill principles of fairness and justice from the moral, ethical and other fundamental values of society ... While the letters of the law are and must remain the core elements of the rule of law, their interpretation and application by the court should be informed by reason and by the fundamental values of the community.[878]

The court's primary role is to administer justice according to the rule of law. "Justice" is a classic term that we cannot streamline. It presents a broad intention that courts should uphold. Nwanbueze further states that, "a

878 Nwanbueze, B. (2004). Constitutional Democracy in Africa, opcit: 29–30, emphasis mine.

narrowly positivist view of the law could only make it sterile, devoid of a proper moral content, and ... judges are eminently well placed to instill into law the necessary moral content based on the notions of reasonableness, fairness, justice, and respect for individual liberty."[879]Judicial interpretation and judicial discretion should be centered on justice, to ensure that the act of judging in Nigeria complies with the rule of law and democratic values. Aguda supports this statement with these words:

> One is bound to suggest that the sensible approach to the matter would be that whenever there appears to be a conflict between what the law dictates and what justice demands, a judge should attempt to resolve the apparent conflict in favor of justice. The ordinary citizen of Nigeria does not expect anything less than this from our judges and lawyers. If Courts lean too much on the side of legalism that may be sure path to the danger of chaos and political instability.[880]

Judges represent justice in any society, hence the title "justice" as appendages to their names.[881] This is why society measures justice from the court's actions and the public's perceptions of judges/courts. The popular aphorism many Nigerian cases cite, which is that justice should not only be done but should manifestly and undoubtedly be seen to be done,[882] is focused on society's standards. So, when judges ignore the justice contemplated by or implicit in the law, then society will be exposed to the danger of chaos and sociopolitical/ socioeconomic instability.

Consequently, the scale of justice shifts like a pendulum, making it unstable, as courts should not get confused between interpreting the law and upholding justice, at the same time, which they often do. In such a quagmire, only the discretion of the judge, which should be applied *socio-judiciously*[883] and *socio-judicially*,[884]can balance or stabilize the scale of justice. Therefore, to connect law and courts to society, and to build public confidence, in the courts, judges should balance the rule of law with social interests through the just exercise of judicial discretion to ensure justice.[885] Judicial discretion is the balancing factor that courts should apply in interpreting statutes to avoid absurdity.[886]

879 Ibid.
880 Aguda, T. A (1986). The Crisis of Justice, Eresu Hill Publishers, Akure, Nigeria, 7.
881 Judges should justify the title in acting justly.
882 Adopted from the English case of *R v. Rand (1988) L.R.I.Q.B 230.*
883 This author's coinage from her theory, socio-judicialism.
884 Ibid.
885 This creates a dilemma for judges all over.
886 See *Oluwabokola v. A.G Lagos State & 4 Ors (supra) at p.39, Hon. Justice Ebiowei Tobi, JCA.*

Applying judicial discretion/ creativity by considering cases through social lenses, as well as the rule of law is fundamental to maintaining the status of equity and justice in Nigeria's justice system or any other justice system for that matter.

Therefore, this book proposes a *socio-judicial approach* to judging with a wide range of discretion in certain cases. This approach combines formalism, realism, and purposeful philosophies of judging. It proposes that Nigerian courts should see the act of judging as a socio-judicial act.[887] This means embracing Social justice, not in the polarized and politicized meaning, but social justice as in justice for society—as judges give effect to law and the interests of the society for which the legislatures allegedly enacted the laws. A court of law is equally a court of justice.[888] This socio-judicial approach to judging can only operate when judges possess a wide latitude of discretion. Where the discretion of a court is restricted, injustice thrives. Socio-judicial judging guarantees the value of judges as human beings who understand and appreciate the value of society, and not computers that can only reproduce what was programmed into them.

Human discretion is not just fundamental to judging; it is necessary and most valuable to the development of democracy as it invokes the phrase "*We the People.*"[889] This is as good for the people as it is for democracy. The foundation of the courts, and public confidence in the judiciary determines the growth and development of any democracy because the judiciary is the institution that solely deals with the dispensation and administration of justice in any democratic state. Therefore, the effects of judicial discretion on society give value to Nigeria's democracy, which demands that judicial discretion integrate predominant social views and interests in the act of judging.

However, sometimes, the interest of law takes priority over the interest of society, so technical or procedural justice overshadows substantial justice and beclouds the judge's discretion. In such a situation, the judge should apply a socio-judicial approach and broader discretion to ensure that substantial

---

[887] This socio-judicial approach is a preface to this author's socio-judiclaism theory, which the next volume of this book–the role of the judiciary in a democracy, discusses in detail.

[888] See the introductory quote of this chapter.

[889] See the preambles to the Constitution of the Federal Republic of Nigeria and the Constitution of the United States of America.

justice prevails over technical justice. Therefore, even when statutes[890] and strict adherence to precedent restrict judicial discretion, judges should resort to their inherent discretion with equity to do what is fair and just.

Judicial discretion is indispensable in interpreting statutes. Every decision in the act of judging involves the exercise of discretion, one way or the other. The need for judges to apply their discretion in interpreting statutes from a socio-judicial perspective cannot be overemphasized. Interpreting statutes from a socio-judicial perspective demonstrates the relevance of courts to society, as there are gaps in the law or system that the judge's discretion should fill. Judges need to relinquish servitude to precedent when the justice of the case so demands. Ijaiye says:

> Courts should not shy away from their duties to fill the gaps when interpreting provisions, based on the feeble reason that rule of law and separation of powers may not be maintained. Rule of law is not all about procedural fairness. It is also about substantive fairness and interpretation of law ... justice attained when a procedural fairness is accompanied by a substantive fairness. Thus, the theory of rule of law recognizes the role of judges in furthering the goal of justice and fairness through interpretation of matters that come before them. Therefore, judges should not be confined or restricted only to the contents of the laws being reviewed but should actually move out of the strict content of the law to ensure that the policy objects of the law is not defeated. The theory of the rule of law views the independence of judges not as a blanket approval of total indifference and apathy of judges to prevailing social, political and economic conditions in the society but an independence which allows judges to ensure that substantive justice supports the purpose of the legislation is done.[891]

Furthermore, this socio-judicial approach to judging attempts to deter undue adherence to precedent, for a human face to the act of judging. Acknowledging the human factor is an important use of judicial discretion. The human face of the law will assist the court in addressing the reality on the ground. Aguda states:

> Ours is a "human" profession in the sense that every case that confronts us must inevitably affect some human being. Our university Law Faculties and Law School should stop teaching law as if the law is going to operate outside human beings, and outside the society as a whole. We need a more humanly applied law than at present.[892]

---

890 Some statutes give judges unrestricted discretion, and others stipulate how such discretion should be applied.

891 Ijaiye, H.O. (2017) Constitutional Approach to Interpretation of Constitutions in Nigeria, Australia, Canada and India, opcit: 182.

892 Aguda. T.A (1986) The Crisis of Justice, opcit: 43.

In interpreting the law and exercising discretion, courts should consider the logic, morality, social justice, and substantial justice that best suits the humanity of the case. The life of the law is not just precedent; it involves experience and logic.[893] Precedent should be developed and renewed constantly. In certain cases, "old" precedent is getting stale, it is being recycled from case to case; it is time for "new" precedent. The time is overdue to review and revise the Nigerian caselaw. For example, the Apex Court should review the precedent in *Okumagba v. Egbe* (that the office of the judge is to state the law and not give it) and replace it with a socially oriented and more relevant precedent.[894] According to Ijaiye "it must however be noted that the court could make corrections in a statute where the mistake on the face of a statute if uncorrected will depart from the obvious intention of the legislature or where it would otherwise, render the provision meaningless… the judge in performing its legislative function should consider the prevailing social value and context."[895]

It is important to restate that this book does not decry the importance of judicial precedent; nor is it campaigning that lower courts depart from the wise, age-old doctrine of *stare decisis*. Nonetheless, since precedent gets stale as society changes and the relevance of outdated precedents fades, it is vital that new precedent emerges. So, if relevant and new precedent does not emerge, the Nigerian judiciary will fail to uphold justice, while injustice may thrive, causing a travesty of the justice system.

The rules or canons of interpretation are judge-made rules formulated over the years by older judges,[896] that sought to solve the problems they encountered in society. Today's judges can take a similar path. What is the essence of law if precedent remains static? The over-reliance on precedent dispenses with and undermines the courts' relevance to society because precedent can be pre-recorded and installed into a computer program software, or an artificial intelligence algorithm, while the precedent downloads the law's requirement verbatim. Thus, this "software" or "algorithm" of precedents enshrined in the court's database could potentially replace judges and ensure apt delivery of

893 See Larsen, opcit.

894 The National Industrial Court of Nigeria seems to be creating new precedent in many cases, but they are not superior courts of record, as their decisions if overturned by the Supreme Court cannot be precedent.

895 Ijaiye, opcit: 184.

896 They created these canons to guide their duties of interpretation.

opinions, but with no human factor that considers the changes and demands of different people and groups.[897] This is not what society wants, and it is not what the Constitution established the courts to achieve.

We find support in Oshio's remark: "it seems that the categories are not closed and would increase as the need to meet new challenges in the interpretation of statutes would arise … Since neither society nor law is static, there may yet arise the need to develop more rules by judges to deal with more unforeseen complexities in the future."[898] Accordingly, the time has come to recognize the benefit and value of the court's discretion, to deal with the present and prospective complexities of our time. If older judges could be "activists" and create canons of interpretation, today's judges can also be "activists" in reforming, adding to, expounding or extending these rules with prevailing relevant social values and interests.

Hence the need to create new and more relevant precedents cannot be overstated. It is the primary responsibility of the appellate court to create new precedents that is relevant to the times, predominant views, and interests of society.[899] Although lower courts are restricted in creating new precedents, they are not excused, as the lower court judge's detailed judgment forms the basis for the appellate court to establish precedent.[900] However, the bulk of the responsibility is on the apex court to review decisions of lower courts, considering social interests, stipulated law, or an abuse of discretion, and upholding the best decision that serves the justice of the case.

However, appellate courts can only review precedents from the lower courts' records before them. This is where the trial judge's decisions play a vital role. If the trial court fails to state core issues in its decision or fails to express its discretionary reasoning, there may be nothing for the apex or appellate courts to affirm and or establish as new precedents upon appeal. Therefore, it is essential for trial judges to be detailed in their judgments and

---

897 Although this point was written about nine years ago in this author's graduate studies' thesis, she repeated it at a recent conference on AI and the Courts in 2024. See discussion in Chapter 4.

898 Ibid: 13.

899 The supreme courts' holding in *Abdulkarim v. Incar Nigeria Ltd (supra)* on overruling its own decision to keep the stream of justice pure, summarizes my point.

900 Appeals are based on substances from the lower court, so lower court judges or trial court judges have a foundational role to play here.

give concrete reasons for the decisions they make. In any event, the apex court should be willing to create precedent and be more ready to overrule itself in the light of prevailing circumstances.[901] Although it could be a herculean task to ask the court to overrule its previous decision, the onus is on the superior courts to bell the cat through judicial reviews and revise the distinguishing principle,[902] in addition to the other factors.[903] For example, lower courts should also be allowed to depart from precedent where the justice of the case so demands or when the lower court is at liberty to apply socio-judicial discretion to the precedent that best fits the pending case.

Judicial discretion is not consistent, as there is always a shift in judicial opinions due to varying circumstances of cases and changes in society. A dissenting opinion or obiter dictum today may eventually metamorphose to be the *ratio decidendi* in a future case, or a decision that an appeal court overturns may be upheld in another cases' appeal in future, like the case of Mojekwu v Mojekwu,[904] where in the Eastern region of Nigeria, under Igbo customary law, wives and daughters did not have the right of inheritance because of the customary notion that women were chattels and therefore, objects of inheritance themselves.[905] The Supreme Court reinforced this cultural practice in *Nezianya v. Okagbue*,[906] that under the native law and custom of Onitsha, a widow cannot deal with the property of her deceased husband without the consent of his family.[907] This principle of law took a daring turn[908] in the celebrated case of *Mojekwu v. Mojekwu*:[909]

> … We need not travel all the way to Beijing to know that some of our customs, including the Nnewi "Oli-Ekpe" custom relied upon by the appellant are not consistent with our civilized world in which we all live today … On my part, I have no difficulty in

901 See Chapter 4.

902 This is the same as distinguishing the case (the only ground the court is allowed to deviate from precedent). See Chapter 1.

903 Ibid.

904 Mojekwu v Mojekwu (supra).

905 See Tobi-Aiyemo, opcit: 10.

906 *Nezianya v. Okagbue [1963] All NLR 358 SC*

907 See also *Nzekwu v. Nzekwu [1989] 2 NWLR 373.*

908 This was two years after Nigeria joined the rest of the world for a global campaign for women's rights at the Fourth World Conference on Women: Action for Equality, Development and Peace, convened by the United Nations 1995 in Beijing, China.

909 *Supra.*

> holding that "Oli-Ekpe" custom of Nnewi is repugnant to natural justice, equity and good conscience.[910]

Unfortunately, upon further appeal to the Supreme Court in 2004, this decision was criticized on its "general and far-reaching language … which could lead to criticism of all other customs that exclude women."[911] In his lead judgment overturning the Mojekwu decision, Uwaifo, JSC, pronounced:

> The learned Justice of Appeal was no doubt concerned about the perceived discrimination directed against women by the said Nnewi "Oli-ekpe" custom. But the language used made the pronouncement so general and far-reaching …, and is capable of causing strong feelings against, all customs which fail to recognize a role for women. For instance, the custom and tradition of some communities which do not permit women to be natural rulers or family heads. The import is that those communities stand to be condemned without a hearing for such fundamental custom and tradition they practice in their native communities. It would appear for these reasons that the underlying crusade in that pronouncement went too far to stir up a real hornet's nest even if it had been made upon an issue joined by the parties, or properly raised and argued. I find myself unable to allow that pronouncement to stand in the circumstance, and accordingly I disapprove of it as unwarranted.[912]

This reasoning by the Supreme Court may be procedurally correct, but respectfully, substantially unjustified. The Court of Appeal, a lower court, had deviated from the precedent in *Nezianya v. Okagbue*[913] and discretionarily attempted to change the status quo custom that discriminated against women in Igboland. Therefore, the Supreme Court's concern in overturning Mojekwu's case is clearly based on technical justice.[914] Technical justice is a slave to precedent and if not controlled discretionarily, it may eventually result to injustice. According to Oshio, rigid and slavish adherence to the

---

910 *Hon. Justice Niki Tobi, JCA (as he then was).* Ibid: 305.

911 The case involved a property dispute between a deceased man's wife and his nephew. Augustine Mojekwu, the nephew, claimed that as the closest surviving male relative of the deceased, he was entitled to inherit his house. Caroline Mojekwu, the wife, on the other hand, argued that her son, Patrick, who had passed away before her husband, had fathered an infant son who should inherit it. Mrs. Mojekwu also had two daughters, but under the Nigerian Nnewi custom, they were not a consideration. Mrs. Mojekwu passed away before the Supreme Court ruled, leaving one of her daughters Theresa Nwachukwu as party in the case.

912 See *Augustine Nwafor Mojekwu v. Mrs. Theresa Iwuchukwu (2004) LPELR-1903 (SC).*

913 *Supra.*

914 In the United States also, a backlash against *Roe v. Wade* is still raising arguments.

literal rule, the doctrine of precedent, and other legal technicalities in interpreting the Constitution or statutes in all cases, especially novel cases, would inevitably lead to injustice, which will not be the intention of lawmakers.[915]

The strict adherence to precedent is affecting the development of the law and society. This is because Nigerian case law—an ardent devotee to judicial precedent—is not developing at the pace of Nigeria's society, thus making law irrelevant to society, and widening the gap between law and society. As the ultimate focus of the judge is to do justice in the case, judges should apply broader discretion to ensure substantial justice, and not procedural justice. The need for judges to apply discretion with wide latitude in interpreting statutes will be of immense value to the Nigerian society. Moreover, if the judicial and judicious discretion is overturned on appeal or even if the decision of a judge is dissenting and not a majority view, such decisions often build a platform for similar cases in the future. A ready example is the Mojekwu case. Although the reversal of this case stalled the advancement of precedent in this area of law for a while, justice eventually prevailed thirteen years later in the same Supreme Court, before the case Ukeji v Ukeji.[916] Also, in *Motoh v. Motoh*[917] the Court of Appeal reinforced this precedent and in citing *Hon. Justice* Niki Tobi's comment,[918] the apex court declared as follows:

> I will have no hesitation in declaring such customary law which discriminates against female children in terms of inheritance to be repugnant to nature of justice, equity and good conscience. I find support in the case of Mojekwu v. Mojekwu ..., where Tobi, JCA (as he then was) said ... Accordingly, a custom or customary law to discriminate against a particular sex is to say the least an affront on the Almighty God himself. Let nobody do such a thing. On my part, I have no difficulty in holding that the Oli-Ekpe custom of Nnewi is repugnant to natural justice, equity, and good conscience.[919]

In creating new precedents or exercising wider discretion, courts need judicial courage and perseverance. Persistence is the key factor here, when a judge is persistent, someday his or her idiosyncratic yet fair perception will prevail. As long as the judge applies justice in the case, at least one judge on appeal

915 Ibid: 32.
916 Ukeji v Ukeji (2014) LPELR –22724 (SC) affirmed the rights of women to inheritance.
917 *Supra.*
918 Opcit.
919 *Hon. Justice Aboki, JCA. (Pp. 72–73, paras. G-C).*

will give a dissenting view, which from antecedents, eventually becomes the *ratio decidendi* in the future.[920] Although only the Supreme Court (except the case ends at the Court of Appeal) can establish judicial precedent because they are the final court of appeal that can reverse or confirm the decisions of the lower courts; nonetheless, lower courts should not hesitate to state and interpret the law as they see fit with society-oriented discretion.

However, most lower court judges fear the wrath of the Supreme Court, so they would rather shy away from applying discretion to create precedent, than stand the chance of being called judicial rascals. The fear of being overturned on appeal does not aid the development of law and society. Courts should give detailed reasons for their discretion so that the record is clear for all to know. The openness of judicial discretion will encourage public trust.[921] Hine states that keeping the exercise of discretion in the open ensures the ability to monitor discretion and to keep the exercise of discretion above board.[922]

Again, even if overturned on appeal, eventually a decision against precedent based on socio-judicial principles will someday become law. Hon. Justice Oguntade, JSC, in citing Lord Denning,[923] repeated: "what is the argument on the other side? Only this that no case has been found that it has been done before. That argument does not appeal to me in the least. If we never do anything which has not been done before we shall never get anywhere. The law will stand still whilst the rest of the world goes on and that will be bad for both."[924]

It takes a courageous, innovative, risk-taking judge to decide a case according to social values and to take steps to develop the law for society. Thus, where law and justice conflict, the judge should ensure that justice prevails. Since the judges' ultimate focus is to do justice in the case before them, the act of judging should advance with society. According to Barack, the legal norm is not flexible enough, and it fails to adapt to the new reality, so we need a new norm to fill the gap between law and society.[925] Therefore, Nigerian judges should not shy away from creating new norms where the justice of

---

920 Dissenting views have eventually become the locus standi in some cases in Nigeria.
921 Hine, opcit: 1788.
922 Ibid: 1787.
923 *Parker v. Parker(supra)Denning, M. R.*
924 See *Ameachi v. INEC (supra).*
925 Barack, opcit: 4.

the case demands. What is the value of judges if precedent remains static? As stated above, we may as well get computers to replace judges and then we can just download software of precedents into the judicial database to ensure the delivery of opinions. May the day not come for computer judges to take the place of human judges.

The human factor is fundamental to the judiciary's traditional role of interpreting statutes. However, no specific law stipulates that a judicial role is to interpret statutes based on the intent of the legislature alone. Discretion is also useful in interpreting statutes. For example, the Nigerian Evidence Act did not include electronically generated evidence, long before electronically generated cases were filed before Nigerian courts. Thus, prior to the amendment of the Evidence Act, Nigerian judges applied discretion in interpreting the admissibility of electronically generated evidence.[926]

To this end, it is fundamental that judges understand social views and interests in the act of judging, judges need to consider how society interprets and uses specific words, so judges can relate them to the circumstances of a pending case. In other words, courts should consider word semantics and how the use of certain words changes over time and make them relevant to society in interpreting laws. Words often assume meanings from their social contexts and their author's perspective. Therefore, judges should remember that text appeals to communities of listeners and they are used purposively, and also that the meanings of these words could change over time.[927] Therefore, courts should not only interpret words used in statutes with the meaning popularly understood at the time the statute became law, but the word should also be interpreted with its current meaning at the time the statute is being interpreted.[928] Courts should appreciate the fact that the English language also evolves; the meanings of words change with time and their cultural context. For example, the word "paranoid" popularly means to be characterized by or suffering from the mental condition paranoia,[929] but in some parts of the world like the United States, the word "paranoid" also means suspicious, distrustful, or obsessed.

---

926 See *Commissioner of Police v. Jelili Lawal & Anor (Supra)*. A case this author presided over at Tinubu Magistrate Court, Lagos State, Nigeria.

927 Easterbrook, F. H (2004), Judicial Discretion in Statutory Interpretation, opcit: 2.

928 This is more relevant to society.

929 See Google Search and Merriam Webster Dictionary, opcit.

New words are often coined and created out of old words. That is why dictionaries have new editions/versions. Thus, if courts were to read words according to the popular meaning understood at the time the statute became law, the word and the statute would have lost their relevance. English words are subject to semantic change as they can be used either as verbs or nouns. For example, the word "block" could mean a place, an item, or even an action, depending on how the user applies the word. However, "block" originally meant "a compact usually solid item or obstruction."[930] Today, the word "block" popularly carries the meaning to "prevent or hinder access to a personal profile or social media like Twitter,' or from viewing your profile. It is also used in the fashion industry as "color block," to mean toning down a combination of colors. Hence, judges must bear in mind semantics and the constant shifts in the meanings of words. The primary duty of the court is to do justice by interpreting the intention of the legislature based on the Constitution, which manifests the legislature's intentions.[931]

It is tough to gauge the intentions of the drafters of our laws when words bear different meanings.[932] As is typical of human beings (that judges are), there would be diverse views in understanding the meaning or intention of a statute. Some people see the meaning of words from another angle and interpret them narrowly, while others see words from several angles and give them a broader interpretation. In other words, some statutory words may appear to have a plain meaning, while others are contextualized to reach an adequate or correct interpretation. Like liquid, words can take the form of a container. Words can also assume the meaning that the user or observer gives. This was explained in *Federal Republic of Nigeria v. Mike*[933] as follows:

> Definitions are definitions because they reflect the idiosyncrasies, prejudices, slants and emotion of the person offering them, while a definer of a word (concept) may pretend to be impartial and unbiased, the final product of his definition will, in a number of situations be a victim of bias.

930 See Merriam Webster Dictionary, opcit.

931 See *Martin Scbroder and Co. v. Major and Co. (Nig) Ltd (1989) 2 NWLR, at 12; Ifezue v. Mbadagbe (supra).*

932 When you speak with a familiar language, people understand it as their own, and when people feel like part of a process they comply with the process, as a cultural process.

933 *Federal Republic of Nigeria v. Mike (2004)1 SC (pt. II) 27 at 25.*

Furthermore, the English word and indeed the entire English language is an omnibus space. It collects comfortable meanings into its space and makes them at home for a while; the space expands as words, interpretations, and events evolve.[934] Over time the courts' understanding and interpretation of words must also evolve. In the words of Lord Denning:

> Whenever a statute comes up for consideration, it must be remembered that it is not within human powers to foresee the manifold set of facts which may arise, and even if it were, it is not possible to provide for them in terms free from ambiguity. The English Language is not an instrument of mathematical precision. Our literature would be much poorer if it were.[935]

This introduces a fundamental point that Nigerian courts should consider—they should judge with Nigerian culture in mind. They should interpret laws according to Nigerian legal culture and traditions—a law that is common to the Nigerian people. Just as English law arose from the culture and Common Law of England, Nigerian Common Law should incorporate Nigeria's Indigenous culture and where necessary in the interest of justice, borrow from foreign culture, applying judicial discretion. Therefore, when Judges consider the culture/tradition of the Nigerian society, more Indigenous words would replace the English words in the statutes, some of which have still not been amended since Nigeria's independence from the British. Accordingly, instead of the phrase "intention of parliament," Nigerian courts should interpret the "intention of the legislators as relevant to present social circumstances" in Nigeria and let the courts consider Nigerians' social views and interests. Courts should also be consistent in replacing the word "parliament" with "legislators." Parliament is a British term that was used during the colonial era. If the circumstances fit, judging should be more inclusive regarding social considerations.

The act of judging based on precedent alone will continue to expand the gap between law and society and cause injustice until the courts exercise their discretionary act of judging broadly, with social values and interests in mind. Cardozo explains that the rule that misses its aim cannot permanently justify

---

934 For example, the word "mad" could mean a mental condition or an emotional state of anger.

935 Oshio, ibid: 10.

its existence, as the final cause of law is the welfare of society.[936] The court aims to do justice. So, judges should jettison technical justice which constrains the court's discretionary power, and embrace substantial justice.[937] The law is loud enough for a court of law to exercise its discretion judicially and judiciously. Judges should exercise their discretion according to the law, intellectual wisdom, and human reasoning. Judges should not apply discretion arbitrarily.

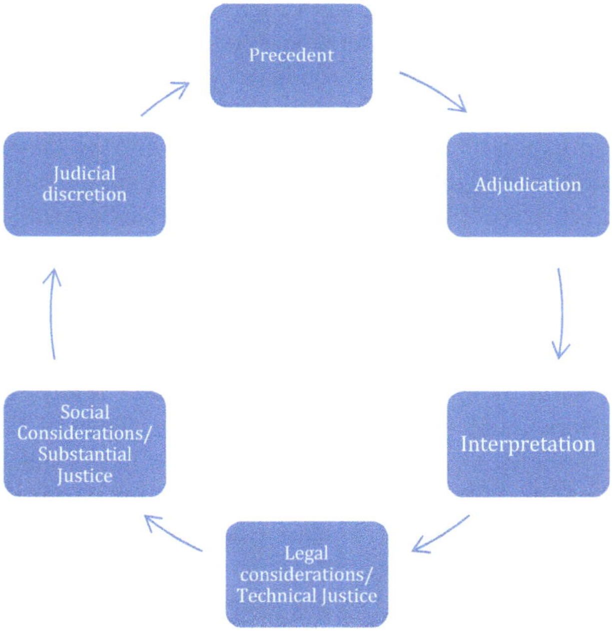

Figure 7.1: The Cycle of Judging in The Nigerian Society

The administration of justice is founded on rules and precedents and not on arbitrariness. This is because judges are human beings who are fallible. According to the Court in *Samuel Ayo Omoju v. The Federal Republic of*

936 Cardozo, B. N. (1921). opcit: 66.

937 *Engineering Enterprises Contractor of Nigeria v. A.G of kaduna State (supra).*

Nigeria,[938] "judges are human beings and like all human beings, are bound to make mistakes and they make mistakes. The appellate system is there to correct mistakes of trial Judges ... a Judge is not a supernatural being. He is a human being and is not infallible." Thus, although discretion should be broadened, judges should be guided to an extent as the use of discretion to interpret statutes is quite dicey.[939]

Accordingly, the judiciary may provide adequate guidelines to assist judges in arriving at judicious and judicial interpretations, in ways to apply wider discretion. The Supreme Court and Chief judges/head judges of various courts should prepare judicial discretionary practice guides to direct judicial discretion.[940] It is pertinent that the judiciary codifies judicial discretion to ensure compliance, albeit making room for checks and balances, in appropriate circumstances.[941] There is need for a uniformity or standard to the extent possible. Although courts cannot direct or control discretion, judges should as much as possible abide by shared principles in exercising discretion to achieve a close to uniform pattern of discretion.

This book challenges judges' strict reliance on precedent and advocates a broader exercise of discretion that incorporates changing societal interests and more just decision-making. As nearly all the principles, precepts, and maxims of statutory interpretation are judge-made,[942] judges may revise them. Therefore, courts should redefine the exercise of judicial discretion to consider relevant social views, values, and interests. Judges should analyze and understand the influence of social norms, values, and interests on judicial pronouncements. Also, the role of judges in appreciating the function of law in society should be emphasized. Incorporating predominant social norms and principles in judging will help the judiciary achieve the law's purpose in people's lives. Hence, the act of judging in Nigeria should advance with the Nigerian culture and society.

---

938 *Samuel Ayo Omoju v. The Federal Republic of Nigeria, (supra) Hon. Justice Muhammed JSC.*

939 According to Lord Denning, "it is not within human powers to foresee the manifold sets of facts which may arise and even if it were, it is not possible to provide for them in terms free from all ambiguity – See *Seaford Estate Ltd v. Asher (supra).*

940 See this author's outline in Chapter 3.

941 By codify, we do not mean legislative intervention as we are aware of how the judiciary frowns on legislative intervention and vice versa.

942 *Awolowo v. Shagari & Ors(supra) Hon. Justice Fatayi-Williams, CJN.*

Hine opines that the idea that laws, not individuals, govern our society is at the core of most citizens' understandings of the American judicial system, so people elect legislatures to enact laws, rather than depend solely on judge-made Common Law.[943] Courts are to remedy a bad situation and not leave society helpless. Aderemi, JSC, summarizes the above pages in *Attorney General of the Federation v, Abubakar*[944] as follows:

> No legal problem or issue must defy legal solution. Were this not to be so, the society, as usual will continue to move ahead, law, God forbid, will then remain stagnant and consequently become useless to mankind. With this unfortunate consequences at the back of his mind, a judge whenever faced with a new situation which has not been considered before, by his ingenuity regulated by law, must say what the law is on that new situation; after all, law has a very wide tentacle and must find solution to all man-made problems. In so doing let no judge regard himself as making or even changing law. He (the judex) only declares it—he considers the new situation, on principle and then pronounces upon it. To me that is, the practical form of saying that the law lies on the breasts of the judges.[945]

Ultimately, every judge should ask the question: "What is the essence of justice if courts fail to justify the 'justness' in the word?" In answering this question, courts should first ruminate on the following words of Hon. Justice Oputa, JSC, (as he then was): "The judge should always ask himself if his decision, though legally impeccable in the end achieved a fair result. 'That may be law, but definitely not justice' is a sad commentary on any decision."[946] Thus, I adopt Ronald Dworkin's apt admonition:

---

943 Hine, (1997) opcit: 1770.

944 *Attorney General of the Federation v. Abubakar (2007)10 N.W.L.R (PT 1041) 1 @ 171–172 (Hon. Justice Aderemi, JSC).*

945 Laws are man-made, and man is not above mistakes or errors; therefore, some provisions of statutes will be ambiguous as the drafters may not foresee future events that may arise after the enactment. Hence, where such events arise and there is no legislation to aid, will the judge turn to the parties and say "sorry, my hands are tied, I do not have the answers as the law has no provision for it, let us all just wait until the legislature through stages of readings and bureaucracy decide to alter and change the law (that is, if it is considered relevant or a legislator is willing to sponsor the Bill), then you can return to get justice"? What a judge that will be! Believe it or not, that is exactly what happens when a judge dares to adhere to letters of law without due consideration of the justice to society.

946 Oshio, ibid: 24.

> Judicial activity is like several co-authors. judges no longer on the bench wrote the earlier chapters. We must now write the continuation of the work; we must ground ourselves in the past while ensuring historical continuity. The chapters that we are writing become, after they are written chapters from the past. New chapters, the creations of new judges, will be written in the future.[947]

Accordingly, "a Judge that is confronted with a legal problem does not have to resign helplessly where the established laws are inadequate in resolving the problem. … Judges are, therefore, encouraged to formulate fresh rules of law or to extend the existing ones."[948] The act of judging must develop as the laws and rules advance. With the liberty of broader discretion, judges should not helplessly resign to seemingly hopeless situations. Instead, they can write "new chapters" that will eventually establish new precedents from an Indigenous Common Law. The appropriate exercise of judicial discretion, and socio-judicial interpretation of the law, which are essential to the act of judging, enables transforming precedent to suit the constantly advancing society. The courts' role in the Nigerian society and other countries has evolved to indeterminate roles, which creates social and judicial dilemmas for all judges. Therefore, what is the role of the judiciary in a democracy of judges engulfed in dilemmas?[949]

---

947 Dworkin, R. (1982). Law as Interpretation, 60, Tex. L. Rev. 527.

948 Aboki, opcit: 113.

949 The role of courts in society and the dilemmas that judges encounter in performing those roles, is the next phase of this research, which this author executed in her dissertation, "The Role of the Nigerian Judiciary in a Democracy: A Judge's Dilemma," which has establsihed a unique Courts & Society Webinar Series.

AN OPEN LETTER TO JUDGES AND ASPIRING JUDGES

January 20, 2025.

Dear Honorable Judges/Justices,

Thank you for investing your time to read this book that I wrote over the years with nostalgia, missing the one judge whose act of judging inspired my research and eventually this book. Congratulations on surviving years of judging different cases at different confusing levels in your respective courts and judicial careers.

You may be reading this book as a judge from other jurisdictions worldwide, but trust me, we are all in the same boat, facing similar challenges. I know this because after about twelve years, as a Nigeran magistrate-judge, with extensive knowledge of Nigerian law, and the Nigerian judiciary, and, six years as a judicial studies student in the U.S., with growing knowledge of the American legal/judicial system, I can tell you *sisi ni sawa* (A Swahili phrase for we are the same). I have also interacted closely with judges from different courts in Nigeria, the United States, and other jurisdictions, and I see that our experiences in court, our concerns about the law, the dilemmas we face, the political challenges, and security issues are the same.

Although I have not served in superior courts as some of you, I was under the tutelage and mentorship of one of your colleagues who served for close to four decades from the High Court to the Supreme Court of Nigeria. I quote the following from his book "The Nigerian Judge," as he said

> ***One of the most misunderstood workers in Nigeria, if not the most misunderstood worker, is the Nigeran Judge. In any litigation, one party likes him, and the other party hates him. In any litigation, one party praises his upright and straightforward attitude, and the other party may accuse him of corruption. In most litigations, the Nigerian Judge is either alleged or suspected of being a bribe taker. In other words, while the party who wins does not see anything bad in the Judge, as he is full of praises for him, the other party who loses, sees everything wrong in the Judge. Such is the fate of the Nigerian judge. Such is the predicament of the Nigerian Judge.***

Therefore, I have an idea of the different levels of challenges, endurance, and occupational hazards that follow judging (some of which are invisible, and beyond the courthouse). I am also aware that this is a lonely and dangerous career, which affects your mental health and puts your life, family, and security at risk. Judgeship is a possessive career that clamours for all your space, time, and life. If you are not deliberate, you will have no life or relationship to return to after retirement. So, as you work hard, play hard, and 'bank' for a life after you retire. However, never mix business with pleasure…. Let your ethical codes guide your 'plays.'

I know it is hard when everyone expects you to be their superhero, but you also struggle with your humanness like everyone. It is especially hard when people misunderstand or misinterpret your good and genuine intentions. Some take you for granted. They judge your decisions even when they have not read the case file and are not conversant with the law or facts of the case. It is distracting and discouraging when they falsely accuse you of corruption, bias, and ignorance of the law, especially if you are a chief justice or head of a court. Your job is a thankless job that only your legacy, and posterity can reward. You will always be a judge even after retirement.

For the newly appointed judges, you have made a good choice, if your intentions are genuine (as I know several people decide to be judges for the wrong reasons). Before you go deep into the case, please note and never forget that your decision, no matter how simple or insignificant it appears, goes a long way to impact more than the litigants before you. It has the potential to lay the platform for a precedent that can either develop or destroy law and society. So, I respectfully admonish you with the words of my mentor, Justice Amina Adamu Augie, JSC, Rtd.– "*We must always have posterity in mind….whatever we are writing, we should remember that one day, in a hundred years' time, one of your great-grandchildren or somebody is reading whatever rubbish you have written, or something sublime that you have written….*"

Accordingly, I employ you to serve with integrity so that posterity will judge you upright. No matter the social or political intimidations, remain consistent on the path of justice. Persevere amidst adversity. I tweak the words of Hon. Justice Augie and hope that long after you have gone, may your words speak for you; may your words teach, motivate, and inspire positive social change.

I end with a quote from one of the most valuable laws of time, a research book that speaks of the act of judging. It says as follows:

> **16 And I charged your judges at that time, "Hear the disputes between your people and judge fairly, whether the case is between two Israelites or between an Israelite and a foreigner residing among you. 17 Do not show partiality in judging; hear both small and great alike. Do not be afraid of anyone, for judgment belongs to God. Bring me any case too hard for you, and I will hear it."**
>
> **–The Holy Bible, NIV Version Deuteronomy 1: 16–17**

May the judicial oath of office that you have taken guide you and so help you, God.

Well done and good luck!

Respectfully

Arinikitobi

Ari Niki-Tobi
atsjconsulting@gmail.com

Bibliography

Abdulwahab, A. A. (2009, September 1). Drama as Court Resumes case on Threat to Adefaye's Life. *Vanguard Newspaper.* Retrieved from <https://www.google.com/url?sa=t&rct=j&q=&esrc=s&source=web&cd=11&cad=rja&uact=8&ved=2ahUKEwiHo-L39JfhAhUriOAKHYW8A_oQFjAKegQIAxAB&url=https%3A%2F%2Fwww.vanguardngr.com%2F2009%2F09%2Fdrama-as-court-resumes-case-on-threat-to-adefayes-life%2F&usg=AOvVaw1W_9-oNoHB5BXH0ZUJ2Dj6>

Abhulimhen-Iyoha, A. (2015). Judicial Discretion of Judges in Criminal Cases in Nigeria: Prospects and Challenges. Retrieved from <https://www.google.com/url?sa=t&rct=j&q=&esrc=s&source=web&cd=1&cad=rja&uact=8&ved=2ahUKEwjC1dWAgIHhAhVBUt8KHbrBBKYQFjAAegQIBxAC&url=http%3A%2F%2Fwww.nigerianlawguru.com%2Farticles%2Fcriminal%2520law%2520and%2520procedure%2FJUDICIAL%2520DISCRETION%2520OF%2520JUDGES%2520IN%2520CRIMINAL%2520CASES%2520IN%2520NIGERIA.pdf&usg=AOvVaw2Arw4TmkrLjOzrDP-IyNBB>

Abiru, H. A. (2018). *The Law as It Is – The Place of Social and Moral Values in Contemporary Nigeria* – Symposium conducted at the at the 60th Birthday Celebration of Professor Imran Oluwole Smith (SAN). Lagos, Nigeria.

Adebayo W. (2014, October 27). Yoruba Precolonial Political System. *Nigerian History.* Retrieved from <https://www.google.com/url?sa=t&rct=j&q=&esrc=s&source=web&cd=1&ved=2ahUKEwj7rKOv6JviAhVO_J4KHYxGBnAQFjAAegQIBBAB&url=https%3A%2F%2Fwaidigbenro.wordpress.com%2F2014%2F10%2F27%2Fyoruba-precolonial-political-system%2F&usg=AOvVaw3zRSVPHmZAG5SfyxU0z4Va>

Ademola, A. (1962). Personal Problems in the Administration of Justice in Nigeria. *Law and Contemporary Problems,* 27 (4), 576–580. Retrieved fro<m <https://www.google.com/url?sa=t&rct=j&q=&esrc=s&source=web&cd=3&ved=2ahUKEwjS5Mn

P1qHfAhVK9YMKHZWXDJwQFjACegQIAhAB&url=http%3A%2F%2Fscholarship.law.duke.edu%2Flcp%2Fvol27%2Fiss4%2F3%2F&usg=AOvVaw30irYUBEnU2jwunHDXmF4R>

Adu, D., Adeola., & Adepoju, B. (2018). Burden of Proof in the Prosecution of Unexplained Wealth in Nigeria – Examining the Similarity Between Daudu v. FRN and Zamira Hajieva's Case. Retrieved from <https://www.google.com/url?sa=t&rct=j&q=&esrc=s&source=web&cd=1&cad=rja&uact=8&ved=2ahUKEwjIzuvR6ZviAhXT6Z4KHRrnBSAQFjAAegQIARAB&url=https%3A%2F%2Fwww.lexology.com%2Flibrary%2Fdetail.aspx%3Fg%3D329b5c8c-627f-4dfc-a44e-66d4d0e594e6&usg=AOvVaw2Dxfj1Ly87ktkvgPr0ikhl>

Aguda, T. A. (1986). *The Crisis of Justice*. Akure, Nigeria: Eresu Hill Publishers.

Agbakoba, O. (2024, August 7) The Threats of Artificial Intelligence (AI) on the Legal and Regulatory Systems – All You Need to Know. Mondaq. <https://www.mondaq.com/nigeria/new-technology/1501938/the-threats-of-artificial-intelligence-ai-on-the-legal-and-regulatory-systems-all-you-need-to-know>

Barak, A. (2006). *The Judge in a Democracy*. Princeton: Princeton University Press.

Brannon, V. C. (2018). *Statutory Interpretation: Theories, Tools, and Trends.* Retrieved from Congressional Research Service: <https://www.google.com/url?sa=t&rct=j&q=&esrc=s&source=web&cd=1&ved=2ahUKEwjO1rP09ufgAhXoYt8KHQkjDV4QFjAAegQICxAC&url=https%3A%2F%2Ffas.org%2Fsgp%2Fcrs%2Fmisc%2FR45153.pdf&usg=AOvVaw38eQKtS7ob6CExDpDSqKM9>

Breyer, S. (2005). *Active Liberty, Interpreting Our Democratic Constitution*. New York: Vintage Books.

Bunker, M. D. (1997). *Justice and the Media*. Mahwah, N.J.: Erlbaum.

Black, H. C. (1968). *Black's Law Dictionary* (4th Edition). Retrieved from <https://www.google.com/url?sa=t&rct=j&q=&esrc=s&source=web&cd=1&cad=rja&uact=8&ved=2ahUKEwis5MSWzurgAhWhTd8KHUbbCS8QFjAAegQICBAC&url=http%3A%2F%2Fheimatundrecht.de%2Fsites%2Fdefault%2Ffiles%2Fdokumente%2FBlack%2527sLaw4th.pdf&usg=AOvVaw0i6MK7kA7STYNu0xG1Crn1>

Cardozo, B. N. (1921). *The Nature of the Judicial Process*. USA: Yale University Press.

Chief Justice Sundaresh Menon, keynote Speech, Inaugural Singapore-India Conference on Technology. SG Courts. <https://www.judiciary.gov.sg/news-and-resources/news/news-details/media-release--supreme-court-of-singapore-and-supreme-court-of-india-hold-inaugural-singapore-india-conference-on technology#:~:text=In%20his%20speech%2C%20Chief%20Justice,will%20affect%20our%20justice%20systems>

Coplan. K. S., Legal Realism, Innate Morality, and the Structural Role of the Supreme Court in the U.S. Constitutional Democracy, 86 Tulane L. Rev. 181 (2011), <http://digitalcommons.pace.edu/lawfaculty/809/.at.p. 206

Duxbury, N. (2001). *Patterns of American Jurisprudence*. USA: Oxford University Press.

Easterbrook, F. H. (2004). Judicial Discretion in Statutory Interpretation. *Oklahoma Law Review*, 57 (1), 1–20. Retrieved from <https://www.google.com/url?sa=t&rct=j&q=&esrc=s&source=web&cd=1&ved=2ahUKEwiBytW5k4HhAhWMMd8KHSl0DtMQFjAAegQICBAB&url=https%3A%2F%2Fchicagounbound.uchicago.edu%2Fcgi%2Fviewcontent.cgi%3Farticle%3D2136%26context%3Djournal_articles&usg=AOvVaw3TdzlToU3o_rjwIVtUghO8>

Eig, M. E. (2014). *Statutory Interpretation: General Principles and Recent Trends.* Retrieved from Congressional Research Service. <https://www.google.com/url?sa=t&rct=j&q=&esrc=s&source=web&cd=1&cad=rja&uact=8&ved=2ahUKEwitr8WVycbgAhUJMt8KHRNCAboQFjAAegQICxAC&url=https%3A%2F%2Ffas.org%2Fsgp%2Fcrs%2Fmisc%2F97-589.pdf&usg=AOvVaw0kMcMLBrEJ6P4Ejx2bFo2q>

Garner, B. A. (2004). *Black's Law Dictionary* (8th Edition). Retrieved from <https://www.google.com/url?sa=t&rct=j&q=&esrc=s&source=web&cd=4&ved=2ahUKEwjvtKfzsZviAhWLqZ4KHemhAS0QFjADegQIBBAC&url=http%3A%2F%2Fwww.republicsg.info%2FDictionaries%2F2004_Black%2527s-Law-Dictionary-Edition-8.pdf&usg=AOvVaw0j68bErKaq5VZxalJkRStz>

Gbamgbose, O. J. (2014). *The Digest of Judgments of the Supreme Court of Nigeria.* (Vol. 3 and 4). Nigeria: Safari Books.

Greenwood, C. Sources of International Law. <https://www.google.com/url?sa=t&source=web&rct=j&opi=89978449&url=https://www.studocu.com/row/document/university-of-zimbabwe/human-rights-law/greenwood-outline-sources/94920012&ved=2ahUKEwifhsSuu7uKAxW8kYkEHUHrAT8QFnoECBoQAQ&usg=AOvVaw2PWY4qJGts67nMgJPMZSUf>

Hine, K. D. (1997). The Rule of Law is Dead, Long Live the Rule: An Essay on Legal Rules, Equitable Standards, and the Debate Over Judicial Discretion. *SMU Law Review, 50* (5), 1770–1788. Retrieved from <https://scholar.smu.edu/smulr/vol50/iss5/12>

Idahosa, C. O. (2016, 21–25 November). *The Doctrine of Stare – Decisis and Judicial Precedent: The Need for Lower Courts to Be Bound by Decisions of The Superior Courts of Record*. Conference of all Nigerian Lower Court Judges, Abuja, Nigeria.

Idem, U. J. (2017). The Judiciary and the Role of Customary Courts in Nigeria. *Global Journal of Politics and Law Research, 5* (6), 34–49, UK: European Centre for Research Training and Development. Retrieved f<rom <https://www.google.com/url?sa=t&rct=j&q=&esrc=s&source=web&cd=2&cad=rja&uact=8&ved=2ahUKEwjus_nji53iAhWMCjQIHU1OBGsQFjABegQIDhAE&url=http%3A%2F%2Fwww.eajournals.org%2Fwp-content%2Fuploads%2FThe-Judiciary-and-the-Role-of-Customary-Courts-in-Nigeria.pdf&usg=AOvVaw1MaOXKIJzme_Z_oGT_Wjo7>

Ijaiya, H. O. (2017). *Constitutional Approach to Interpretation of the Constitutions in Nigeria, Australia, Canada and India*. Lagos, Nigeria: Malthouse Press Ltd.

Imam, I. (2015). Judicial Activism in Nigeria: Delineating the Extend of Legislative-Judicial Engagement in Law Making. *International and Comparative Law Review, 15* (1), 109–127. Retrieved from <https://www.google.com/url?sa=t&rct=j&q=&esrc=s&source=web&cd=2&ved=2ahUKEwjS182xyJffAhXoRd8KHR6vBi4QFjABegQICRAC&url=http%3A%2F%2Ficlr.upol.cz%2Fwp-content%2Fuploads%2F2016%2F06%2Ficlr_1_2015.pdf&usg=AOvVaw3jIcsOtYSo-d3mIe4vZ3sr>

Kana, A. A. (2014). Perspectives and Limits of Judicial Discretion in Nigerian Courts. *Journal of Law, Policy and Globalization, 29*, 157-166. Retrieved from <https://www.google.com/url?sa=t&rct=j&q=&esrc=s&source=web&cd=1&ved=2ahUKEwiHy7u7vIPhAhVI2oMKHaPgB_UQFjAAegQIARAC&url=https%3A%2F%2Fwww.iiste.org%2FJournals%2Findex.php%2FJLPG%2Farticle%2Fdownload%2F15935%2F16403&usg=AOvVaw04sB_Q41d82vEGXYjxc5Yo>

Kelso, R. R (1994) Styles of Constitutional Interpretation and the Four Main Approaches to Constitutional Interpretation in American Legal

History. *Valparaiso University Law Review, 9* (1), 121–223. Retrieved from <https://www.google.com/url?sa=t&rct=j&q=&esrc=s&source=web&cd=14&ved=2ahUKEwj78L-8lcrgAhUNPN8KHSk0B2EQFjANegQIBRAC&url=https%3A%2F%2Fscholar.valpo.edu%2Fcgi%2Fviewcontent.cgi%3Farticle%3D1924%26context%3Dvulr&usg=AOvVaw1cytGf8-fQHX9XzqGJbZTg>

Konrad-Adenauer, S. (2003). UNODC Working Paper "Selection and Appointment of Judges in Nigeria, Analysis and Recommendations" p. 6.

Kopp, L. Q. (2018, February 20.). *Replacing Judges with Computers is Risky* [Web log post]. Retrieved from <https://Www.Google.Com/Url?Sa=T&Rct=J&Q=&Esrc=S&Source=Web&Cd=1&Cad=Rja&Uact=8&Ved=2ahukewjdiolf09lfahxd5omkhw93cseqfjaaegqiaxab&Url=Https%3a%2f%2fblog.Harvardlawreview.Org%2freplacing-Judges-With-Computers-Is-Risky%2f&Usg=Aovvaw3gjdebvhvqf_Yzte7fngsr>

Larsen, J. H. (2018). *How to Use Images to Draw Conclusions in Legal Reasoning* (master's thesis). University of Nevada, Reno. Available from <http://hdl.handle.net/11714/3344>

Lessig L., Scalia: The Legal Sociologist. *Harvard Journal of Law & Public Policy Per Curiam. No.4 Winter 2023.*

Miller, A. S. and Howell, R. F. (1960). The Myth of Neutrality in Constitutional Adjudication. *University of Chicago Law Review, 27* (4), 661–695. Retrieved from< <https://www.google.com/url?sa=t&rct=j&q=&esrc=s&source=web&cd=1&ved=2ahUKEwj6_MT92qHfAhUE94MKHS3ZDMcQFjAAegQICRAC&url=https%3A%2F%2Fchicagounbound.uchicago.edu%2Fcgi%2Fviewcontent.cgi%3Farticle%3D3205%26context%3Duclrev&usg=AOvVaw1Be-Q9mGSou1dtE_0KCyDw>

Monahan, J. & Walker, L. (2014). *Social Science in Law* (8th Edition). New York, NY: Thompson Foundation.

Murgan, M. G, Kwagyang, G. U., & Azeez Bello, S. A. (2015). Judicial Precedent and the Prevention of Contradictory Judgments: An Expository Study of Compliance with Judicial Precedent in Malaysian and Nigerian Courts. *Journal of Humanities and Social Science, 20* (11), 65–75.

Murrill, B. J (2018). *The Supreme Courts Overruling of Constitutional Precedent*. Retrieved from Congressional Research Service: <https://www.google.com/url?sa=t&rct=j&q=&esrc=s&source=web&cd=21&cad=rja&uact=8&ved=2ahUKEwiPsLm_urLgAhVGmeAKHfpIAMgQFjAUegQICBAC&url=https%3A%2F%2Ffas.

org%2Fsgp%2Fcrs%2Fmisc%2FR45319.
pdf&usg=AOvVaw2o-4aTrsVN3_-rWmirTqSe>

Murrill, B. J. (2018). Modes of Constitutional Interpretation. Retrieved from Congressional Research Service: <https://www.google.com/url?sa=t&rct=j&q=&esrc=s&source=web&cd=1&cad=rja&uact=8&ved=2ahUKEwiJtufn9pviAhUFrp4KHW3MCS0QFjAAegQIABAC&url=https%3A%2F%2Ffas.org%2Fsgp%2Fcrs%2Fmisc%2FR45129.pdf&usg=AOvVaw13xjfsmv8uUYolf_N_yQZS>

Mustapha, D. (2011). *The Nigerian Judiciary: Towards Reform of the Bastion of Constitutional Democracy.* Lagos, Nigeria: Nigerian Institute of Advanced Legal Studies.

Newman, T. R. & Ahnuty, J. S. (2015, May 7). Urging a Change in the Law: When to set Aside Precedent? *Duane Morris*. Retrieved from <https://www.google.com/url?sa=t&rct=j&q=&esrc=s&source=web&cd=1&cad=rja&uact=8&ved=2ahUKEwiO6qqk95viAhUXrp4KHQZjB5gQFjAAegQIARAB&url=http%3A%2F%2Fwww.mondaq.com%2Funitedstates%2Fx%2F395454%2Ftrials%2Bappeals%2Bcompensation%2FUrging%2Ba%2BChange%2Bin%2Bthe%2BLaw%2BWhen%2Bto%2BSet%2BAside%2BPrecedent&usg=AOvVaw03iZfnMIAXuo4w6EbOn8W8>

Nigeria-United Nations. *Sustainable Urban Development and Good Governance in Nigeria*. Retrieved from <https://www.google.com/url?sa=t&rct=j&q=&esrc=s&source=web&cd=12&ved=2ahUKEwikwLaq4qbhAhUlTd8KHcitC40QFjALegQIABAC&url=http%3A%2F%2Fwww.un.org%2Fga%2FIstanbul%2B5%2F12-Nigeria.doc&usg=AOvVaw0SUEU43cXONo3qsBapqKNO>

Niki-Tobi, A. AI and Courts: A Socio-Judicial Dilemma. International Association of Court Administrators Conference, Singapore. November 12, 2024.

Niki-Tobi, A. (2022, April 25). "The Impact of Judicial Precedent on Societal Development." (Courts & Society Webinar Series, 1st Edition) A.T. Socio-Judicial Consulting. Available at <https://youtu.be/KfQytGfFexE>

Niki-Tobi, A. (2022, July 21) *The Courts as Agents of Social Change* (Courts & Society Webinar Series, 2nd Edition) A.T. Socio-Judicial Consulting. https://atsjconsulting.com/

Niki-Tobi, A. (2024, December 12). The Court's Role in Implementing Human Rights (Courts & Society Webinar Series, 10th Special Edition)

A.T. Socio-Judicial Consulting. also available <https://atsjconsulting.com/>

Nwanbueze, B. (2004). *Constitutional Democracy in Africa*, (Vol. 3), Nigeria: Spectrum Books.

Ogbuagu, U and Takuru, K. (n.d.). Innovations for the development of remote justice in Nigeria.

Ojomo, E. *History of the Nigerian Judicial System, Introduction to Law* [PDF Document]. Retrieved from Lecture notes outline website: <https://www.google.com/url?sa=t&rct=j&q=&esrc=s&source=web&cd=2&cad=rja&uact=8&ved=2ahUKEwjhv5WewvrhAhVqmeAKHZ_gCgkQFjABegQIARAC&url=http%3A%2F%2Fwww.yararena.org%2Fuploads%2FTopic%2520Two%2520-%2520History%2520of%2520the%2520Nigerian%2520Judicial%2520System.pdf&usg=AOvVaw3ppQcNnQesk6nazn4_SejL>

Olong, A. M. (2007). *The Nigerian Legal System, An Introduction* (2nd edition). Lagos, Nigeria: Malthouse Press Limited.

Oniha, B. (n.d.). Legality of Euthanasia and The Right to Die in Nigeria. P.12, available at <https://edojudiciary.gov.ng/wp-content/uploads/2017/07/LEGALITY-OF-EUTHANASIA-AND-THE-RIGHT-TO-DIE-IN-NIGERIA-BY-BRIGHT-E.-ONIHA-CORRECTED.pdf>

Oshio, P. E. (n.d.). Towards a Purposeful Approach to the Interpretation of the 1999 Constitution. Retrieved from< <https://www.google.com/url?sa=t&rct=j&q=&esrc=s&source=web&cd=1&cad=rja&uact=8&ved=2ahUKEwi7xuuYjfrhAhWDJjQIHWZ-A3sQFjAAegQIABAC&url=http%3A%2F%2Fwww.nigerianlawguru.com%2Farticles%2Fconstitutional%2520law%2FTOWARDS%2520A%2520PURPOSIVE%2520APPROACH%2520TO%2520THE%2520INTERPRETATION%2520OF%2520THE%25201999%2520CONSTITUTION.pdf&usg=AOvVaw1WG8IfxzpIkXYKfNhwBVxw>

Osipitan, T. (2018). Supreme Court of Nigeria and Stare Decisis. Paper presented in Honor of professor Akin Oyebode at University of Lagos: Nigeria.

Posner, R. (2012). The Incoherence of Antonin Scalia. <https://www.law.nyu.edu/sites/default/files/Posner%2C%20Richard%20A.%2C%20%27The%20Incoherence%20of%20Antonin%20Scalia%27%20The%20New%20Republic.pdf>

Posner, R. A. (2013). *Reflections on Judging*. USA: Harvard University Press.

Prasad, B. B. “Sources of International Law” International Journal of Scientific Research in Multidisciplinary Studies, Vol.5, Issue.11, pp.80–88, November (2019) at p. 81.

Prestidge, A. (2010). “Semantic Change in Supreme Context: Semantics in the Privacy Line and Originalist Interpretation,” *Brigham Young University Prelaw Review: 24* (26). Retrieved from <https://scholarsarchive.byu.edu/byuplr/vol24/iss1/26>

Posner, R. A. & Gluck, A. R. (2019). Statutory Interpretation on the Bench: A Survey of Forty-Two Judges on the Federal Courts of Appeal. *Harvard Law Review,* 131(1298),1298–1378. Retrieved fr<om <https://www.google.com/url?sa=t&rct=j&q=&esrc=s&source=web&cd=2&cad=rja&uact=8&ved=2ahUKEwjX_b2ftNfhAhXB1lkKHdwFBF4QFjABegQIABAB&url=https%3A%2F%2Fharvardlawreview.org%2F2018%2F03%2Fstatutory-interpretation-on-the-bench-a-survey-of-forty-two-judges-on-the-federal-courts-of-appeals%2F&usg=AOvVaw30b4XmJLjQng0tdVip9Bg1>

Simmons, B “International Law” Handbook of International Relations, <https://www.google.com/url?sa=t&rct=j&q=&esrc=s&source=web&cd=&ved=2ahUKEwiogaey_O71AhVwRN8KHXuMBb4QFnoECAYQAw&url=https%3A%2F%2Fscholar.harvard.edu%2Ffiles%2Fbsimmons%2Ffiles%2Fch_14_-_international_law.pdf&usg=AOvVaw00ILhm2I--9ZsowZ_6o6Nr>

Smithburn, J. E. (2006). *Judicial Discretion*. Reno, Nevada: NJC Press.

Sokefun, J. & Njoku, N. C. (2016). The court System in Nigeria: Jurisdiction and Appeals. *International Journal of Business and Applied Social Science*, 2(3). Retrieved from <https://www.google.com/url?sa=t&rct=j&q=&esrc=s&source=web&cd=1&cad=rja&uact=8&ved=2ahUKEwip4tbi5crgAhVyUN8KHV-pAEkQFjAAegQICRAC&url=https%3A%2F%2Fijbassnet.com%2Fstorage%2Fapp%2Fpublications%2F56fcacaab8e9511459399850.pdf&usg=AOvVaw0gxxnTWhuWDTzf6wuHWtGZ>

Stumpf, F. F. (2008). *Inherent Powers of the Court*. Reno, Nevada: NJC Press.

Sule, I., Olurunyemi, F., Ajah, J., & Usman, A. (2024) Virtual Court Proceedings in Nigeria: Some Legal Matters Arising. European Journal of Law and Political Science Vol 3 | Issue 3 | May 2024 ISSN 2796–1176 at PP 17–22

Sutherland, E.H, "Differential Association Theory and Differential Social Organization." Encyclopedia of Criminological Theory. (2010) Sage Publications.

Tobi, A. "Right to Adequate Housing" The Guardian National Daily Newspaper (December 2, 2003) p. 56

Tobi-Aiyemo, A. (2016). Mainstreaming Gender in the Development of Family Law in a Borderless World; The Nigerian Perspective. *Commonwealth Magistrates' and Judges Association Gender Section Newsletter.* 3(2), 5–11.

Tobi-Aiyemo, A. (2017). The Intermediate Obligation of a Judge Vis a Vis Law and Society: A Matter of Interpretation. Unpublished manuscript, Department of Judicial Studies, University of Nevada, Reno.

Tobi-Aiyemo, A. (unpublished), *International Law in a Borderless World: The Role of a Judge* the International Law and Organizations Seminar, State University of New York, Oneonta. September 17th, 2019, at 109 Schumacher Hall, SUNY Oneonta, New York State.

Tobi-Aiyemo, A. (2022). "The Role of Courts in Shaping Human Rights in a Borderless World." The City University of New York, Slide 8

Tobi, N. (1992). *The Nigerian Judge*. Nigeria: A.T.&T Professional Publishers.

Uchechukwu, C. U. (2024) The Administration of Bail in the Nigerian Legal System. SSRN Electronic Journal. 10.2139/ssrn.4795594

Ukeje, R. N. (2018). *Intrinsic and Extrinsic Aids to the Interpretation of the Constitution, Statutes and Private Documents*. Lagos, Nigeria: ECOWATCH Publications (Nig.) Ltd.

UN News (2016, September 20). Corruption is A Major Obstacle to Achieving Agenda 2030.*UN News.* Retrieved from <https://www.google.com/url?sa=t&rct=j&q=&esrc=s&source=web&cd=6&cad=rja&uact=8&ved=2ahUKEwiNt4jswMHhAhVNT98KHUzSAGAQFjAFegQIAxAB&url=https%3A%2F%2Fnews.un.org%2Fen%2Fstory%2F2016%2F09%2F539632-corruption-major-obstacle-achieving-agenda-2030-nigerian-leader-tells-un&usg=AOvVaw3BMpmVWyCh_CdhVArsuOrF>

UN Press 8962nd MEETING. SC/14788. <https://press.un.org/en/2022/sc14788.doc.htm> 7 February 2022

Van Boom, W. H. (2004). Some Remarks on the Decline of Rylands v. Fletcher and the Disparity of European Strict Liability Regimes. *SSRN Electronic Journal*. Doi:10.2139/ssrn.694241.

Wex Legal Dictionary. (n.d.). <https://www.google.com/url?sa=t&rct=j&q=&esrc=s&source=web&cd=10&cad=rja&uact=8&ved=2ahUKEwiGmJaao8PkAhUk01kKHRpjBu4QFjAJegQIARAB&url=https%3A%2F%2Fwww.law.cornell.edu%2Fwex%2Finternational_law&usg=AOvVaw1UtKwdipT8c_Y11a8TJIm8>

Walker, J. M. (2016). The Role of Precedent in United States: How Do Precedents Lose Their Binding Effects? *Stanford Law School*. Retrieved from <https://www.google.com/url?sa=t&rct=j&q=&esrc=s&source=web&cd=11&cad=rja&uact=8&ved=2ahUKEwiPsLm_urLgAhVGmeAKHfpIAMgQFjAKegQIABAB&url=https%3A%2F%2Fcgc.law.stanford.edu%2Fcommentaries%2F15-john-walker%2F&usg=AOvVaw3tlVfRof4bjWp7lzqqhRAu>

Merriam Webster Dictionary. (2019). Retrieved from <https://www.google.com/url?sa=t&rct=j&q=&esrc=s&source=web&cd=12&cad=rja&uact=8&ved=2ahUKEwiryuCw3qvgAhUpWN8KHWoqCS4QFjALegQICRAB&url=https%3A%2F%2Fwww.merriam-webster.com%2Fdictionary%2Fcontext&usg=AOvVaw1SR9RjidizGjJz1t3g1M6m>

Zonay, T. A. (2015). *Judicial Discretion: Ten Guidelines for its use*. The Judicial Edge, The Reno, Nevada: National Judicial College. Retrieved from <https://www.judges.org/judicial-discretion-ten-guidelines-for-its-use/>

Appendix

List of Legislations

The Constitution of the Federal Republic of Nigeria
The Constitution of the United States of America
The Federal Republic of Nigeria Code of Conduct for Judicial Officers
The Independence Constitution of 1960
The Interpretation Act, Cap 17, Laws of the Federation of Nigeria (LFN) 2004
The Federal Capital Territory Courts (Sentencing Guidelines) Practice Direction, 2016
The Compulsory, Free Universal Basic Education Act, 2004
The National Judicial Commission Rules
The Guidelines of the Supreme Court of Nigeria
The Fundamental Human Rights Procedure Enforcement Rules, 2009
The Lagos High Court Rules
The International Court of Justice (ICJ)
The African Charter on Human and Peoples' Rights
The Discrimination (Employment and Occupation) Convention, 1958 (No 111)
Lagos State Judiciary (Sentencing Guidelines) Practice Directives, 2018

List of Cases

Nigerian Cases

Abacha v. Fawehinmi (2000) 4 FWLR 533
Abacha v. The State (2002) 11 NWLR (pt779) 437 at 484
Abegunde v. The Ondo State House of Assembly & Ors (2014) LPELR-23683 (CA)
Abiodun v. FRN (2018) LPELR-43838(SC) Pp. 18–19, Paras. C-A
Adedeji v. The State (1992) 4 NWLR (Pt. 234) 248 at 265
Adeleke v. Oyo State House of Assembly (2006) 6 NWLR (Pt 1006) 608
Abdulkarim v. INCAR Nigeria Ltd (1992) 7 SCNJ P.366
Abubakar & Ors. v. Yar'Adua & Ors. (2008) LPELR-51 (SC)

AC & Anor v. INEC (2007) LPELR-66 (SC)
A.C.B. Ltd. v. Nnamani (1991) 4 NWLR (Pt. 186) 486
Adejumo v. Military Governor Lagos State (1972) 3 SC 45
Adelaja v. C.M.S. Grammar School Bariga & Ors (2017) LPELR-42729(CA) at 11
Adebayo v. Okonkwo (2002) 8 NWLR (pt. 768) 1
Adegbenro v. Akintola (1963)3W.L. R 63
Adeyemi & Ors. v. O. Achimu/Ndic/Assurance Bank Ltd & Ors, supra, at p.17 Abiru, JCA
Adisa v. Oyinwola (2000) 10 NWLR (Pt. 674) 116 at P.168
Asims (Nig) Limited v. Lower Benue River Basin (2002) 8 NWLR (Pt. 769) 349
Afro-Continental (Nigeria) Ltd. v. Co. Operative Association of Professionals Inc. (2003) 5 NWLR (Pt. 813) 303
Agwuna v. A.G. Federation (1995) LPELR-258(SC)
Adegoke Motors Ltd. v. Dr. Babatunde Adesanya & Anor (1989) LPELR-94(SC)
Action Congress (Ac) And Anor v. INEC (2007) 12 NWLR (PT. 1048) 222 at 259
A.G Abia State v. A.G Federation (2002) 3 SC 106 at 164
A.G Abia State v. A.G Federation (2006) 16 NWLR (pt. 1005) 265
A.G Lagos State v. Mamman Keita (2016) LPELR-40163 (CA) 15–16
A.G. Federation v. Abubakar (2007) 10 NWLR (pt.1041) 1 at 118, G-H
Alkamawa v. Bello (1998) 8 NWLR (pt.561) 173
A.G of Lagos v. A.G Of federation & 35 Ors (2003) 35 W.R.N97
A.G. Lagos State v. A.G. Federation (2013)16 NWLR (pt. 1380)383, Para D-E
A.G. Ogun State v. Aberuagba (1985) 1 NWLR (pt. 3) 395
A.G Bendel Sate v. A.G federation (1981) SC 1
A.G Bendel State v. A.G Federation and 22 Ors (1983) NCLR 1 at 40
Attorney General, Federation v. Attorney General, Lagos State (2013) 16 NWLR (Pt 1380) 249
A.G Federation v. Alhaji Atiku Abubakar (Appeal No. CA/A/21/07, delivered on 5th April 2007)
A.G Bendel Sate v. A.G federation, supra
A.G Ogun State and Anor v. Dr. L.C. Egenty (1986) 1 C.A. (pt. 11) page 162
Attorney General of the Federation v. Abubakar (2007)10 N.W.L.R (PT 1041) 1 @ 171–172
Agbaje v. Fashola (2008) All FWLR (pt.443) 1302 at 1337 B-C

Akeredolu v. Abraham & Ors (2018) LPELR- 44067 (SC)
Akinyemi v. Odu'a Inv. Co. Ltd (2012) LPELR 3270 (SC) 39
Akpamgbo-Okadigbo v. Chidi & 7 Ors (2015) LPELR-25464 (SC) 28
Akpughunum v. Akpughunum (2007) ALL FWLR (Pt. 376) 746 at 758 Paras. B-D (CA)
Ajuwa v. SPDC Ltd. (2011) 18 NWLR (Pt.1279) 787
Ali v. Albishir (2008) 3 NWLR (Pt. 1073) 94 at Pp. 130–131, paras. H-A
Alhaji Isiyaku Yakubu Ent Ltd v. Tarfa & Anor (2014) LPELR-24223 (CA)
Alioke v. Oye & Ors (2018) LPELR-45153 (SC)
Amos Motors Nigeria Limited & Anor v. Agboola (2012) LPELR-8011 (CA)
Archbishop Anthony Okogie and Others v. The Attorney General of Lagos State (1981) 2 NCLR 350
Awolowo v. Shehu Shagari (1979) 6–9 SC51 at 64
Achi v. Ebenighe (2014) 4 NWLR (Pt.1397) 380
Aboseldehyde Lab. Plc. v. U.M.B. Ltd. (2013) 13 NWLR (Pt.1370) 91 @ pp. 97–98
Araka v. Egbue (2003) 3 WRN 20
Aroh v. PDP (2013) 13 NWLR (Pt.1371) 235
Abiodun v. CJ. Kwara State (2007) 18 NWLR (Pt.1065) 109 @ p.152
Adeniji v. Adeniji (2013) 15 NWLR (Pt.1376) 102 @ p. 125
Anyah v. African Newspaper of Nig. Ltd (1992) LPELR-511 (SC)
Amobi v. Nzegwu & Ors (2013) vol. 12 MJSC Pt. 1 at page 1
Adeyemi & Ors. v. O. Achimu/Ndic/Assurance Bank Ltd & Ors (2015) LPELR-24379 (CA) pp.43–47
APC & Ors. v. In Re: CPC & Ors (2014) LPELR-24036 (SC)
Adegoke Motors Ltd v. Adesanya (1989) 3 NWLR (pt109) at 266
Alioke v. Oye & Ors (2018) LPELR-45153(SC) Hon. Justice Bage, JSC (P. 24, Paras. A-B)
Agu v. Nicon Ins Plc. (2009) 11 NWLR (PT. 677) 187 @ P. 194
Airhiavbere v. Oshiomhole & Ors (2012) LPELR-19787 (CA)
Artra Industries Nigeria Ltd v. The Nigerian Bank for Commerce and Industries (1998) 4 NWLR (Pt. 546) 381 SC
Atiku v. The State (2002) 4 NWLR (Pt. 757) 265
Augustine Nwafor Mojekwu v. Mrs. Theresa Iwuchukwu (2004) LPELR-1903 (SC)
Awani v. Erejuwa 11 (1976) H SC 307
Awojugbagbe Light Industries Ltd. v. P. N. Chinukwe & Anor (1995) 4 NWLR (Part 390) 379; (1995) 4 SCNJ 1
Awure & Anor. v. Iledu (2007) LPELR-3719 (CA)

Awuse v. Odili (2003) 18 NWLR (Pt. 851) 116 at 179, C.
Awosika v. State (2018) LPELR-44351(SC)
Bassey v. A.G Akwa Ibom State & Ors (2016) LPELR-41244 (CA)
Balogun v. Salami (1963) 1 All NLR 129
Board of Customs and Excise v. Bolarinwa (1968) NMLR 350 at 352,
Bronik Motors Ltd & Anor v. Wema Bank (1983) 1 SCNLR 296,
Brooks v. Canada Safeway Ltd (1989) 1S.C. R
Busari v. Ose (1992) LPELR-14981 (CA)
British American Tobacco (Investments) Ltd v. A.G. Of Lagos State & Ors (2014) LPELR-23200 (CA)
Busari & Ors v. Oseni & Ors (1992) LPELR-14981 (CA) Paras B-C
Buhari v. Obasanjo (No.3) (2004) 1 W.R.N. Page 1 at 46
Caribbean Trading & Fidelity Corporation v. Nigerian National Petroleum Corporation (2002) 5 SC (Pt. I) at page 21
Celtel Nig B.V v. ECONET Wireless Ltd & Ors (2014) LPELR 22430 (CA)
Chibuike Amaechi v. INEC (2008) 5 NWLR (Pt 1080)Chief Awolowo v. Alhaji Shagari (1979) 6–9 SC 51
Chief Nicholas Banna v. Telepower Nigeria Ltd (2006) 7 SCNJ 182
Chief Emma Onuorah Emesim v. Hon. Calista Nwachukwu (Mrs.) & Ors (1999) LPELR-6573(CA)PP.33–34, para-D-B
Commissioner of Police v. Yahaya Sheriff-Aminu, (Unreported) Case No. CR/43/2020.Dada v. Commissioner of Police v. Jelilie Lawal & Kehinde Oyelara (Unreported), Charge No. L/8/2009. Igbosere Magistrate Court, Lagos State, Nigeria
Davies & Ors v. Odofin & Ors (2017) LPELR-41871(CA)
Daudu v. FRN (2018) 10 NWLR (Pt.1626) 169, 183 E -F (2018) LPELR-43637 (SC)
Dasofunjo v. Ajiboye (2017) LPELR-42354 (CA)
Dalhatu v. Turaki (2003) 15 NWLR Pt. 843 page 310 at 323
Dantsoho v. Mohammed (2003) 6 NWLR (pt.817) 457 at 492
Dickson v. Sylva & Ors (2016) LPELR-41257 (SC) P.78, para-C -F
Doherty v. Doherty (1960) 1 All NLR 299
Dingyadi v. INEC (2011) 10 NWLR (1255) 347
Dapianlong & Ors v. Dariye & Anor (2007) LPELR-928 (SC)
Deen Mark Constr. Co Ltd v. Abiola (2002) 3 NWLR (PT. 754) 418 @ PP. 449 – 450
Dyeris v. Mobil Oil Nigeria Limited (2010) 1 NWLR (PT. 1175) 309
D.Y.S. Trocca Valsesia & Co. v. Osaghae (2008) ALL FWLR (Pt.413)1313 at P. 1335, paras C – E A

Eboreime v. Olagbegi & Ors (2018) LPELR-44816 (CA)
Egbo v. Agbara (1997) 1 NWLR (Pt.481) 293 at 321
Engineering Enterprise Contractor Co. of Nigeria v. Attorney- General of Kaduna State (1987) 1 NSCC 601
Elabanjo v. Dawodu (2006) 15 NWLR (Pt 1001) 76 at 138H
Ehuwa v. Ondo State I.E.C & Ors (2006) 10 NWLR (pt1012) 544 at 595, paras A-C
Ekwere v. The State (1981) LPELR-1103 (SC)
Ejike Okoye v. Commissioner of Police (2015) LPELR, SC 279/2011
Ekweghiariri v. Unachukwu & Ors (2013) LPELR-22074 (CA)
Etokhana v. Progress Bank of Nigeria Plc. (1997) LPELR-6258 (CA)
Eronini v. Iheuko (1989) 2 NWLR (101) 46 at (Pp. 64–65, paras. B–D)
Enakhimion v. Edo Trans Services (2006) All FWLR (pt391) 1683 at 1696
Enemuo & Anor v. Ezeonyeka & Ors (2016) LPELR-40171 (CA)
Enekebe v. Enekebe (1964) 1 ALL NLR 102.
Emueze & Ors v. Governor of Delta State & Ors (2014) LPELR-23201 (CA)
E.F.P.C. Ltd. v. NDIC. (2007) All FWLR (pt. 367) 793 @pp. 825–826.
Ewa Ekeng Inyang v. Efana Ekeng Ita & Ors (1929)9 N.L.R.84
Etokhana v. Progress Bank of Nigeria Plc (1997) LPELR-6258(CA)
Falomo v. Banigbe (Supra) at 695 paragraphs C – G.
Faleye (2007) ALL FWLR (Pt. 349) 1134 at 1146 Paras. A – B (CA)
Fawehinmi v. I.G.P & Ors (2002) LPELR-1258 (SC) 36, Hon. Justice Uwaifo, JSC
Federal University of Technology, Akure & Anor v. Asuu (2013) LPELR-20323(CA)
Federal Republic of Nigeria v. Mike (2004) 1 SC (pt. II) 27 at 25
Federal Republic of Nigeria v. Osahon (2005) 25 NSCQR512 at537
Fidelity Bank Plc. v. Monye & Ors. (2012) 3 SC. (PT.73).
Folarin Oreka Maiya v. The Incorporated Trustees of Clinton Health Access Initiative, Nigeria & 2 Ors (2012) 27 NLLR (Pt. 76) 110 NIC
Flour Mill of Nigeria Ltd v. Ogunbayo (2014) LPELR-24264 (CA)
Gani Fawehinmi v. The State (1990) 1 NWLR PT 127 at 486.
Garba Kyos & Anor v. Kwaturu & 41 Ors (Unreported APPEAL NO CA/K/EPT/SHA/01/2015. At p.16 Delivered September 21, 2016
Global Excellence Communications Limited & Ors v. Mr. Donald Duke (2007) LPELR-1323(SC);
Honey Crown *Products Ltd v. Shell Electric Manufacturing (2013) Lpelr-20077 (CA)*
ICAN v. Attorney Gen. Federation (2004) 3 NWLR (Pt. 859) 186

Iche v. State (2013) LPELR-22035 (CA)
Ibrahim v. Mohammed (2003) LPELR-1409 (SC) at 23
Ibidapo v. Lufthansa Airlines (1997) LPELR-1397(SC) at PP 30–31, paras G-C
Idris v. A.N.P.P. (2008) 8 NWLR (Pt.1088) 1 at 75, paras. E-H
Inakoju v. Adeleke (Ladoja's case) (2007) 4 NWLR (Pt. 1025) 423
Isaac Madubuago v. Dr. Mudiaga Odje & Ors (1985) 10 SC 267 at pages 268–269
Ifediora v. Umeh (1988) 2 NWLR page 5 at 13
Ifezue v. Mbadugha & Anor (1984) LPELR-1437 (SC)
Iwuju v. Federal Commissioner for Establishment and Anor (1985) LPELR-1568 (SC)
IPCO Nigeria Ltd. v. NNPC (2013) LPELR-22083 (CA)
I.G.P. v. A.N.P.P (2007) 18 NWLR (Pt. 1066) 457 at 496 – 497, paras. G – E (CA)
Irepodun-Ifelodun Local Government v. Balemo (2007) LPELR-8439 (CA)
Johnson v. Mobil Producing (Nig) Unlimited (2010) 7 NWLR (Pt 1194) 462
Johnbull Adams Nig. Ltd & Ors. v. Isoko Community Bank Ltd (2013) LPELR-20730 (CA)
Johnson v. Lawanson (1971) 1 All NLR P. 56
Kobia Osumanu v. Kofi Amadu & 2ors (1949) 12 WACA 437
Kolawole v. Alberto (1989) 1 N.W.L.R (pt98) 382
Latinde & Anor. v. Bella Lajunfin (1989) 5 SC 59; (1989) 5 SCNJ 59
Lawal v. GB Ollivant (1972) 2 SC 124
Legal Defence and Assistance Project (LEDAP) GTE & LTD v. Federal Ministry of Education & Another (Judgement) (FHC/ABJ/CS/978/15) [2018] NGFCHC 1 (17 April 2018)
Likita v. C.O.P. (2002) 11 NWLR (Pt. 777) 145
Mbas Motel Ltd. v. Wema Bank Plc (2013) LPELR-20736 (CA) at P. 26, Paras. E-G
Mercantile Bank (Nig) Plc v. IMESCO Enterprises Ltd (supra)
Mobile v. F.B.I.R (1977) 3 SC 53
Mobil Producing (Nig) Unltd v. Ajanaku & Ors (2007) LPELR-8758(CA
Motoh v. Motoh (2010) LPELR-8643(CA)
Mokelu v. Fed. Comm. Works & Housing (1976) NSCC 187
Mohammed v. FRN & Ors (2009) LPELR-8364 (CA)
Moghalu v. Ngige (2005) 4 NWLR (pt. 914)
Motel Kaduna Ltd. v. Deyemo (2006) LPELR-11596 (CA)

Maclean v. Inlaks (1980) 8–11 SC 1
Medical and Dental Practitioners Disciplinary Tribunal v. Dr. John Emewulu Okonkwo 58 (2001) 3 SC 76
Monye v. Abdullahi (2012) LPELR-20103(CA)
Makeri Smelting Co. Ltd v. Access Bank (Nig.) Plc (2002) 7 NWLR (Pt.766) 411 at 476–417
Martin Scbroder and Co. v. Major and Co. (Nig) Ltd (1989) 2 NWLR, at 12
Mwana v. UBN (2003) 28 W.R.N 62
Nafiu Rabiu v. The State (1981)2 NCLR 326
NEPA v. Atukpor (2000) LPELR-5931 (CA)
Nasi & Ors. v. Haruna (2001) LPELR-7023 (CA)
National Electric Power Authority v. Onah (1997) 1 NWLR (Pt. 484), Page 680 at 688
Nezianya v. Okagbue [1963] All NLR 358 SC
Nzekwu v. Nzekwu [1989] 2 NWLR 373
Nemi v. The State (1994) 1 LRC 376
Nicon Hotel Inter. S. A. v. Nicon Hilton Hotels & Anor. (2007) 7 NWLR (pt. 1032) 86 at 113–114
Nigeria-Ara Bank Ltd v. Nze A.U. Ogueru (1990) 6 NWLR (Pt. 159) 751
Nwali v. Ebsiec & Ors (2014) LPELR-23682 (CA)
Nwangwu v. Nwangwu (2000) Pt. 2 FWLR Page 273
Nigerian Navy v. Lambert (2007) LPELR-2026(SC)
Nigerian Navy & Ors v. Labinjo (2012) LPELR-7868 (SC)
Nwosu v. Imo State Environmental Sanitation Authority & Ors. (1990) 2 NWLR (pt.135) 688 at 723
Nkwocha v. Governor of Anambra State & Ors (1984) LPELR-2052 (SC)
NURTW & Anor v. RTEAN & Ors. (2012) LPELR-7840 (SC)
Nwaukoni v. Bielonwu & Ors. (2008) LPELR-4648 (CA)
Nwobodo v. Nwobodo (1995) 1 NWLR (Pt. 370) 203 at (Pp. 214–215
Nwannewuihe v. Nwannewuihe (2007) LPELR-8247 (CA)
Obayuwana v. Governor Bendel State & Anor. (1982) 12 SC. 147
Obidiegwu Onyesoh v. Nze Christopher Nnebedun & Ors (1992) LPELR-2742 (SC)
Odutela Holdings v. Ladejob (2006) 12 NWLR (ot.994) SC 321
Odusote v. Odusote (1971) All NLR 219
Olatubosun v. Texaco Nigeria Plc (2012) 14 NWLR (Pt.1319) 200;
Oguneyehun & Ors. v. The Governor Ondo State & Ors (2007) LPELR-4239 (CA)
Ogbunyiya v. Okudo (1976) 6–9 Sc.32

Ogunmade v. Fadayiro (1972) 8–9 SC.1
Ojukwu v. Agupusi & Anor (2014) LPELR-22683(CA) Hon. Justice Agube, JCA, at pp 41–41, paras F-A
Oke v. Nwizi (2013) LPELR-21252(CA)
Okon Bassey Ebe v. Commissioner of Police (2008) LPELR-984 (SC)
Okotie-Eboh v. Manager & Ors. (2004) LPELR-2502 (SC)
Okumagba v. Egbe (1965)1 All NLR 62 at 65
Okpalaeke v. NEPA (2003) 14 NWLR (pt.840) 383 at p.403
Olatunbosun v. Odunjo & Ors (2016) LPELR-40542 (CA)
Ola Animashaun v. Attorney General of Lagos State & Ors at p.29
Olafisoye v. Federal Republic of Nigeria (2004) 4 NWLR (Pt 864) 580
Oladeji (Nig.) LTD v. Nigeria Breweries PLC (2007) 5 NWLR (Pt. 1027) P. 415 at P. 436
Onashile v. Idowu (1961) All NLR 313
Ola Animashaun v. Attorney General of Lagos State & Ors (Unreported) Appeal No: CA/L/1046/2015, delivered on 30/10/2018
Okoh & Ors. v. University of Lagos & Anor. (2010) LPELR-4719 (CA)
Onovo & Ors v. Mba & Ors (2014) LPELR-23035(SC)
Onuoha v. Okafor (1983) 2 SCNLR 244
Omoju v. FRN (2008) 7 NWLR (Pt.1085) 38 at 57
Orhiunu v. FRN (2005) 1 NWLR (Pt.906) pg. 55 paras B-D
Osakwe v. FGN (2004) 14 NWLR (Pt.893) 305
Osakwe v. Federal College of Education (Technical) Asaba (2010) NWLR (pt.1201) at34
Oyekanmi v. NEPA (2000) 15 NWLR (pt. 690) 414
Ozigbu Engr Co Ltd v. Iwuamadi (2009) 16 NWLR (PT.1116) 44 @ 79
Olusanya v. UBA Plc (2017) LPELR-42348 (CA)
Oruobu v. Anekwe (1997) 5 NWLR (Pt. 506) 618
Odi v. Osafile (1987) 2 NWLR (PT. 57) 510;
Peenok Investment Ltd. v. Hotel Presidential Ltd. (1982) 12 SC 1 at 25
PDP v. Ugba & Ors (2011) LPELR-4838 (CA)
PDP v. Sherrif & Ors (2017) LPELR-42736 (SC) (P. 54, Paras. A-B),
PDP v. INEC (1999) 7 SC (pt11) 30
PDP v. CPC. & Ors (unreported) SC.272/2011
PDP v. INEC & Ors. (2012) LPELR-9724 (SC)
Plateau State Health Services Management Board & Anor. v. Goshwe (2012) LPELR-9830 (SC)
Rabiu v. State (1981) 2 NCLR 293 at 326
Rivers State Government v. Specialist Konsult (2005) 7 NWLR (Pt 923) 145.

Rida National Plastics Ltd v. Artee (Ind.) Ltd (2017) LPELR-43132(CA)
Registered Trustees Of The Airline Operators Of Nigeria v. Nigerian Air Space Management Agency (2014) 8 NWLR (PT. 1408) 1 @ PP. 30–31
R v. Bangaza (1960) 5 FSC 1
R v. Princewill (1963) 2 All NLR
Samuel Ayo Omoju v. The Federal Republic of Nigeria (2008) LPELR-2647 (SC)
Saleh v. Abah & Or (2017) LPELR-41914 (SC)
Sarakatu v. Nigerian Housing Development Society Ltd (1984) 4 SC 26
Seaford Estate Ltd v. Asher (1949) 2 K.B 481
Stabilini Visinoni Ltd v. Mallinson & Partners Ltd (2014) LPELR-23090 (CA)
Sebelius v. Cloe 569 U.S. 369 (2013)
SETRACO (Nig) Ltd v. Kpaji (2017) LPELR-41560(SC) PP 25–26 paras D-A
Skye Bank v. Iwu (2017) LPELR-42595(SC)
Simon Edibo v. The State (2007), 13 NWLR (Pt. 1051) 306
SPDC (Nig) Ltd v. KATAD (Nig) Ltd (2006) 1 NWLR (PT.960) 216 PARA D-G
Standard Trust Bank Plc v. Olusola (2007) LPELR-4978 (CA)
Suleiman v. Commissioner of Police (2008) 3 SCNJ 1 at 9 – 10; Johnbull Adams Nig. Ltd & Ors. v. Isoko Community Bank Ltd (2013) LPELR-20730 (CA)
State v. Gwonto (1983) 1 SCNLR 142;
Sha v. Kwan (2000) 8 NWLR (Pt. 670) 685;
Tejumade A. Clement & Anor v. Bridget J. Iwuanyanwu & Anor (1989) LPELR-872 (SC)
The Prosecutor v. Dominic Ongwen (ICC-02/04-01/15) <https://www.icc-cpi.int/uganda/ongwen>
Tinubu v. I.M.B Securities (2001) 8 NWLR (PT 740) 192
Tell Communications Limited v. Colonel Mohammed Buba Marwa (2005) LPELR-6148(CA)
The Resident Ibadan Province v. Olagunju (1954) 14 WACA 552,
The Admin. & Exec. Of The Estate Of Abacha v. Eke-Spiff &Ors. (2009) LPELR-3152(SC),
Total Engineering Services Team Inc. v. Chevron Nigeria Ltd. (2010) LPELR-5032(CA)
Thimnu v. UBN Plc. & Ors. (2013) LPELR 22127 (CA) @ pp. 20–21
T.M. Lewin (Nig) Ltd v. Smartmark Ltd (2017) LPELR-43136 (CA)
UBN Plc. v. Astra Builders (W.A.) Ltd (2010) LPELR-3383 (SC)

Ugoji & Ors v. Iwuagwu (2013) LPELR-20810 (CA)
Ugwu v. Ararume (2007) 12 NWLR (pt1048) 367 at 498, 31
Ukiri v. Geco – Prakla (Nig.)
University of Lagos & Ors. v. Professor Luke Uka Uche (2008) LPELR-5073(CA)
Unity Bank & Anor. v. Edward Bonari (2008) 2 SCM 193 at 240
University of Lagos v. Aigoro (1985) 1 NWLR (Pt.1) 143
Union Bank of Nigeria Plc. v. Ikwen (2000) 3 NWLR (Pt. 648) 223)
Ugwu v. Arurume (2007) 31 WRN 1 at 60–61
Ude v. Nwara & Anor. (1993) LPELR-3289(SC) P.24, Paras. B-C.
Udeze v. Onuniju (2001) 3 NWLR (pt. 700) 216
UBN Plc. v. Astra Builders (W.A.) Ltd (2010) LPELR-3383(SC)
Uwazuruike v. A.G. Federation (2013) 10 NWLR (Pt.1361) 105
Wilson v. A.G of Bendel state (1985) 1 N.W.L.R (pt. 17) 572
Williams v. Hope Rising Voluntary Funds Society (1982) 2 SC 145
Yusuf v. Adegoke & Anor (2007) LPELR – 3534 (SC)

Foreign Cases
Alleyne v. United States, 570 U.S. 99, 118 (2013)
Brown v. Board of Education, 347 U.S. 483
Buckley v. City of New York 56 N.Y.2d 300, 305 (1982)
Bowers v. Hardwick,478 U.S. 186 (1986)
Citizens United v. FEC,558, U.S. 310, 378 (2010)
Corley v. United States, 556 U.S. 303 (2009)
Darby v. Cisneros, 509 U.S. 137, 147 (1993)
Daubert v. Merrell Dow Pharmaceuticals, Inc. 509 U.S. 579, 113 S.Ct. 2786, 125 L.Ed.2d 144 (1987)
Dobbs, State Health Officer of the Mississippi Department of Health et al. v. Jackson Women's Health Organization et al., 597 U.S. (2002)
Green v. Bock Laundry Machine Co., 510 U.S. 200, 209 (1994)
Gideon v. Wainwright, 372 U.S. 335
Griswold v. Connecticut, 381 U.S. 479 (1965)
Janus v. American Federation of State, County and Municipal Employees, 585, U.S (2018), No.16, 1466, slip opt at 43–35
Kasabian v. Chichester, 72 A.D.3d 1141; 898 N.Y.S.2d 293 (3rd Dept., 2010)
Knowlton v. Moore, 178 U.S 41 (1990)
Korematsu v. United States, 323 U.S. 214
Louisiana v. Hayes, 806 So.2d 816 (La. App. 2001.)
Lawrence v. Texas, 539 U.S. 558(2003)

Marbury v. Madison, 5 U.S. (1 Cranch) 137 (1803)
Magor and St Mellons Rural District Council v. Newport Corporation (1951) 2 All E.R 839
Montana v. Nelson, 48 P.2d 739 (Mont.2002)
Payne v. Tennessee, 501 U.S. 808, 827 (1991)
Planned Parenthood of Southeastern PA. v. Casey, 505 U.S. 833 (1992)
Pepper (Inspector of Taxes) v. Hart (1993) 1 All E.R 42
People v. Bing, 76 N.Y.2d 331, 337–338 (1990)
R v. Susses Justices Ex Parte Marcathy (1924) 1 K.B, 256
R v. Rand (1988) L.R.I.Q.B 230
R v. Susses Justices Ex Parte Marcathy (1924) 1 K.B, 256
Rylands v. Fletcher (1868) L.R.3 H.L.330
Roe v. Wade, 410 U.S. 113 (1973)
Shell Oil Co. v. Iowa Dep't of Revenue, 488 U.S. 19,26 (1988)
Sebelius v. Cloe, 569 U.S. 369 (2013)
Seaford Estates Ltd v. Asher, Denning (1947) 2 K.B 481.498
Southeastern PA. v. Casey 505 U.S. 833 (1992)
Transco Plc (formerly BG plc and BG Transco plc) v. Stockport Borough Council (2004) 1 All E.R. 589 29
The House of Lords in Pepper (Inspector of Taxes) v. Hart (1993) 1 All E.R 42
Thunder Basin Coal Co. v. Reich, 10 U.S. 200, 209 (1994)
United Sav. Ass'n of Tex v. Timbers of in wood Forest Assocs Ltd, 484 U.S 365, 371 (1988)
United States v. Locke 471 U.S, 84 (1985)
United States v. Morrison 529 U.S. 598 (2000)
United States v. Locke 471 U.S. 84 (1985)
United Sav. Ass'n of Tex v. Timbers of in wood Forest Assocs Ltd, 484 U.S. 365, 371 (1988)
U.S v. Noriega 917 F.2d 1543 (11th Cir. 1990)
United States v. Morrison 529 U.S. 598 (2000)
Hilton v. SC Pub. Rys. Comm'n, 502 U.S. 197, 202 (1991)
Vasquez v. Hillery, 474 U.S. 254, 265–66 (1986)
Willard v. State, 244 Ga. App. 469, 535 S.E.2d 820 (2000)
Wirtz v. Bottle Blowers Ass'n, 389 U.S. 463, 468 (1968)

Index

www.ingramcontent.com/pod-product-compliance
Ingram Content Group UK Ltd.
Pitfield, Milton Keynes, MK11 3LW, UK
UKHW020714071026
15590UKWH00011B/594

9 783631 877524